WRITE

for BUSINESS

A Compact Guide to Writing & Communicating in the Workplace

Second Edition

Meyer / Sebranek / Van Rys

Verne Meyer • Pat Sebranek • John Van Rys

UPWRITE PRESS®

www.upwritepress.com

Acknowledgements

The authors wish to thank the many business people in for-profit and not-for-profit organizations across the United States and Canada who contributed samples of business writing for this project. In addition, we want to thank the following people for sharing their valuable time, energy, and ideas by reviewing *Write for Business* at various stages of its development: Julia Blackmore, Bernard De Wit, Jim Evers, Tip Haagsma, Erik Hoekstra, Richard Kobes, Heidi Mosher, Gloria Pickering, Marcy Stravers, Pam Ten Napel, Jon Van Gorp, Keith Van Rys, Loren Veldhuizen, and Daniel Walker.

UpWrite Press

Administration

Owner/President:
  Christopher Erickson
Owner/Vice President: Janae Sebranek
Director of Operations: Steve Augustyn
Customer Service Manager:
  Jean Varley

Editorial

Editor in Chief: Rob King
Author/Senior Writer: Dave Kemper
Writer/Technologist: Lester Smith
Writer/Editor: Tim Kemper
Copy Editor: Lois Krenzke

Production

Manager: Colleen Belmont
Design Consultant:
  Christian R. Krenzke
Designer/Developer:
  Mark Lalumondier
Designer/Developer: April Lindau
Senior Software Developer:
  Jason Reynolds

Printed in the U.S.A.

Library of Congress Control Number: 2003104597

ISBN (smythe): 978-1-932436-32-7

ISBN (spiral): 978-1-932436-33-4

5 6 7 8 9 —LSC— 18 17

Right for Business

How often do you receive confusing e-mails from colleagues or clients? Imagine how much more successful those folks would be if they improved their communication skills.

Now imagine that you have a terrific idea you want to present to a supervisor or client. Do you call the person, send an e-mail, or write a proposal? The way you communicate your idea may mean the difference between success and failure.

Whatever your communication need, *Write for Business* is here to help. In these pages, you'll find

- **guidelines** for quickly creating winning proposals, effective e-mails, polished presentations, and much more.
- **models** of every important type of business document.
- **checklists** to help you quickly revise and refine writing.
- **rules** for punctuation, capitalization, usage, and grammar.

This second edition of *Write for Business* includes all-new chapters on social media, communication options, and management writing, as well as over 60 trait-based solutions to common writing problems. There are even three new chapters to help English language learners!

Good communication is good business. When communication counts—and it always does—turn to *Write for Business.*

shutterstock.com

Using *Write for Business*

Do you need to fix a document that isn't working? Turn to Section 1 for common problems and concrete solutions. Do you need to quickly create an effective document? Turn to Sections 2 or 3 for guidelines, models, and checklists. Do you need to find a rule of grammar? Turn to Section 4: The Proofreader's Guide. Here is a quick overview of the parts of *Write for Business*.

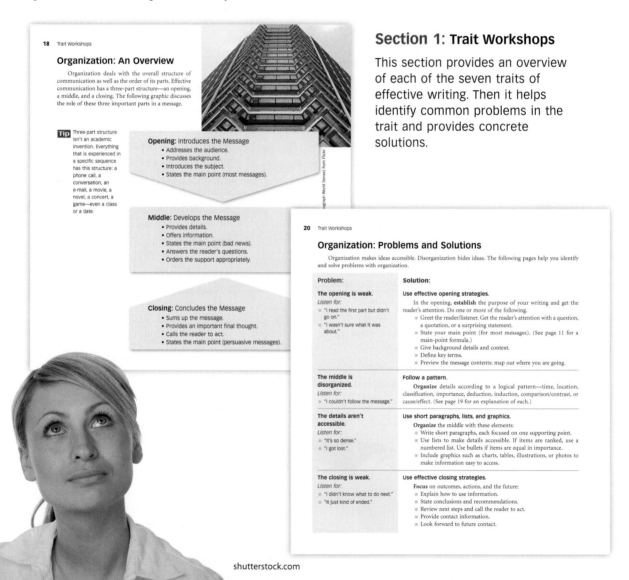

Section 1: Trait Workshops

This section provides an overview of each of the seven traits of effective writing. Then it helps identify common problems in the trait and provides concrete solutions.

shutterstock.com

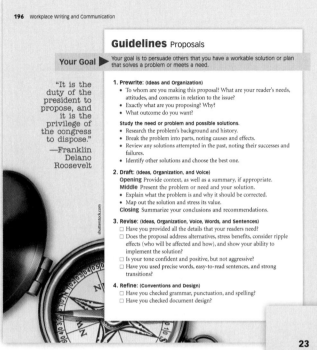

Guidelines Proposals

Your Goal ▶ Your goal is to persuade others that you have a workable solution or plan that solves a problem or meets a need.

"It is the duty of the president to propose, and it is the privilege of the congress to dispose."
—Franklin Delano Roosevelt

1. Prewrite: (Ideas and Organization)
- To whom are you making this proposal? What are your reader's needs, attitudes, and concerns in relation to the issue?
- Exactly what are you proposing? Why?
- What outcome do you want?

Study the need or problem and possible solutions.
- Research the problem's background and history.
- Break the problem into parts, noting causes and effects.
- Review any solutions attempted in the past, noting their successes and failures.
- Identify other solutions and choose the best one.

2. Draft: (Ideas, Organization, and Voice)
Opening Provide context, as well as a summary, if appropriate.
Middle Present the problem or need and your solution.
- Explain what the problem is and why it should be corrected.
- Map out the solution and stress its value.
Closing Summarize your conclusions and recommendations.

3. Revise: (Ideas, Organization, Voice, Words, and Sentences)
☐ Have you provided all the details that your readers need?
☐ Does the proposal address alternatives, stress benefits, consider ripple effects (who will be affected and how), and show your ability to implement the solution?
☐ Is your tone confident and positive, but not aggressive?
☐ Have you used precise words, easy-to-read sentences, and strong transitions?

4. Refine: (Conventions and Design)
☐ Have you checked grammar, punctuation, and spelling?
☐ Have you checked document design?

Sections 2 and 3:
Guidelines, Models, and Checklists

Clear, helpful guidelines take you step-by-step through writing a specific business form. Models show examples of each form, and checklists help you revise and refine your work.

Section 4: Rules

The Proofreader's Guide provides rules and examples for punctuation, mechanics, usage, grammar, and sentences, with special help for English language learners.

23
Punctuation

Period

To End a Sentence

- Use a **period** to end a sentence that makes a statement, requests something, or gives a mild command.

(Statement) **"A gold mine is a hole in the ground with a liar at the top."**
—Mark Twain

(Request) **Please arrange an on-site meeting.**
(Mild Command) **"Concentrate on finding your goal; then concentrate on reaching it."**
—Michael Friedsam

Note: Omit a period after a statement that has parentheses around it if it is part of another sentence.
These early entrepreneurs (some of them were true visionaries) often met skepticism.

After an Initial or an Abbreviation

- A period should be placed after an initial and after most abbreviations.

Ms.	Inc.	O.D.	M.A.
C.E.	a.m.	U.S.A.	Joan Q.

Note: When an abbreviation is the last word in a sentence, do not add a second period.
Tom recently received his M.B.A.

After an Indirect Question

- Use a period, not a question mark, after an indirect question.
I wonder how much that will cost us.

Ellipsis

To Show Omitted Words

- Use an **ellipsis** (three spaced periods) to indicate that words have been omitted in a quoted passage. Leave one space before and after each period.

(Original) **All new employees must fill out the standard work forms—Social Security, insurance, and payroll. The forms, which maybe obtained from your immediate supervisor, should be completed before beginning work. If you have any questions, please contact Rosa for assistance.**

(Quotation) **"All new employees must fill out the standard work forms . . . which may be obtained from your immediate supervisor . . . before beginning work."**

At the End of a Sentence

- If words from a quoted passage are omitted at the end of a sentence, the ellipsis follows the period.

"All new employees must fill out the standard work forms—Social Security, insurance, and payroll. . . . If you have any questions, please contact Rosa for assistance."

If the quoted material is a complete sentence (even if it was not in the original), use a period and then an ellipsis.

"All new employees must fill out the standard work forms. . . . Please contact Rosa for assistance."

Note: The first word of a sentence following a period and an ellipsis may be capitalized, even though it was not capitalized in the original.

* * * Success occurs when opportunity meets preparation. —Zig Zigler * * *

Table of Contents

Section 2: Writing Three Message Types   91

Section 3: Workplace Writing and Communicating   135

Section 4: Proofreader's Guide   255

shutterstock.com

Getting Started

Good business writing is informative, clear, and convincing. It helps facilitate business transactions and strengthen business relationships. To produce better business writing—and communicating as a whole—follow the bottom-line principles listed below.

Bottom-Line Writing Principles

1. **Use the seven traits to solve problems with writing.** Practice quality control by measuring your writing in each document against these traits: ideas, organization, voice, words, sentences, correctness, and design. (See pages 1-70.)

2. **Set positive goals.** To complete each document successfully,
   - establish a reasonable deadline,
   - decide what you want to accomplish, and
   - align your writing goals with the company's mission and values.

3. **Write directly to readers.** Think about each reader's knowledge, motivation, and position. How will he or she react to your message? How can you build common ground? Consider the diversity of your audience and then write respectfully to that audience. (See pages 38-39.)

4. **Master the writing process.** Be prepared to do the necessary work—prewriting, drafting, revising, and refining. Develop efficient writing habits. (See pages 71-90.)

5. **Follow good models.** To save time and money, avoid starting each document from scratch. Keep a file for samples of good writing and check the models in this book. Then copy, paste, and modify models to fit any given situation.

6. **Produce a professional look.** The appearance of your writing is almost as important as the content. So always use appropriate stationery, inks, fonts, logos, envelopes, and so on.

7. **Be a team writer.** Work together for the benefit of the project, the company, and the reader. Test important documents before sending or distributing them. Ask for and give honest feedback in order to improve each piece of writing.

shutterstock.com

Introduction
The Seven Traits of Effective Writing

Effective writing is clear, concise, and compelling. It communicates the writer's ideas to the world. Ineffective writing is confusing, long-winded, and unconvincing. It clouds the writer's ideas. But what makes writing effective?

Effective writing exhibits seven traits, or qualities, listed below. This chapter introduces you to the seven traits, and the chapters that follow outline specific strategies for improving each trait in your writing:

1. Ideas
2. Organization
3. Voice
4. Words
5. Sentences
6. Correctness
7. Design

The Seven Traits of Effective Writing

What makes writing effective? Ask that question, and you'll receive a hundred different answers—clear sentences, correct spelling, good details, a professional voice, no dropped words, nice-looking letterhead, no logical errors, a great anecdote. . . .

Effective writing is subjective, right?

Wrong. The hundreds of things that make writing effective are summed up in the seven traits. Here is the trait-based profile of writing that works:

Trait	
Ideas	The writing focuses on an important subject, has a clear main point, provides effective details, and achieves its purpose.
Organization	The writing has a strong beginning, middle, and ending and orders information well.
Voice	The tone is appropriate for the subject, purpose, and audience, reflecting well on the writer and connecting with the reader.
Words	The writing uses precise nouns and verbs, avoids slang expressions and colloquialisms, and defines technical terms as needed.
Sentences	The sentences read smoothly, varying in length, pattern, type, and beginnings.
Correctness	Punctuation, capitalization, spelling, usage, and grammar are correct.
Design	Typography, color, white space, lists, visuals, and other elements convey the message clearly and suit the subject and purpose.

The Seven Traits in *Write for Business*

Write for Business—and all materials from UpWrite Press—use the seven traits to improve writing and communication. In this book, you'll find the seven traits in

- trait workshops, pointing out common problems with each trait and offering concrete solutions.
- writing guidelines, helping you focus on each trait as you develop writing.
- model annotations, helping you understand how each trait works best.
- revising and editing checklists, helping you improve and discuss your message.

How the Traits Can Work for You

Understanding and employing the seven traits will give you an advantage in all of your business communications. The traits can *guide writing* projects, *diagnose problems* in writing, *solve problems* in writing, and give you a platform from which to *discuss writing* (reports, bids, fliers, and so on) with your coworkers.

To Guide Writing:

How often do you get writer's block? It may happen because you are overwhelmed, thinking about everything at once instead of taking it a step at a time. The trait-based guidelines throughout *Write for Business* allow you to focus on one thing at a time.

To Diagnose Problems:

How can you tell whether a message is working? The traits remove the guesswork. They zero in, telling you what works— and what does not work—in writing. The trait workshops and checklists throughout *Write for Business* help you pinpoint problems in every form of communication.

To Solve Problems:

When there's a problem with a message, how do you fix it? The traits provide specific, concrete solutions for everything from clarifying your main point to putting modifiers where they belong. The first section of *Write for Business* features over 60 trait-based solutions for common problems.

To Discuss Writing:

The traits provide a common language that businesspeople can use to discuss writing. Whether you need to advertise a product in a flier, convince a client to give your company some repeat business, break bad news to valued employees, or deliver some other important message, the traits can help you work with others to produce effective communications.

shutterstock.com

Using the Traits
To Guide Writing

The traits can guide you as you start a writing task.

1. **Prewrite:** When you begin writing, focus on ideas and organization.
   - **Ideas:** Decide on a main point and gather ideas to support it.
   - **Organization:** Decide on the best order for your ideas.
2. **Draft:** When you write a first draft, continue to focus on ideas and organization and also consider voice.
   - **Voice:** Use a tone that fits your subject, audience, and purpose.

Guidelines Letters

Your Goal ▶ In a letter, your goal is to communicate your message and give a positive impression of yourself and your organization.

1. **Prewrite:** (Ideas and Organization)
   - Ask yourself what you want the letter to accomplish.
   - Consider the reader's concerns about, knowledge of, and history with your organization.

   Gather information.
   - Gather files and other necessary resources.
   - Jot down your main points in a logical order.
   - Use the letter format (full-block, semiblock, or simplified) that your company prefers.

2. **Draft:** (Ideas, Organization, and Voice)
   Opening State the situation (reason for writing, background).
   Middle Give the full explanation, supporting points, and details. If your message is good or neutral news, make your key point early. For a bad-news or persuasive message, build up to the main point.
   Closing End with a call to action (who should do what, when), and, if appropriate, mention future contact.

3. **Revise:** (Ideas, Organization, Voice, Words, and Sentences)
   - ☐ Are all names, dates, and details accurate?
   - ☐ Is information presented in a logical order?
   - ☐ Do you use a conversational but professional tone?
   - ☐ Do you emphasize the reader's perspective?
   - ☐ Have you used precise wording?
   - ☐ Have you used personal pronouns in a positive way?
   - ☐ Do you have smooth sentences that pass the "read aloud" test?

4. **Refine:** (Conventions and Design)
   - ☐ Have you checked spelling (especially double-checked names)?
   - ☐ Have you checked grammar, punctuation, and mechanics?
   - ☐ Have you checked format and design?

Invite sales reps:
- Welcome
- Rankin's 25th anniv.
  - open house (June 1)
  - ribbon-cutting ceremony
  - refreshments
- Directions
- Contacts

Using the Traits
To Diagnose and Solve Problems

After you write a first draft, the traits can help you diagnose problems and implement solutions.

3. **Revise:** When you review your first draft, continue to focus on the first three traits and also consider words and sentences.

- **Words:** Replace general nouns and verbs and cut wordiness.
- **Sentences:** Adjust sentences until they read smoothly.

Guidelines Letters

Your Goal ▶ In a letter, your goal is to communicate your message and give a positive impression of yourself and your organization.

1. Prewrite: (Ideas and Organization)
- Ask yourself what you want the letter to accomplish.
- Consider the reader's concerns about, knowledge of, and history with your organization.

Gather information.
- Gather files and other necessary resources.
- Jot down your main points in a logical order.
- Use the letter format (full-block, semiblock, or simplified) that your company prefers.

2. Draft: (Ideas, Organization, and Voice)
Opening State the situation (reason for writing, background).
Middle Give the full explanation, supporting points, and details. If your message is good or neutral news, make your key point early. For a bad-news or persuasive message, build up to the main point.
Closing End with a call to action (who should do what, when), and, if appropriate, mention future contact.

3. Revise: (Ideas, Organization, Voice, Words, and Sentences)
- ☐ Are all names, dates, and details accurate?
- ☐ Is information presented in a logical order?
- ☐ Do you use a conversational but professional tone?
- ☐ Do you emphasize the reader's perspective?
- ☐ Have you used precise wording?
- ☐ Have you used personal pronouns in a positive way?
- ☐ Do you have smooth sentences that pass the "read aloud" test?

4. Refine: (Conventions and Design)
- ☐ Have you checked spelling (especially double-checked names)?
- ☐ Have you checked grammar, punctuation, and mechanics?
- ☐ Have you checked format and design?

May 27, 2011

Ms. Lorraine Scott
Sales Representative
206 West Dundee Street
Chicago, IL 60614

Dear Lorraine:

We are celebrating Rankin's 25th anniversary. Our office expansion is finished, and sales grew by 16 percent. On Wednesday, June 1, there is an open house from 8:30 a.m. to 4:00 p.m. with hourly tours of the new office, engineering, and manufacturing facilities. There is a ribbon-cutting ceremony at 4:00 p.m. on the west lawn, with refreshments served at 4:30 p.m.

It would be a shame to put all this effort in and find out you are too busy.

If you need directions, transportation, or other information, speak with Rebecca Wright or call Matthew Nicolai at 555-1980, extension 4, or send him an e-mail at mnicolai@rankin.com.

Sincerely,

Sharissa Hershey

Sharissa Hershey
Vice President of Sales

Ideas
I need a clear main point and better details.

Organization
I need a better beginning.

Voice
I'll make this sound friendlier.

shutterstock.com

Using the Traits **To Discuss Writing**

After the letter is revised, it needs refining, or editing. Then you can prepare a finished piece like the one below. The traits help you discuss the writing with other team members.

4. **Refine:** When you edit your work, focus on the last two traits.
   - **Correctness:** Check punctuation, capitalization, spelling, and grammar.
   - **Design:** Present your work in the accepted format.

Guidelines Letters

Your Goal ▶ In a letter, your goal is to communicate your message and give a positive impression of yourself and your organization.

1. **Prewrite: (Ideas and Organization)**
   - Ask yourself what you want the letter to accomplish.
   - Consider the reader's concerns about, knowledge of, and history with your organization.

   Gather information.
   - Gather files and other necessary resources.
   - Jot down your main points in a logical order.
   - Use the letter format (full-block, semiblock, or simplified) that your company prefers.

2. **Draft: (Ideas, Organization, and Voice)**
   Opening State the situation (reason for writing, background).
   Middle Give the full explanation, supporting points, and details. If your message is good or neutral news, make your key point early. For a bad-news or persuasive message, build up to the main point.
   Closing End with a call to action (who should do what, when), and, if appropriate, mention future contact.

3. **Revise: (Ideas, Organization, Voice, Words, and Sentences)**
   - ☐ Are all names, dates, and details accurate?
   - ☐ Is information presented in a logical order?
   - ☐ Do you use a conversational but professional tone?
   - ☐ Do you emphasize the reader's perspective?
   - ☐ Have you used precise wording?
   - ☐ Have you used personal pronouns in a positive way?
   - ☐ Do you have smooth sentences that pass the "read aloud" test?

4. **Refine: (Conventions and Design)**
   - ☐ Have you checked spelling (especially double-checked names)?
   - ☐ Have you checked grammar, punctuation, and mechanics?
   - ☐ Have you checked format and design?

May 27, 2011

Ms. Lorraine Scott
Sales Representative
206 West Dundee Street
Chicago, IL 60614

Dear Lorraine:

Welcome to the Sales Seminar! I hope that you will have a productive week. While you are here, please help us celebrate Rankin's 25th anniversary.

This year, we have a lot to celebrate. Our office expansion is finished, and sales grew by 16 percent. On Wednesday, June 1, we would like you to be our guest at the following events:
- An open house from 8:30 a.m. to 4:00 p.m. with hourly tours of the new office, engineering, and manufacturing facilities
- A ribbon-cutting ceremony at 4:00 p.m. on the west lawn, with refreshments served at 4:30 p.m.

You are a big part of Rankin's success, Lorraine. I hope that you can take a break from your busy seminar schedule and join us. If you need directions, transportation, or other information, please speak with Rebecca Wright or call Matthew Nicolai at 555-1980, extension 4, or send him an e-mail at mnicolai@rankin.com.

Sincerely,

Sharissa Hershey

Sharissa Hershey
Vice President of Sales

Correctness
I'll have Jack proof this.

Design
I'll print on letterhead.

shutterstock.com

Section 1:
Trait Workshops

In this section

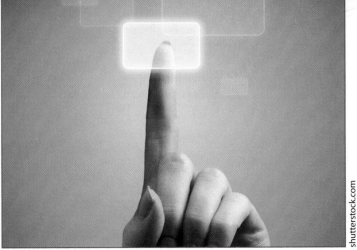

shutterstock.com

1
Trait 1: Ideas

Just before the turn of the millennium, a pair of Ph.D. students had an idea. Sergey Brin and Larry Page wanted to create a search engine that would make information accessible to everyone, everywhere. Their idea gave birth to Google—and freed up ideas for the whole world.

That's the power of ideas. They are the soul of business: Google, YouTube, and Apple all began with an idea and a garage. Ideas are also the soul of communication. The whole point of writing or speaking is to transfer ideas from one person to another. Strong ideas result in meaningful communication.

This chapter provides an overview of ideas, points out specific problems with ideas, and gives concrete solutions.

Ideas: An Overview

Ideas are the soul of any message, written or spoken. To successfully communicate your ideas, you need first to understand the communication situation.

The Communication Situation

The communication situation involves five elements: a **sender**, a **message**, a **medium** that bears the message, a **receiver**, and the **context** in which the message is sent. Consider the diagram below.

shutterstock.com

Five Elements

1. Sender
Who is speaking or writing?

David Sheffield, Plant Manager

2. Message:
What is being said and why?

A new alarm code and procedure must be implemented.

3. Medium:
How is the message sent?

Company-wide e-mail and announcement at staff meeting

4. Receiver:
Who is listening or reading?

All employees

5. Context: How does the message fit in? Where and when will it be received?

Recent false alarms have caused trouble for staff, police, and the alarm company. Employees will receive the message this morning via e-mail and this afternoon at a staff meeting.

shutterstock.com

Tip Understanding the situation will help you choose the best medium of communication. While some messages are best delivered face-to-face, others may require a phone call or an e-mail. The medium should be appropriate for the rest of the communication situation.

Main Point (the Big Idea)

Effective messages have a main point—the subject and purpose of the message expressed in a single sentence. A simple formula can help you state your main point.

Subject a new alarm code and procedure	**+**	**Purpose** I want everyone to use them.	**=**	**Main Point** Starting tonight, everyone must use the new code and procedure for setting the alarm.

Supporting Details (Ideas That Answer)

Effective messages answer the receiver's basic questions about the main point. These answers are supporting details. Make sure your message answers these basic questions: *who? what? where? when? why?* and *how?*

(1) **Who?**

(2) **Where?**

(3) **When?**

(4) **What?/ How?**

(5) **Why?**

The last person in the building should do the following when leaving:

1. Do an "all call" to make sure no one else remains in the building.
2. Check that the copiers are turned off.
3. Shut off all coffee makers.
4. Set the answering machine light to the "Night" setting.
5. Punch the new code (3613) into the alarm system and press "On."
6. Exit the building, making sure the door is closed and locked.

Following this procedure will help us avoid future false alarms.

Answering Objections (Opposing Ideas)

If receivers are resistant to the message, they may have objections to your main point. Just as you answered the receivers' questions, you should answer any objection they may have. First, acknowledge the objection, and then give a reason that addresses the issues raised.

Acknowledgment
Some people think that only evening shift needs to worry about the alarm, but many of the false alarms have been caused by day-shift workers.   **Answer**

Ideas: Problems and Solutions

In business, a great idea is worth its weight in gold, but first an idea has to be communicated. When there are problems with ideas, try these solutions:

Problem:

People don't know what to do with the message.

Listen for:

- "Why did you send that?"
- "What did you want?"
- "What do you want me to do?"
- "How should I respond?"

Solution:

Communicate with purpose in mind.

Ask yourself what you want to accomplish and what you want the reader to do. The answer is your purpose. If you know your purpose, you can clearly state it for readers and listeners. Skim the list of options below and select the one that best describes your purpose. The third column shows a page where a model message has the same purpose.

I want to . . .	I want the reader to . . .	Model
ask for information.	**provide** information.	99
ask for permission.	**grant** permission.	128
ask for help.	**provide** help.	129
provide information.	**understand** the information.	95
invite the person.	**accept** the invitation.	100
give encouragement.	**be** encouraged.	179
give instructions.	**follow** the instructions.	212
solicit ideas.	**suggest** ideas.	130
present options.	**choose** an option.	167
propose a solution.	**approve** the solution.	201
convince the reader	**be** convinced.	201
sell a product or service	**buy** the product or service.	131
say, "yes."	**hear**, "yes."	102
say, "no."	**hear**, "no."	109
complain.	**make** the situation right.	111
apologize.	**forgive**.	105
thank.	**appreciate**.	104

Tip As you formulate your main point, clearly state your purpose. Stating it flat out—"I want to _____"—is much better than not stating it at all. (See page 11.)

Problem:	**Solution:**

The main point is unclear.

Listen for:

- "What does this all mean?"
- "What's the point?"

Check your main point for subject and purpose.

Check that your main point (1) names your subject (what you are writing about) and (2) states your purpose (why you are writing). Use the formula below to write your main point.

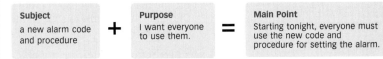

| **Subject** a new alarm code and procedure | **+** | **Purpose** I want everyone to use them. | **=** | **Main Point** Starting tonight, everyone must use the new code and procedure for setting the alarm. |

A detail is unclear.

Listen for:

- "What does that mean?"
- "Give an example."

Provide a definition or an example.

Define any terms that may be unclear:

> The alarm code is the four-digit number you press into the keypad to activate or deactivate the alarm.

Provide an example of what you mean to further clarify your message.

> For example, the old alarm code was 1993, the year the company was incorporated.

The main point needs more support.

Listen for:

- "Can you prove it?"
- "Why is this an issue?"

Use facts, statistics, and graphs.

Use facts to provide support for your main point.

> Each time that the alarm goes off, whether due to a security breach or a false alarm, the plant manager and the police have to meet on site.

Use statistics to quantify your support.

> Each false alarm costs the company $100.

Use a graph to make statistics visible.

Cost of False Alarms

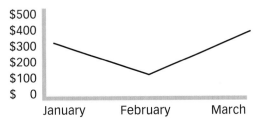

Problem:	**Solution:**

People think the message isn't relevant.

Listen for:
- "Why should I care?"
- "Does this even matter?"

Give an anecdote or a prediction.

Use an anecdote (a short story with a point) to connect your main point to real life.

Anecdote: Last week, the plant manager and his family were awakened at 3:00 a.m. by an automated phone call indicating that the alarm was going off. The machine called again every two minutes for the next twenty minutes until he was able to shut off the alarm. It was a false alarm caused by employee error.

Use a prediction to indicate possible outcomes.

Prediction: Those who do not learn the new alarm code and procedure will have a conversation with the plant manager.

People are resistant.

Listen for:
- "You're forgetting . . ."
- "What about . . . ?"
- "Yeah, but . . ."

Address needs/answer objections.

List what the receiver needs. Then **address** those needs in your message.

Needs: To keep our workplace secure and to make sure you are confident in setting the alarm, please follow the procedure listed below.

> Employees need . . .
> —A secure workplace.
> —Confidence when setting the alarm.
> —To stop hearing us complain about false alarms.

List the objections the receiver is likely to have. **Acknowledge** those objections and **answer** them.

Acknowledge and Answer: Some may feel that only second-shift workers need to know how to set the alarm. However, many false alarms are caused by first-shift workers.

> Employees might object that . . .
> —Only second-shift workers need to know how to set the alarm.

shutterstock.com

Problem:	Solution:
The options are not clear.	**Compare and contrast options clearly.**

Listen for:
- "What's the difference?"
- "I can't decide which to choose."

Compare and contrast the similarities and differences between options, helping the receiver choose between them.

Similarities and Differences: If you accidentally set off the alarm, turn it off immediately and call the plant manager's office. If he is not available, call his cell phone. If you are unable to reach him, wait on site until he arrives. Each option is acceptable, but the latter two options will be less enjoyable.

The message lacks authority.

Listen for:
- "Why is this from you?"
- "Who says?"

Refer to an authority.

Provide a reference or quotation from a higher authority to add authority to a message.

Authoritative Reference: President Jackson said, "Anyone who causes a false alarm in the future will need to discuss it with me."

The message isn't engaging.

Listen for:
- "I didn't read it."
- "Sorry, I drifted off for a second."

Use sensory details.

Use sensory details—sights, sounds, smells, textures, and tastes—when you want to engage the audience (this strategy is not suitable for more matter-of-fact communications). Create a sensory chart on a piece of scrap paper and use some of the senses in the message.

Sight	carnations, blue, red, card signed by all
Sound	playing "Wake Up, Sweet Susy"
Smell	sweet, fresh
Taste	chocolate-caramel truffles
Touch	smooth ribbon

Details Employed: Thanks to all who sent me the beautiful bouquet of blue and red carnations, the card that said, "Get some sleep!" and the chocolate-caramel truffles. I will get more sleep with the new alarm-code procedure!

—David Sheffield, Plant Manager

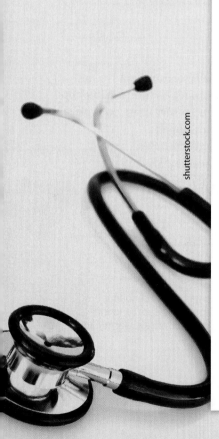

shutterstock.com

Checklist Ideas

Your goal is to provide a main point that names your subject and purpose and then to support the main point effectively.

____ **1.** Is my **subject** important and relevant?

____ **2.** Does my message have a solid **purpose**?

____ **3.** Is my **main point** clear?

____ **4.** Have I **qualified** my main point, if necessary?

____ **5.** Does my support **answer** the reader's main questions (5 W's and H)?

____ **6.** Have I used a variety of **details** to support my main point?

- ☐ Definitions to clarify meanings
- ☐ Examples to demonstrate ideas
- ☐ Facts, statistics, and graphs to create credibility
- ☐ Anecdotes to connect to life
- ☐ Predictions to imagine outcomes
- ☐ Needs of the audience to persuade them
- ☐ Answers to objections to convince the audience
- ☐ Comparisons to show similarities
- ☐ Contrasts to show differences
- ☐ Quotations to appeal to authority
- ☐ Sensations to engage my audience

shutterstock.com

2
Trait 2: Organization

It's no mistake that a business may also be called an organization. A business that is well organized will most likely be profitable, and a business that is poorly organized will most likely fail.

The same goes for communication. A well-organized message clearly and convincingly communicates its ideas, while a poorly organized message only confuses and frustrates the reader or listener.

Organization deals with the overall structure of a message, the order of its parts, and the transitions that tie it all together. This chapter focuses on organization, outlines specific problems with organization, and provides concrete solutions.

Organization: An Overview

Organization deals with the overall structure of communication as well as the order of its parts. Effective communication has a three-part structure—an opening, a middle, and a closing. The following graphic discusses the role of these three important parts in a message.

U-g-g-B-o-y (Photograph World Sense) from Flickr

Tip Three-part structure isn't an academic invention. Everything that is experienced in a specific sequence has this structure: a phone call, a conversation, an e-mail, a movie, a novel, a concert, a game—even a class or a date.

Opening: Introduces the Message
- Addresses the audience.
- Provides background.
- Introduces the subject.
- States the main point (most messages).

Middle: Develops the Message
- Provides details.
- Offers information.
- States the main point (bad news).
- Answers the reader's questions.
- Orders the support appropriately.

Closing: Concludes the Message
- Sums up the message.
- Provides an important final thought.
- Calls the reader to act.
- States the main point (persuasive messages).

Patterns of Organization

When arranging details within the middle of a message, you have many options. Choose the organizational pattern that best fits your content. Here are common patterns and transitions.

Pattern	How It Works	Transition Groups		
Time	Move chronologically from start to finish.	first second third last	start by continue with be sure to finish by	to begin afterward next finally
Location	Move from near to far, left to right, or top to bottom.	in front beyond that next in line at the back	on the left next to it in the middle on the right	at the top in the middle below that at the bottom
Classification	Split topic into categories and deal with one at a time.	one type another type the third type the last type	group 1 group 2 group 3 group 4	a common variety a second variety a rare variety the rarest variety
Importance	Move from most important to least or from least to most.	the biggest reason another reason in addition a final reason	first of all secondly furthermore most importantly	to begin additionally significantly certainly
Deduction/ Induction	Move from specific to general or from general to specific.	generally in some cases an example one specific	a case study similar studies studies agree we can conclude	the rule states we would expect looking closer the evidence shows
Compare/ Contrast	Examine the similarities of and the differences between two subjects.	as/like similarly in the same way likewise also	however in contrast nevertheless though but/yet/still	both neither on the one hand on the other hand by comparison
Cause/Effect	Outline the causes and effects of a situation.	because due to the reason the catalyst	as a result consequently the outcome the conclusion	whenever once from then on in consequence

Organization: Problems and Solutions

Organization makes ideas accessible. Disorganization hides ideas. The following pages help you identify and solve problems with organization.

Problem:	Solution:
The opening is weak. *Listen for:* ▪ "I read the first part but didn't go on." ▪ "I wasn't sure what it was about."	**Use effective opening strategies.** In the opening, **establish** the purpose of your writing and get the reader's attention. Do one or more of the following. ▪ Greet the reader/listener. Get the reader's attention with a question, a quotation, or a surprising statement. ▪ State your main point (for most messages). (See page 11 for a main-point formula.) ▪ Give background details and context. ▪ Define key terms. ▪ Preview the message contents: map out where you are going.
The middle is disorganized. *Listen for:* ▪ "I couldn't follow the message."	**Follow a pattern.** **Organize** details according to a logical pattern—time, location, classification, importance, deduction, induction, comparison/contrast, or cause/effect. (See page 19 for an explanation of each.)
The details aren't accessible. *Listen for:* ▪ "It's so dense." ▪ "I got lost."	**Use short paragraphs, lists, and graphics.** **Organize** the middle with these elements: ▪ Write short paragraphs, each focused on one supporting point. ▪ Use lists to make details accessible. If items are ranked, use a numbered list. Use bullets if items are equal in importance. ▪ Include graphics such as charts, tables, illustrations, or photos to make information easy to access.
The closing is weak. *Listen for:* ▪ "I didn't know what to do next." ▪ "It just kind of ended."	**Use effective closing strategies.** **Focus** on outcomes, actions, and the future: ▪ Explain how to use information. ▪ State conclusions and recommendations. ▪ Review next steps and call the reader to act. ▪ Provide contact information. ▪ Look forward to future contact.

Problem:

I have trouble with overall organization.

Listen for:

- "I had to review the message a couple times to get it."
- "What's the point of this message?"

Solution:

Start with your main point and provide support.

For good or neutral news, **organize** your message this way:

- **Opening:** State your main point.
- **Middle:** Explain your main point, supporting it with details.
- **Closing:** Call the reader or listener to act: lay out next steps.

▶ Main Point

Remember **SEA**—**S**ituation (main point), **E**xplanation, **A**ction.

| Send | Attach | Fonts | Colors | Save As Draft |

To: Grant Bostwick

Cc:

Subject: Your Credit Approved at Cottonwood Hills Greenhouse

Dear Mr. Bostwick:

Thank you for requesting a credit account at Cottonwood Hills Greenhouse and Florist Supply. We are pleased to extend you $100,000 in credit based on Dale's Garden Center's strong financial condition. Congratulations!

Here are some details concerning your account:
1. You will be billed the first day of the month.
2. The balance is due within 30 days, interest free.
3. Any balance owed beyond 30 days will be subject to a 15 percent annual finance charge.

Attached is a document describing in more detail our credit policies and procedures. Please call me (655-555-3321) if you have any questions.

Because you indicated that you plan to expand your sales of bedding plants and silk flowers, I am also sending by mail our spring catalog with these sections flagged. Mr. Bostwick, we look forward to filling your orders and satisfying your customers. Count on us to help Dale's flourish!

Sincerely,

Salome Nguru
Sales Manager

Problem:

I have a hard time delivering bad news.

Listen for:

- "You could've been nicer about it."
- "Your message made me furious."

Solution:

Place your main point in the middle.

To deliver bad news, don't start with your main point (the bad news). **Use** the following structure:

- **Opening**: Start with a buffer, a neutral statement that focuses on the positive.
- **Middle**: Provide an explanation leading up to the main point (the bad news).
- **Closing**: Exit cleanly, looking toward future collaboration or ending the relationship politely.

Remember **BEBE**—**B**uffer, **E**xplanation, **B**ad news (main point), **E**xit.

MEMORANDUM

Date: July 21, 2010
To: All Staff
From: Lawrence Durante, President   *LD*
Subject: Recent FDA Plant Inspection

As you know, this past Friday, July 16, the FDA came to our plant for a spot inspection. I'm writing to share the inspection results and our response.

The good news is that the FDA inspectors did not find problems warranting a shutdown of Premium Meats. The bad news is that the inspectors cited us for three major violations resulting in a fine of $90,000.

The FDA is sending us a clear message. We must take immediate steps to protect our customers, our jobs, and our company. To that end, I have taken the following steps:

1. The Executive Committee met with me to review the FDA report and determine the problem areas in our production process.
2. I have directed the Production Management Team to review quality-control procedures and conduct two retraining sessions immediately.
3. I have appointed a Quality Task Force of both management and production staff to study the production process and make further recommendations.

If you have suggestions or questions, please speak to your immediate supervisor. Together, we can correct these problems.

Problem:

I have a hard time persuading people.

Listen for:

- ▪ "I don't buy it."
- ▪ "Nice try, but I'm not interested."

Solution:

Lead up to your main point at the end.

To persuade, don't start with your main point (your persuasive pitch). **Build up** to it. Use the following structure:

- ▪ **Opening:** Grab the reader's attention, focusing on her or his needs.
- ▪ **Middle:** Build interest and desire.
- ▪ **Closing:** Call the reader to act, giving your main point (the persuasive pitch).

▶ Main Point

Remember **AIDA**—**A**ttention, **I**nterest, **D**esire, **A**ction (main point).

March 15, 2010

Ms. April Wadsworth
Belles Lettres Books
The Harbor Mall
Bar Harbor, ME 04609-3427

Dear Ms. Wadsworth:

Does your store or office have a bare wall or corner that needs a painting, photograph, or sculpture? We can help!

For 14 years, your Hancock County Arts Council has sponsored ArtBurst—a fair in which artists sell their work. Last year, ArtBurst attracted more than 90 artists and 15,000 visitors. This year, the fair will be in Central Park on Saturday, May 1.

The Purchase Awards Program, supported by local businesses, is key to ArtBurst's success. Business people like you join the program by agreeing to purchase artwork. Your commitment helps us attract better artists and more visitors. And you personally win in two ways. First, you get a beautiful print, painting, drawing, photograph, or sculpture of your choice to decorate your business. Second, all ArtBurst publicity materials advertise your business.

So please join the Purchase Awards Program! Just complete the enclosed form and return it in the postage-paid envelope by April 15.

Yours sincerely,

Lawrence King

Lawrence King, Director

Enclosure: Purchase Awards Program form

"Don't agonize.
Organize."

—Floryne
Kennedy

Checklist Organization

Your goal is to organize the overall structure of your message as well as the individual details in it.

_____ **1.** Does my message include an **opening**, a **middle**, and a **closing**?

_____ **2.** Does my message use the best formula? (**SEA, BEBE,** or **AIDA**)?
- **Most Messages: SEA**—Situation, Explanation, Action
- **Bad News: BEBE**—Buffer, Explanation, Bad News, Exit
- **Persuasion: AIDA**—Attention, Interest and Desire, Action

Organization

| Opening |
| Middle |
| Closing |

_____ **3.** Does the **opening** grab attention and state my purpose?
- Addressing the audience
- Providing background
- Introducing the subject

_____ **4.** Does the **middle** use a clear **pattern of organization**?
- Developing the main point
- Providing details
- Answering questions the audience may have
- Using an appropriate organization plan

_____ **5.** Do transitions help the reader follow my message?

_____ **6.** Have I included **lists** as appropriate?

_____ **7.** Does the **ending** focus on outcomes?
- Revisiting the main point
- Providing an important final thought

shutterstock.com

shutterstock.com

3
Trait 3: Voice

Voice may be hard to define, but it's easy to recognize. "Don't use that tone of voice" is often our response to a sarcastic, angry, or otherwise inappropriate tone. We may also respond negatively to an e-mail with an unprofessional voice.

A professional voice, on the other hand, reflects well on the subject, audience, and writer and elicits a positive response from the reader. To achieve such a voice, use natural language and avoid negativity.

This chapter provides an overview of voice and then focuses on specific problems with voice and solutions for fixing the problems.

Voice: An Overview

Human beings are hardwired to read facial expressions. Just by looking at people's faces, we can tell who they are and what they are feeling. And it's the same with people's "voices." Whether in speech or in writing, the voice is unique, revealing personality, intelligence, and self-image. Voice also reveals a wealth of information about each part of the communication situation, as shown in the following chart.

Andrew Wippler from Flickr

Voice in the Communication Situation

1. Sender: Voice reveals personality and position, telling who the person is or thinks he or she is. Business-like voice is positive and professional.

2. Message: Voice reveals how the person feels about the main point of the message. Businesslike voice is confident and in control.

3. Medium: Voice reveals the sender's mastery and comfort level with the medium. Businesslike voice is natural.

4. Receiver: Voice reveals the sender's relationship with the receiver, how close they are, and what roles they play. Businesslike voice is constructive and courteous.

5. Context: Voice reflects the history of the situation and the current climate. Businesslike voice is engaged and practical.

Fyi Voice can be described using adjectives that distinguish personality—*friendly, confident, humorous, clever,* and so on.

Three Levels of Formality

Like business attire, business voice comes in three levels of formality: formal, semiformal, and informal. Just as you would match clothing to an event—whether a formal meeting or an informal office picnic—you should match voice to the situation as well.

Formal	Semiformal	Informal
A formal voice is serious, dignified, deliberate, and objective. It avoids contractions and uses few if any personal pronouns.	A semiformal voice is friendly, natural, personable, and conversational. It uses occasional contractions and some personal pronouns.	An informal voice uses frequent contractions and personal pronouns and may contain humor or slang; avoid it in business writing
Sender • Any employee	**Sender** • Any employee	**Sender** • Any employee
Message • Official business • Legal business • Bad news	**Message** • Everyday business • Good news • Persuasion	**Message** • Personal business • Prewriting • Thoughts
Medium • Major document • Formal letter • Résumé • Report • Proposal • Instructions • Memo	**Medium** • Minor document • Sales letter • E-mail • Blog post • Podcast • Meeting minutes • Forums	**Medium** • Unofficial document • Personal notes • List • Sketch • Text message • Social media • Chat room
Receiver • Superiors • Unfamiliar people outside company	**Receiver** • Subordinates • Familiar people outside company	**Receiver** • Colleagues • Close contacts outside the company
Context • Serious situations	**Context** • Typical situations	**Context** • Social situations

 Tip Analyze the writing situation and see which voice best matches the message, medium, receiver, and context. Avoid using an informal voice in business writing.

Voice: Problems and Solutions

An effective voice matches the communication situation and gets your point across. An inappropriate voice can get you fired. The following pages will help you diagnose problems with voice and solve them.

Problem:

People say I come across as negative.

Listen for:

■ "Why are you so annoyed?"

■ "How about some team spirit?"

■ "You're making a bad situation worse."

Look for:

■ Youngstown Microchip used to know how to pack an order, but now you can't get a single shipment out on time with the right stuff in it. Your warehouse supervisor, Nick Luther, ought to be fired, or maybe Rankin Technologies will fire your whole company. We don't have to work with clowns who can't even fill an order. You guys better make this right.

Solution:

Focus on the positive.

Focus on what can be done, not what can't. Even in a bad situation, a voice that focuses on the positive rather than on the negative helps keep business moving forward.

Focus ON

■ **the subject—not on** the personalities. Avoid a judgmental tone.

■ **solutions—not on** problems. Be the solution person, not the problem person.

■ **the future—not on** the past. Use the past merely to provide a context for moving forward.

■ **strengths—not on** weaknesses. Capitalize on the opportunity to bridge or address any weak spots.

■ **cooperation—not on** antagonism. Move beyond personal agendas and consider how you can help resolve the situation.

■ **suggestions—not on** threats. Avoid threatening language, which hampers clear thinking. Suggestions cultivate new ideas.

■ **positive words—not on** negative words. Foster the "can do" attitude by marking successes and using encouraging words.

Positive Voice: Rankin Technologies has always valued our partnership with Youngstown Microchip. Within the last six months, however, late shipments and incorrectly filled orders have impacted our working relationship. Rankin Technologies would appreciate an opportunity to discuss future shipments with the warehouse supervisor.

Tip When the message includes bad news, avoid personal pronouns, especially *you* and *your.* They can create an accusatory tone. Notice how the use of *you* and *your* in the "Look for" example above pits the writer against the reader.

Problem:	**Solution:**
People say I sound arrogant.	**Tone down your message.**

Problem:

People say I sound arrogant.

Listen for:

- "You're full of yourself."

Look for:

- Forget those other carpet-cleaning services with their so-called experts and shoddy machines. We get every carpet clean.

People think I lack confidence.

Listen for:

- "You sound doubtful."

Look for:

- You probably haven't heard of Cooper's Carpet Cleaners, but if you want to, maybe you could give us a try.

I sound overly emotional.

Listen for:

- "Calm down."

Look for:

- I said no more two-hour meetings! That costs a fortune! Stick to the agenda, and if you don't have one, MAKE ONE!

Solution:

Tone down your message.

Do the following to create a reasonable voice:

- Avoid praising yourself.
- Avoid absolute claims.
- Focus on facts.
- Provide what the receiver needs.
- Don't tear others down.

Reasonable Voice: Cooper's Carpet Cleaners use continuous-flow extraction with power wands to guarantee the best results.

Create confidence.

Do the following to sound confident:

- Avoid an apologetic tone.
- Focus on facts.
- Avoid unnecessary qualifiers (*maybe, probably*).
- Stand behind your statements and your work.

Confident Voice: Cooper's Carpet Cleaners are the new kids on the block, but we're determined to prove our value with clean carpets and friendly service.

Focus on business, not on feelings.

Control your emotions, especially in challenging situations. Becoming emotional only decreases your power rather than increasing it.

Controlled Emotion: In order to keep meetings short and productive, the chair must have a prepared agenda. Please provide the agenda prior to the meeting.

Problem:
My voice sounds stiff.

Listen for:

accordingly	so
according to our records	our records show
acquaint	tell
adhere	stick
afford an opportunity	allow/permit
along the lines of	like
applicable to	apply to
apprise	tell
are in receipt of	have received
are of the opinion that	think that
ascertain	learn/find out
as per	according to
as regards	regarding
awaiting your instructions	please let me know
call your attention to	please note
case in point	example
ceased functioning	quit working
cognizant	aware
commence	begin
concur	agree
configuration	shape
disbursements	payments
do not hesitate to	please
due consideration	careful thought
endeavor	try
enumerate	list
evacuate	leave
expedite	speed up
fabricate	make
facilitate	make easier
finalize	settle/finish
fluctuate	vary
herein	in this
heretofore	until now
in accordance with	as

Solution:
Use natural expressions.

Listen for:

inasmuch as	as/because
increment	amount/step
indispensable	vital
in lieu of	instead of
in the amount of	for
kindly	please
manifest	show
manipulate	operate
modification	change
necessitate	require
on a daily basis	daily
paradigm shift	major change
parameter	limit
per se	as such
personnel reduction	layoffs
per your request	as requested
precipitate	cause
preliminary to	before
prioritize	rank
procure	buy/get
pursuant to	following up
quantify	measure/count
ramification	result
recapitulate	review
remuneration	pay
reproduction	copy
salient	important
strategize	plan/solve
subsequent	later/after
terminate	end
under separate cover	separately
utilize	use
vacillate	waver
visualize	picture
wherewithal	means

Problem:	**Solution:**

People's feelings get hurt when I offer criticism.

Listen for:

■ "You think I'm stupid."

Look for:

■ Don't you guys have any idea how to create a good carton? You sure don't change the color scheme and hide the logo!

Make your criticism constructive.

Focus on improving processes and building teams, not on derailing processes and tearing down teams.

■ Focus on issues, not personalities.
■ Expect improvement.
■ Create a team atmosphere.
■ Begin with the positive before you criticize.

- - - - *Constructive Criticism:* The team's carton design is eye catching, but the color scheme needs to match that of the competition and needs to more clearly include the logo.

I've been told I'm too abrupt.

Listen for:

■ "Don't be rude."
■ "You're so insensitive."

Look for:

■ To Whom It May Concern:

Boniface specializes in waste removal and recycling. Our rates are available on our Web site. You need better garbage removal. From what I heard, the recycling guys are ripping you off.

Give me a call: 303-555-2356.

Think of your audience and use courtesy.

Think first of the receiver. How will the person feel about your message? Encouraged? Discouraged? Helped? Threatened? Informed? Overwhelmed? Energized? Write with the receiver's feelings in mind.

■ Use *please* and *thank you.*
■ Use *we, us,* and *ours* to include (not exclude) the audience.
■ Use appropriate courtesy titles (*Mr., Ms., Dr.*)
■ Treat names with respect and spell them properly.
■ Focus on the receiver's needs.

- - - - *Sensitive Voice:*

Dear Ms. Grey:

Thank you for the chance to bid on Millwood Inc.'s waste removal and recycling needs. We are pleased to offer

• one eight-cubic-yard container for regular refuse, serviced twice a week.
• one eight-cubic-yard container for cardboard, serviced once a week.
• one billing a month at $169.

We would like to add you to our list of satisfied customers. Please call me at 303-555-2356.

"A loud
voice cannot
compete with
a clear voice,
even if it's a
whisper."

—Barry Neil
Kaufman

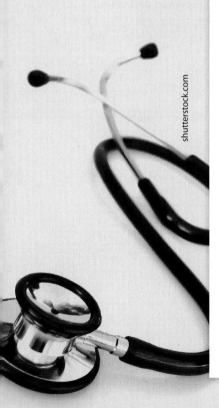

shutterstock.com

Checklist Voice

Your goal is to use a voice that matches the communication situation: sender, message, medium, receiver, and context.

_____ **1.** Does the voice represent **me** well?
 ☐ Professional and polished
 ☐ Smart and committed

_____ **2.** Does the voice show my connection to the **subject**?
 ☐ Knowledgeable and clear
 ☐ Positive and serious

_____ **3.** Does the voice show my **purpose**?
 ☐ Informative or persuasive
 ☐ Engaging

_____ **4.** Does the voice show mastery of the **medium**?
 ☐ Natural and easy
 ☐ Effective and accomplished

_____ **5.** Does the voice connect with the **reader**?
 ☐ Polite and friendly
 ☐ Formal or semiformal

_____ **6.** Does the voice fit the **context**?
 ☐ Routine or unique
 ☐ Public or confidential

_____ **7.** Is the voice **professional**?
 ☐ Positive
 ☐ Confident
 ☐ Constructive
 ☐ Calm

shutterstock.com

4
Trait 4: Words

Take a lesson from the three little pigs: Just as a house built of straw or sticks cannot stand against the wind, writing containing poor, dull words cannot deliver a strong message. A house built of bricks, however, stands firm; and writing containing rich, interesting words delivers a powerful message.

Work at building your messages with "bricks"—words that are concrete, strong, and well-connected to other words around them. Cut out deadwood, slang, cliches, redundancy, and puffed-up language.

This chapter will help you recognize which words to cut from your writing and which words to add.

Words: An Overview

The fewer words you use to express an idea, the better. That kind of economy necessitates careful choosing. Certainly, you can write down or key in the first words that come to mind, but always be willing to change them.

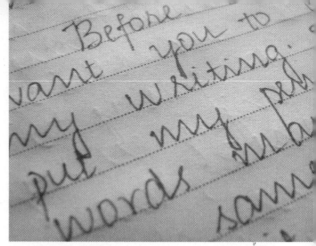

Specific Nouns, Verbs, and Adjectives

When selecting words for a message, choose the most precise word for each situation. General nouns, verbs, and modifiers create vague, confusing messages. Specific language makes your message clear and effective.

Manoj Vasanth from Flickr

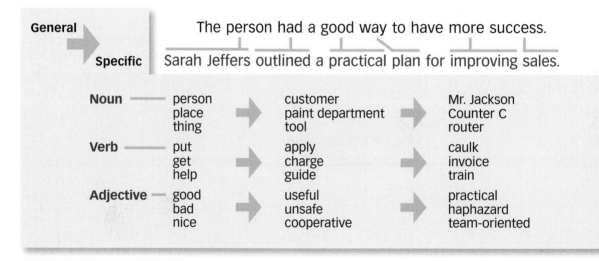

General → The person had a good way to have more success.

Specific → Sarah Jeffers outlined a practical plan for improving sales.

Noun	person place thing	→	customer paint department tool	→	Mr. Jackson Counter C router
Verb	put get help	→	apply charge guide	→	caulk invoice train
Adjective	good bad nice	→	useful unsafe cooperative	→	practical haphazard team-oriented

Active/Passive Verbs

- A verb is active when the subject of the sentence performs the action. —— The committee recommends a new marketing approach.
- A verb is passive when the subject of the sentence receives the action. —— A new marketing approach is being recommended.
- Use active verbs for most messages. —— All Farm Insurance seeks to serve you. (direct)
- Use passive verbs for bad news or to direct attention away from the subject. —— Your insurance coverage is being canceled. (indirect)

Words: Problems and Solutions

Strong word choice creates clear communication. Weak word choice derails your message. The following pages help you recognize and fix problems with word choice.

Problem:	Solution:
The message isn't clear. *Listen for:* ■ "Can you be more specific?"	**Use specific nouns, verbs, and adjectives.** **Select** the most specific word for each situation. See the facing page for examples of general and specific words and the way they affect writing.
The words are sluggish. *Listen for:* ■ "This is boring."	**Change passive voice to active voice.** **Revise** the sentence so that the subject performs the action. See the facing page for examples.
The bad-news messages sound too blunt. *Listen for:* ■ "You're insensitive."	**Use a passive voice to soften the message.** **Use passive voice** for bad news, diverting emphasis from the sender onto the message.
The writing sounds unprofessional. *Listen for:* ■ "Take out the slang." *Look for:* ■ Our goal is to cut you in on some cool deals and hot service. *Listen for:* ■ "That's a cliche." *Look for:* ■ The lawn application includes fertilizer and insecticide, killing two birds with one stone.	**Avoid slang and cliches.** **Avoid slang,** which is informal language that becomes popular, is widely used, and then falls out of style. Using it undercuts your thinking, excludes receivers unfamiliar with the expression, and quickly dates the message. Also avoid overused expressions, or cliches. *Professional:* Our goal is to provide you the best service at the best price. *Professional:* The lawn application both fertilizes the ground and kills insect pests.

Problem:
The message is wordy/artificial.

Listen for:

advance forward	**advance**
advance planning	**planning**
a majority of	**most**
any and all	**any/all**
are of the opinion that	**believe**
ask the question	**ask**
assembled together	**assembled**
at an early date	**soon**
attach together	**attach**
at the conclusion of	**after/following**
at the present time	**now**
based on the fact that	**because**
basic essentials	**essentials**
both together	**together**
brief in duration	**brief**
close proximity	**close**
combine together	**combine**
completely unanimous	**unanimous**
connect together	**connect**
consensus of opinion	**consensus**
descend down	**descend**
despite the fact that	**although**
disregard altogether	**disregard**
due to the fact that	**because**
during the course of	**during**
end result	**result**
engaged in a study of	**studying**
few in number	**few**
filled to capacity	**filled**
final conclusion	**conclusion**
final outcome	**outcome**
first and foremost	**first/foremost**
foreign imports	**imports**
for the purpose of	**for**
for the reasons that	**because**
free gift	**gift**

Solution:
Use plain language: Avoid long, wordy phrases.

Listen for:

free of charge	**free**
having the capacity to	**can**
in connection with	**about**
in light of the fact that	**since**
in order to	**to**
in spite of the fact that	**although**
in the amount of	**for**
in the event that	**if**
in the vast majority	**most**
in view of the fact that	**because**
it is often the case that	**often**
it is our opinion that	**we believe that**
it is our recommendation	**we recommend**
it is our understanding	**we understand**
joint cooperation	**cooperation**
join together	**join**
joint partnership	**partnership**
main essentials	**essentials**
make reference to	**refer to**
meet together	**meet**
mutual cooperation	**cooperation**
of the opinion that	**think that**
on a daily basis	**daily**
on a weekly basis	**weekly**
on the grounds that	**because**
over again	**again**
personal in nature	**personal**
personal opinion	**opinion**
pertaining to	**about**
plan ahead	**plan**
postponed until later	**postponed**
present status	**status**
prior to	**before**
repeat again	**repeat**
until such time as	**until**
with regard to	**about**

Problem:	Solution:
The language sounds pompous and fake.	**Use plain English.**

Use plain English.

Avoid pompous language, which some people use to sound "important." Pompous language actually makes you sound fake and silly. Plain English does a much better job of communicating.

Listen for:

- "Sounds like a lecture."

Look for:

- In accordance with managerial policy, attached hereto is an enclosure that contains highly informative delineations of policies and procedures pertaining to credit.

– – – – *Plain:* I have enclosed a brochure that describes our credit policies and procedures in more detail.

There are too many words.

Listen for:

- "Your message is bloated."

Look for:

- The plant must go through a thorough retooling process necessary for producing the most recent additions to the new line of competitive products.

Cut deadwood.

Watch for and cut irrelevant information, obvious statements, and awkward phrases. Also cut wordy phrases or clauses that could be replaced by concise words.

– – – – *Concise:* The plant must retool to produce competitive products.

The message is confusing.

Listen for:

- "The message has inaccuracies."

Look for:

- I completed the installment of the 200-watt electrical server for the customer at 311 Marten Luthar King Drive.

Double-check fact-words.

Double-check fact-words—names, key terms, and other facts. A message that makes mistakes with fact-words confuses instead of communicating.

– – – – *Correct:* I completed the installation of the 220-amp electrical service for the customer at 311 Martin Luther King Jr. Drive.

Problem:	Solution:

People say the message is ageist.

Listen for:
- "That's ageism."

Use accepted words when you refer to age.

Use terms of respect when referring to age. Mention age only when it is necessary to the issue.
- **boys, girls** (up to ages 13 or 14)
- **youth, young people** (between 13 and 17)
- **young adults** (late teens and 20's)
- **adults** (30's to 60's)
- **older adults** (60 and older)

People say the message is sexist.

Listen for:
- "That's sexism."

Use accepted words when you refer to gender.

Use terms of respect when you refer gender. Mention gender only when it is necessary. Take special care when dealing with occupations, courtesy titles, and salutations.
- **chair, presiding officer, moderator** (not chairman)
- **sales representative, salesperson** (not salesman)
- **mail carrier, postal worker** (not mailman)
- **executive, manager, worker** (not businessman)

People say the message is racist.

Listen for:
- "That's racism."

Use accepted words when you refer to race.

Use respectful language that gives equal value and respect to all races and ethnicities. Mention race only when it is central to the issue.

General	Specific
Native Americans	Cherokee people, Inuit people
Asian Americans	Chinese Americans, Korean Americans
Hispanic Americans	Mexican Americans, Cuban Americans
African Americans	This term has wide acceptance, though the term "black" is preferred by some individuals. "Person of color" is also used to mean "nonwhite."

People say the message is insensitive to those with disabilities.

Listen for:
- "That's insensitive."

Use accepted words when you refer to ability.

Refer to the person first and to the disability second. Mention ability only when it is the central issue. Use the following accepted terms.
- **person with HIV/AIDS** (not AIDS victim)
- **person with autism** (not autistic)
- **person with a disability** (not handicapped)

Problem:

Bilingual people don't understand the message.

Listen for:

- "I don't understand."

Solution:

Use clear language and avoid cultural pitfalls.

Here are tips for communicating with those who come from different language and cultural backgrounds:

- **Avoid cultural references.** Be careful with references to people, places, and events specific to a culture. These may confuse or alienate your reader. Specifically, avoid sports, pop culture, religious, and military references.

- **Avoid jargon, slang, idioms, acronyms, and abbreviations.** Such shorthand has a restricted use that may confuse bilingual readers. Use plain English instead.

- **Use simple, objective words.** Avoid words that have emotional or historical baggage. Use nouns with clear meanings and verbs that express a clear action. However, don't confuse simplicity with a condescending tone: Don't write as if your reader were a child.

- **Use clear, obvious transitions.** At the beginnings of paragraphs and sentences, use obvious transitions like *however, in addition, first, second,* and so on, whenever appropriate. Such transitions highlight relationships between statements and help bilingual readers follow your thoughts.

- **Be grammatically correct.** Spelling errors, misplaced modifiers, sentence fragments, and faulty comma usage can confuse bilingual readers. Be especially careful with spelling. When a name or word includes accents or other diacritical marks, make sure that you use them.

- **Keep sentences and paragraphs short**. Avoid long, complex sentences (more than 15 words) and big, intimidating paragraphs (8 lines or longer). Such sentences and paragraphs are challenging for some bilingual readers.

- **Use Standard English.** Not all English is the same. For example, American English is different from Canadian, British, and Australian English. Bilingual readers will have the most success reading Standard English.

- **CAUTION: Avoid humor.** Cultural differences present ready opportunities for unintended offense. Humor does not translate well from one culture to another.

shutterstock.com

> "In good writing, words become one with things."
>
> —Ralph Waldo Emerson

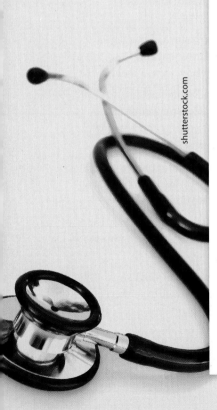

shutterstock.com

Checklist Words

Your goal is to select words that best express your ideas, using plain English and respecting diversity.

____ **1.** Have I used **specific nouns, verbs,** and **adjectives**?

____ **2.** Have I used **active verbs** to be direct and **passive verbs** to be indirect?

____ **3.** Have I used **concise rather than wordy** phrasing?

____ **4.** Have I **avoided unprofessional expressions**?

- ☐ Rewording slang
- ☐ Stating cliches in fresh language
- ☐ Avoiding euphemisms

____ **5.** Do I use **plain English**?

- ☐ Avoiding pompous language

____ **6.** Have I used **fair, respectful language**?

- ☐ Respecting age
- ☐ Respecting ability
- ☐ Respecting gender
- ☐ Respecting ethnicity

____ **7.** Have I used **plain, clear wording** for bilingual readers?

____ **8.** Have I **cut unnecessary phrases** and clauses?

- ☐ Removing deadwood

____ **9.** Have I used **correct key terms,** names, numbers, facts, and easily confused words?

____ **10.** Have I **avoided humor** or other nuanced and potentially misleading language?

shutterstock.com

5
Trait 5: Sentences

Sentences are the workhorses of communication. Any unit that is smaller than a sentence contains only a fragment of thought:

in infamy   shall live   this day

But a sentence combines those fragments into a complete thought:

This day shall live in infamy.

A sentence can be short or long. It can state a fact or ask a question, make a command or express emotion, or even show the relationship between two situations. That's a lot for the lowly sentence to accomplish. This chapter will show how it's done.

Sentences: An Overview

A sentence is basically a connection between a noun (the subject) and a verb (the predicate). The subject tells what the sentence is about, and the predicate tells what the subject is doing or being. All of the other words in a sentence simply modify the subject or the predicate. Sentences have different functions and structures.

shutterstock.com

How Sentences Function

Sentences perform different jobs—they make statements, ask questions, give commands, and so on. Here are the basic functions.

Function	
Statement A statement tells something about a person, a place, a thing or an idea.	The fourth-quarter earnings report has improved.
Question A question requests information from the reader or listener.	Does the report reflect the company's new marketing effort?
Command A command tells people what to do, using the understood subject *you*. **Note:** A command is the only kind of sentence that can have an understood subject.	Review the report in detail.
Exclamation An exclamation expresses emotion or surprise.	This is a great report!
Conditional A conditional sentence shows that one circumstance depends on another. It uses a word such as *if, when,* or *unless* to show the dependent relationship.	If the first-quarter earnings continue to improve, we should reinvest.

How Sentences Are Structured

Sentences have different structures. They can be simple, compound, complex, or compound-complex. Here are the basic structures.

Structure

Simple A simple sentence is made up of a subject (or subjects) and a predicate (or predicates). A simple sentence is an independent clause.	The meeting concluded. 　(Single subject: *meeting*; single verb: *concluded*) Anika and Tamlyn nearly fell asleep. 　(Compound subject: *Anika* and *Tamlyn*; single verb: *fell*) Bob and Tom talked and debated endlessly. 　(Compound subject: *Bob* and *Tom*; compound verb: *talked* and *debated*)
Compound A compound sentence is made up of two simple sentences. They are joined by either a semicolon or a comma and a coordinating conjunction *(and, but, or, nor, for, so, yet)*.	We reached a decision; we should have fewer meetings. 　(Two simple sentences joined with a semicolon) Bob agreed with this idea, but Tom debated it. 　(Two simple sentences joined with a comma and the coordinating conjunction *but*)
Complex A complex sentence contains one simple sentence (independent clause) and one or more dependent clauses, which begin with a subordinating conjunction *(though, because, whenever,* and so on) or a relative pronoun *(who, which, that).*	Whenever we asked Tom to stop debating, he objected. 　(Dependent clause beginning with the subordinating conjunction *whenever*) Tom, who can craft a good argument, had more to say. 　(Dependent clause beginning with the relative pronoun *who*)
Compound Complex A compound-complex sentence contains two or more independent and one or more dependent clauses.	Though Tom was still talking, Bob called to adjourn, and I seconded. 　(One dependent and two independent clauses)

Sentences: Problems and Solutions

Sentences are the pack mules of communication: They carry meaning. Strong sentences get your meaning across, and weak sentences leave it behind. These pages provide strategies for solving sentence problems.

Problem:	Solution:
The sentences are repetitive. *Listen for:* ▪ "They all start alike."	**Vary the beginning of sentences.** **Start** some sentences with the **subject**, others with a prepositional or verbal **phrase**, and others with a dependent **clause**. Vary the beginnings so that your writing doesn't sound predictable.
The writing is halting. *Listen for:* ▪ "This isn't smooth."	**Vary the length of sentences.** **Use short** sentences to make a point. Use **medium** sentences for most information. Use **long** sentences for more complex ideas.
The sentences don't engage the reader. *Listen for:* ▪ "I lost interest."	**Vary the function of sentences.** **Use** a variety of sentence functions. (See page 42.) If your sentences are all statements—providing information—the receiver may become bored. ▪ **Statements** (present facts) ▪ **Questions** (elicit information) ▪ **Commands** (call the receiver to act) ▪ **Exclamations** (express [positive] emotion) ▪ **Conditionals** (show relationships between situations)
The sentences all sound the same. *Listen for:* ▪ "This sounds repetitive."	**Vary the structure of sentences.** **Use** a variety of sentence structures. (See page 43.) If you have too many simple sentences, your writing will sound choppy and your thinking will seem limited. ▪ **Simple sentences** (present information in the most direct way) ▪ **Compound sentences** (connect two equal ideas) ▪ **Complex sentences** (show a relationship between two ideas) ▪ **Compound-complex** (show relationships between three or more ideas)

Problem:	Solution:
Two sentences sound choppy. *Listen for:* ▪ "Smooth this down." *Look for:* ▪ The inspector checked the roof. Some shingles had moss.	**Combine two equal ideas.** If you want two sentences to have equal importance, **connect** them with a comma and a coordinating conjunction (*and, but, or, nor, for, so, yet*). *Combined:* The inspector checked the roof, and some shingles had moss.
Three sentences sound choppy. (equal ideas) *Listen for:* ▪ "That sounds choppy and confusing." *Look for:* ▪ Some shingles had moss. A few were cracked. The flashings were worn out.	**Combine three or more equal ideas.** If you want three or more sentences to have equal importance, **make a series**. Place a comma after each sentence (except the last), and insert a coordinating conjunction (*and, but, or, nor, for, so, yet*) before the last sentence. *Combined:* Some shingles had moss, a few were cracked, and the flashings were worn out.
The sentences sound simplistic. *Listen for:* ▪ "What's the point of this?" *Look for:* ▪ We need a new roof. I will get quotes.	**Combine two unequal ideas.** If you want to emphasize one sentence over the other, **combine** them using a subordinating conjunction. Place the conjunction at the beginning of the less important sentence. If that sentence comes first, place a comma after it. *Combined:* Because we need a new roof, I will get quotes. ———— or ———— I will get quotes because we need a new roof. **Subordinating Conjunctions:** *after, although, as, as if, as long as, as though, because, before, if, in order that, provided that, since, so that, that, though, till, unless, until, when, where, whereas, while*

Problem:	Solution:

The sentences feel sluggish.

Listen for:

- ▪ "This part is just blah."

Look for:

- ▪ We had a discussion of the incident and made the discovery that accidents were frequent.

Use strong verbs.

Avoid weak verbs such as *do, have,* and *make.* They often hide a more interesting verb in the direct object. Turn the direct object into a verb form, and eliminate the weak verb.

Strengthened: We discussed the incident and discovered that accidents were frequent.

The sentences are passive.

Listen for:

- ▪ "This sounds tired."

Look for:

- ▪ If a meeting is missed, Richard should be notified.

Use active verbs.

Change *be* verbs and passive verbs into active verbs. An active verb tells what the subject is doing. A passive verb tells what is happening to the subject.

Energized: If you *miss* a meeting, you *should notify* Richard.

The sentences lack information.

Listen for:

- ▪ "Be specific."

Look for:

- ▪ The department will meet to discuss changes in procedures.

Expand the sentences.

Expand sentences by adding details that answer the 5 W's and H—who? what? where? when? why? and how?

Expanded: On Monday, August 23, at 2:00 p.m., the Production Department will meet with President Harre in Conference Room B to discuss changes in project-turnover procedures.

Fyi You can also create strong sentences by patterning a sentence off a strong model:

Model: Thank you for your thoughtful note about our company.

New: Thank you for your insightful comment about our competition.

shutterstock.com

Problem:

The modifiers are confusing.

Listen for:
- "That sentence sounds funny."

Look for:
- The committee has nearly been arguing for two hours. (misplaced modifier)
- After waiting for two hours, the meeting was cancelled. (dangling modifier)

Solution:

Fix misplaced and dangling modifiers.

Place the modifier as close as possible to the word it modifies. When the modifier is connected to the wrong word in a sentence, the modifier is misplaced. When it is connected to no word in the sentence, the modifier is dangling. For the dangling modifier, reword the sentence.

Well Placed: The committee has been arguing for nearly two hours.

Well Placed: After waiting for two hours, we found out that the meeting was cancelled.

The comparison is confusing.

Listen for:
- "It's better than what?"

Look for:
- The T180 water extractor has 20 percent more suction.

Complete the comparison.

Make sure a comparison names both things being compared. Otherwise, the comparison is incomplete.

Complete: The T180 water extractor has 20 percent more suction than the T160.

The sentence could mean two things.

Listen for:
- "What do you mean?"

Look for:
- You can never pour too much soap in the laundry machine.

Reword ambiguous sentences.

Rewrite a sentence if it could be read in more than one way. Make sure your meaning is clear.

Clear: Avoid pouring extra soap into the laundry machine.

shutterstock.com

Problem:

The sentences are fragmented.

Listen for:

▪ "That's incomplete."

Look for:

▪ Missing Subject:
  Need to complete the application.

▪ Missing Predicate:
  The whole department.

▪ Missing Subject and Predicate:
  From the beginning.

▪ Incomplete Thought:
  After Shakira spoke.

Solution:

Add what is missing to make a sentence.

Make sure each sentence includes a subject and a predicate and expresses a complete thought. Otherwise, the group of words is a fragment. Fix fragments by supplying what they lack—a subject, a predicate, or a complete thought.

Complete: We need to complete the application.

Complete: The whole department will attend the meeting.

Complete: From the beginning, we liked this new product.

Complete: After Shakira spoke, she answered the audience's questions.

The sentences run together.

Listen for:

▪ "These sentences aren't joined correctly."

Look for:

▪ The prototype has arrived everyone should take a look. (run-on)

▪ The prototype has arrived, everyone should take a look. (comma splice)

Use both a comma and conjunction to join sentences.

If two sentences are joined without any punctuation or conjunction, a **run-on** results. If the sentences are joined with only a comma, a **comma splice** occurs. These errors can be fixed by joining the sentences with a semicolon, with a semicolon and a conjunctive adverb, or with a comma and a coordinating conjunction (*and, but, or, nor, for, so, yet*). The errors could also be fixed by making two sentences.

Corrected: The prototype has arrived; everyone should take a look.

The prototype has arrived; however, everyone should take a look.

Corrected: The prototype has arrived, so everyone should take a look.

The prototype has arrived. Everyone should take a look.

Problem:	**Solution:**
The tenses shift.	**Stay in one tense.**
Listen for:	**Avoid** using more than one tense in a sentence when only one is needed.
▪ "You go from past to present."	
Look for:	
▪ I answer phones and will update patients' records.	*Corrected:* I answer phones and update patients' records.
The pronouns shift.	**Don't shift the person of pronouns.**
Listen for:	**Avoid** improperly mixing first person (*I, we, us*), second person (*you, your*), and third person (*he, she, they*) in a sentence.
▪ "Stay in third person here."	
Look for:	
▪ Clients can check their status online or when you call in.	*Corrected:* Clients can check their status online or when they call in.
The voice shifts.	**Do not mix active and passive voice.**
Listen for:	**Avoid** mixing active and passive voice within a sentence.
▪ "The voice changes."	
Look for:	
▪ If you review the account, a lot of action will be seen.	*Corrected:* If you review the account, you will see a lot of action.
A series sounds awkward.	**Use parallel structure.**
Listen for:	**Make sure** all elements in a list are the same part of speech (all nouns, all adjectives, all prepositional phrases, and so on).
▪ "This isn't parallel."	
Look for:	
▪ We specialize in costume design, tailoring, alterations, and to clean costumes. (nonparallel)	*Parallel:* We specialize in costume design, tailoring, alterations, and cleaning.

"A sentence is a noun and a verb—matter and energy. You can catch the whole universe in a sentence."

—J. Robert King

Checklist Sentences

Your goal is to use a variety of sentences, to create a smooth flow of thought, and to make sentences error free.

_____ **1.** Do I use a variety of sentence **functions**?
- ☐ Statement
- ☐ Question
- ☐ Command
- ☐ Exclamation
- ☐ Conditional

_____ **2.** Do I use a variety of sentence **structures**?
- ☐ Simple
- ☐ Compound
- ☐ Complex
- ☐ Compound-complex

_____ **3.** Do I use a variety of sentence **beginnings**? (subject, transition, phrase, clause)

_____ **4.** Have I combined choppy sentences?

_____ **5.** Have I energized tired sentences?

_____ **6.** Have I reworked rambling sentences?

_____ **7.** Have I corrected fragments?

_____ **8.** Do my sentences read smoothly overall?

shutterstock.com

shutterstock.com

6
Trait 6: Correctness

Imagine that you are getting ready for a big event and you want to look your best. You check yourself in the mirror: Does your hair look good? Are your teeth free of broccoli bits? Is your collar straight? Are your clothes pressed and spot free? What about the cat fur? You check these details because you would be embarrassed to show up in public with any of these glaring gaffes.

In the same way, checking correctness is the last step before you share your writing with another person. Just as you wouldn't want to go out with buttons missing or hems unraveling, you wouldn't want to publish with agreement errors, misspellings, and other embarrassing mistakes.

Correctness: An Overview

The conventional use of punctuation, capitalization, spelling, words, grammar, and sentences all converge into the error-free communication that business needs and expects. The Proofreader's Guide at the end of this book provides detailed rules and examples for each of these important areas. These two pages provide a general overview of conventions, and the rest of the chapter focuses on solutions for common convention problems.

Takomabibelot from Flickr

Punctuation

Punctuation marks are like road signs, telling the reader where to pause or stop. Without them, the reader can easily get lost; and once that happens, the writing has failed to deliver its message. See pages 256-272 for information on the following:

- end punctuation (periods, question marks, and exclamation points) __ **257, 265**
- commas _____ **258-261**
- colons, semicolons, hyphens, and dashes _____ **262-264**

- quotation marks _____ **266-267**
- italics, slashes _____ **268**
- parentheses, brackets _____ **269**
- apostrophes _____ **270-272**

Mechanics

Mechanics covers capitalization, numbers, abbreviations, and spelling. The capital letter that begins a sentence serves a high purpose, signaling a new thought or idea. Capitals also highlight the importance of names—names of people, corporations, official documents, localities, and so on. Using numbers and abbreviations in a consistent way is especially important in business writing. And spelling speaks for itself. See pages 273-284 for the rules of mechanics along with numerous examples.

Usage

The English language seems to be full of words that are so close in appearance or pronunciation that you may have trouble telling them apart—*your/you're, there/their/they're, advise/advice,* and so forth. Each of these words has its own meaning, and it's up to the writer to use each in the right way. Naturally, misusing a word creates confusion. The minute a reader says, "Does the writer really mean that, or did he or she mean to say this instead," the message has been interrupted and perhaps lost. See pages 285-302 for a complete listing of the most commonly misused words, with definitions and examples of each.

Grammar

Grammar involves using the eight parts of speech together in conventionally acceptable ways. One says, correctly, "The packages have arrived," not "The packages they has arrived." Correct, standard grammar is expected in business writing. Correctness is not a matter of being stuffy but of being understood. See pages 303-316 for information about the following parts of speech:

Constructing Sentences

Effective sentences have style—which means that they not only express ideas well, but engage the reader and reflect well on the writer. In addition to discussing subjects, predicates, phrases, and clauses, pages 317-322 provide the basics of creating sentence style:

Avoiding Sentence Errors

Effective sentences also are correctly created. To communicate, a sentence needs to be free of basic errors. See pages 323-328 for explanations and examples of the following types of sentence errors:

Tip The following pages provide an overview of the most-common problems that arise with punctuation, mechanics, usage, grammar, and sentences. Use these pages as a quick guide, and refer to the Proofreader's Guide (pages 256-352) for more depth and coverage.

Correctness: Problems and Solutions

Correctness ensures that nothing will derail your message. It also ensures that your message reflects well on you and your company. The following pages provide a quick guide to the most common correctness problems—and solutions to them.

Problem:

I have trouble with end punctuation.

Listen for:

- "This question should end with a question mark."
- "No more exclamation points."

Solution:

Match the punctuation to the kind of sentence.

Use periods for statements, conditionals, and most commands. Use question marks for questions and use exclamation points (sparingly) for exclamations.

Statement:	We open the meeting with introductions.
Conditional:	If we start on time, we should be done in an hour.
Command:	Please see the attached agenda.
Question:	Does everyone agree with the main points?
Exclamation:	Excellent job!

Commas are confusing.

Listen for:

- "A comma goes here."
- "You have too many commas."

Apply four basic comma rules.

Use commas in the following four key places:

1. *In Compound Sentences:* When joining two sentences, use a comma and a coordinating conjunction (*and, but, or, nor, for, so, yet*).

   The new catalog arrived, but the order form was missing.

2. *After Introductory Phrases:* Use a comma after an introductory phrase of four or more words at the beginning of a sentence.

   When making travel arrangements, use the Human Resources travel service.

3. *Around Nonessential Words:* If a phrase or clause could be removed from a sentence without changing the basic meaning, set off the words with commas.

   My supervisor, who enjoys chess, is a master of the boardroom.

4. *Between Equal Adjectives:* If two adjectives modify a noun equally, place a comma between them. (If the order of the adjectives can be switched, they modify equally.)

   Juan submitted a thorough, thoughtful analysis of the problem.

Problem:	Solution:

I have trouble with capitalization.

Listen for:

- "Your capitalization seems random."
- "You capitalize too much."

Capitalize first words and names.

Follow these two basic capitalization rules:

1. *First Words:* Capitalize the first word of each sentence as well as the first word of a quoted sentence.

   The applicant asked, "**D**o you offer a flex-time schedule?"

2. *Proper Nouns and Adjectives:* Capitalize names or words used as names (such as Dad and Mom). Also capitalize the names of days, months, holidays, titles, organizations, and adjectives formed from proper nouns.

   I asked **S**andy **N**ovak if she could work **S**unday, **M**arch 6, to benefit the **Y**oung **R**eader's **A**ssociation. This year's fund-raiser has an **O**lympic theme.

Note: Do not type in ALL CAPS unless you are typing a WARNING.

I always get it wrong when adding *s, ing,* or *ed*.

Listen for:

- "Drop the *e* before adding that."
- "Double the last letter."

Learn and apply three mechanics rules.

Remember these three basic mechanics rules:

1. *Forming Plurals:* Form the plurals of most nouns by adding *s* to the singular form. If the noun ends in *ch, s, sh, x,* or *z,* form plurals by adding *es.* If the noun ends in a *y* that follows a consonant, change the *y* to *i* and add *es.*

   The lad**ies** from the church**es** tell stor**ies** to **children**.

Note: Words such as *child* or *mouse* have special plural forms—*children, mice.*

2. *Doubling Final Consonants:* If a word ends in a consonant after a single vowel and the syllable is accented, double the consonant before adding a suffix that starts with a vowel.

   Oh, I was plan**ning** to remove the price tag before I wrap**ped** the present.

3. *Using the Silent e:* If a word ends in a silent *e,* keep the *e* when adding a suffix beginning with a consonant. Drop the *e* when adding a suffix beginning with a vowel.

   I'm hope**ful** that I won't be driv**ing** in a snowstorm tomorrow. Hop**ing** may not change the forecast, however.

Problem: I get words mixed up.	Solution: Learn these differences.
Look for: bring, take	*Bring* refers to movement toward the writer or speaker; *take* refers to movement away from the writer or speaker. Please *take* this note to President Jones and *bring* back her rely.
fewer, less	*Fewer* refers to countable units; *less* refers to quantity, value, or degree. *Fewer* complaints mean *less* customer dissatisfaction.
it's, its	*It's* is the contraction of "it is" or "it has." *Its* is the possessive form of "it." *It's* too bad this copier leaves streaks on *its* copies.
lay, lie	As verbs, *lay* means "to put or place something" while *lie* means "to rest or recline." (However, the past tense of *lie* is *lay*.) You *lay* your coat on the chair and *lie* down to rest.
lend, borrow	*Lend* means "to give the use of temporarily"; *borrow* means "to obtain for temporary use." You can *borrow* my pencil if you will *lend* me a pen.
real, very, really	*Real* is usually an adjective meaning "authentic." Do not use it in place of the adjectives *really* or *very*. *Real* cheese is *really* delicious.

Look for: than, then	*Than* (conjunction) indicates a comparison; *then* (usually an adverb) refers to time. The work environment is more relaxed now *than* it was back *then*.
there, their, they're	*Their* is a possessive pronoun. *There* is an adverb indicating place; *there* is also an expletive used to introduce a sentence. *They're* is the contraction of "they are." *There* is the hall where *they're* giving *their* presentation.
to, too, two	*To* is a preposition indicating direction; *to* also is used to form an infinitive. *Too* is an adverb that means "also," "very," or "excessively." *Two* is the number 2. *Two* of my friends are *too* busy *to* go *to* the concert.
your, you're	*Your* is a possessive pronoun showing ownership. *You're* is the contraction of "you are." *You're* right. This is *your* coat.

Problem:

I struggle with subject-verb agreement.

Listen for:

- "Your subjects and verbs don't agree."

Solution:

Follow basic subject-verb agreement rules.

Use these three basic rules for subject-verb agreement:

1. *With Most Subjects:* A singular subject takes a singular verb, and a plural subject takes a plural verb.

   > **President Mitchell plans** to speak. The three **vice presidents plan** to take notes.

2. *With Compound Subjects:* Compound subjects joined by *and* take a plural verb. When compound subjects are joined by *or*, the verb should agree with the last subject.

   > **Lupita and Jacob work** the day shift. Either **Ted or Lynne works** the night shift.

3. *With Indefinite Pronouns:* Some indefinite pronouns are singular, some are plural, and some can be singular or plural depending on the object of the preposition that follows it.

Singular
anybody, anyone, anything, everybody, everyone, everything, nobody, no one, nothing, somebody, someone, something

---

Plural
both, few, many, others, several

Singular or Plural
all, any, more, most, none, some
All of the **pie is** gone. (singular)
All of the **pies are** gone. (plural)

 Fyi Sometimes a subject is separated from the verb by other words. Make sure to match the number of the actual subject:

> The **president**, who works with all departments, **is** very busy.
>   singular   singular

"Bad spellers
of the world,
untie."

—Graffito

Checklist Correctness

Your goal is to create a document that uses correct punctuation, mechanics, usage, and grammar and includes correctly constructed sentences.

____ **1.** Have I used end punctuation correctly?

____ **2.** Have I used commas in compound sentences?

____ **3.** Have I used commas after introductory phrases?

____ **4.** Have I used commas to set off nonessential words?

____ **5.** Have I used commas between equal adjectives?

____ **6.** Have I capitalized first words?

____ **7.** Have I capitalized proper nouns (names) and proper adjectives?

____ **8.** Have I formed plurals by adding *es* to nouns ending in *ch, s, sh, x,* or *z*?

____ **9.** Have I followed the rules for doubling final consonants and using the silent *e*?

____ **10.** Have I checked use of commonly confused words?
- ☐ bring, take
- ☐ fewer, less
- ☐ it's, its
- ☐ lay, lie
- ☐ lend, borrow
- ☐ real, very, really
- ☐ than, then
- ☐ there, their, they're
- ☐ to, too, two
- ☐ your, you're

____ **11.** Do my subjects and verbs agree?

shutterstock.com

shutterstock.com

7
Trait 7: Design

Strong design in business documents is not about producing a splash or using color for color's sake. Instead, design needs to serve content. As with every other trait, the goal of design is clear communication, and the only way for design to succeed is for it to make the message clearer.

This chapter focuses first on the basics of designing business documents, including page layout, format, and typography. Then, the chapter shows different types of graphics and how to incorporate them in a document. Last, you'll find a checklist to help with design.

Design: An Overview

Your goal is to create a page design that is attractive and easy to read and reflects well on you and your company. To achieve a reader-friendly design, use the tips below.

shutterstock.com

Elements of Document Design

A document design should (1) follow company standards, (2) make information accessible, and (3) look inviting to the reader. Smart choices about format, page layout, and typography will lead to a successful design.

Page Layout

Produce pages that are open, balanced, and readable.

- Balance your pages with an effective combination of print, graphics, and white space.
- Introduce headings to separate blocks of text; keep headings consistent in size and presentation (**boldfaced**, centered, or <u>underlined</u>).
- Use visual cues (like numbers, bullets, or indents) to help distinguish between main and secondary points.
- Maintain a ragged right margin unless full justification is required.
- Do not place headings, hyphenated words, or the first lines of paragraphs at the very bottom of a page or column.
- Avoid placing single words or lines at the top of a page.
- Keep all items in a list on the same page.

Typography

Choose attractive, easy-to-read typefaces and type sizes.

- Select 10-12 point type for regular text,14-16 for subheadings, and 16-20 for major headings and titles.
- Choose a readable serif typeface such as Times New Roman, Bookman, Schoolbook, or Garamond (**like this type**).
- Use sans serif type such as Arial or Helvetica (**like this type**) for special text, including headings and on-screen documents.
- Try special type styles and treatments for emphasis: underlining, highlighting, *italics*, boxes, UPPERCASE, and color.

Format

Use an appropriate design.

- Follow the rules for the type of document you are writing (memo, letter).
- Plan the overall design by considering the number and the width of columns.
- Consider using graphics. (See pages 62–69.)
- Organize each page by using numbers, headers, lists, bullets, and so on.

Creating Strong Design

The document below is designed simply but effectively. Headings, lists, boldface type, white space, and margins are used to make each part of the message clear and easy to follow.

Lines are a moderate length, flush left, and ragged right.

Boldface type is used to draw attention to key information.

White space helps break text into readable units.

Headings and lists separate blocks of text.

Main text is serif; headings are sans serif.

Appropriate margins are used on all sides.

Family and Children Coalition
Confidentiality Procedures

The Family and Children Coalition Confidentiality Policy states that all clients have the right to confidentiality. Conduct your work in keeping with this policy by following the procedures below.

Client Intakes:
During the client intake, the Coalition counselor should discuss conditions of confidentiality with the client. The counselor should explain the following:

1. Information will never be shared unless the client has given written permission using the Consent to Release Form.

2. Confidentiality may be limited or canceled if Coalition staff have serious concerns about child abuse or neglect.

Outside Requests for Information:
Coalition counselors will handle outside requests for client information.

1. No client information will be shared without the client's written permission.

2. Clients will be notified of any outside requests for information. If the client gives permission, he or she must sign the Consent to Release Form and indicate what information may be released and to whom.

Breaches of Confidentiality:
If a client believes that Coalition staff have not observed the confidentiality policy and procedures, he or she should be directed to follow the Client-Grievance Process.

By carefully following the procedures above, the Coalition staff can help our clients while also respecting their rights to confidentiality.

Design: Problems and Solutions

You've heard that form should follow function. That's especially true when designing a document. Design's role is to make communication clearer and more compelling. The following pages outline common design problems and ways to solve them.

Problem:

Every document I create looks the same.

Listen for:

- "Another boring document."
- "Words, words, words."

Solution:

Experiment with page design.

Select an appropriate page design for the document as a whole. Consider the amount of text and the number of graphics you plan to use, and select a layout to balance the two. Choose from the following designs:

- A single column with a large graphic (**A**).
- Two even columns with a small graphic (**B**).
- Two even columns, one text and one graphics (**C**).
- Two uneven columns, one text and one graphics (**D**).

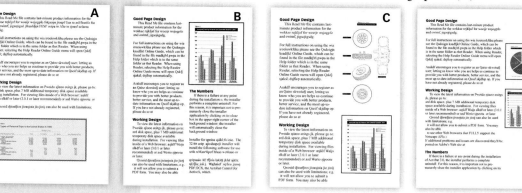

I'm not sure where to put graphics on a page.

Listen for:

- "Where's the figure?"
- "What does this table go with?"

Place graphics to aid the reader.

Position graphics logically. Insert a graphic close to the first reference to it—preferably after the reference.

- Place a *small* graphic on the same page as the reference.
- Place a *large* graphic on a facing page in a double-sided document, or on the page following the reference in a single-sided document.
- Make a less *important* or a *very large* graphic an attachment or an appendix item.
- Refer to the graphics in text.
- If there are many graphics, consider using a numbering system and including a caption.

Problem:

I need to show a lot of raw data.

Listen for:

▪ "There are too many numbers in the text."

Solution:

Use a table.

Create a table to arrange raw data in rows and columns, allowing readers to easily compare figures. Use tables to

▪ categorize data for easy comparison.

▪ provide many exact figures in a compact format.

▪ present raw data that are the foundation of later graphs.

I don't know how to set up a table.

Use a table maker and follow these tips.

1. **Set up rows and columns in a logical order.** Make tables easy to read by using patterns of organization: *category, time, place, alphabet, ascending,* or *descending order.* Make the columns or rows containing totals clear and prominent.

2. **Label information.** Identify columns at the top and rows at the left. Use short, clear headings and set them off with color, screens (light shades of color), or rules (lines).

3. **Present data correctly.** In a numerical table, round off numbers to the nearest whole (if appropriate) and align them at their right edge. Otherwise, align numbers at the decimal point. Indicate a gap in data with a dash or n.a. (not available). In a text table, use parallel wording.

Sample Numerical Table

- Organize and label columns.

- Organize and label rows.

- Align numbers at the right edge or at the decimal point.

Table 1: Fourth Quarter 2010 Sales Comparison for Full-Spectrum Lights

Full-Spectrum Lights	Item	Price	Fourth Quarter Sales			Total	Revenue
			Oct.	Nov.	Dec.		
Floor Lamp (Black) 70w	FLB70	$199.00	320	343	415	1,078	$214,522
Floor Lamp (Chrome) 70w	FLC70	$199.00	311	315	398	1,024	$203,776
Desk Lamp (Black) 70w	DLB70	$169.00	421	441	505	1,367	$231,023
Desk Lamp (Chrome) 70w	DLC70	$169.00	414	408	480	1,302	$220,038
Hobby Lamp (Black) 70w	HLB70	$139.00	231	212	248	691	$96,049
Hobby Lamp (Chrome) 70w	HLC70	$139.00	202	214	231	647	$89,933
Floor Lamp (Black) 42w	FLB42	$129.00	422	448	495	1,365	$176,085
Floor Lamp (Chrome) 42w	FLC70	$129.00	399	414	498	1,311	$169,119
Desk Lamp (Black) 42w	DLB70	$99.00	452	441	511	1,404	$138,996
Desk Lamp (Chrome) 42w	DLC70	$99.00	514	517	571	1,602	$158,598
Hobby Lamp (Black) 42w	HLB70	$69.00	312	321	348	981	$67,689
Hobby Lamp (Chrome) 42w	HLC70	$69.00	317	341	361	1,019	$70,311
Totals:			4,315	4,415	5,061	13,791	$1,836,189

Problem:

I need to show the changes in amounts over time.

Listen for:

- ▪ "What have the trends been?"

Solution:

Use a line graph.

Create a line graph to show relationships between numbers—differences, proportions, or trends. A line graph shows changes in quantity over time.

- ▪ Typically, the horizontal axis measures time (days, months, years), and the vertical axis measures a quantity (costs, products sold).
- ▪ The quantity for each time period creates a "data point." When joined, these points create the lines that show the trends.

I don't know how to make a line graph.

Follow these tips for creating a line graph.

1. **Start the vertical axis at zero.** If it's impractical to show all increments, show a break on the axis.
2. **Use all available data points** (no skipping). Make sure vertical and horizontal units match well (roughly equal in scale or ratio).
3. **Identify each axis.** Label units measured (years, dollars), and use consistent increments. Print all words horizontally, if possible.
4. **Vary data lines.** Make data lines heavy, axis lines light, and background graph lines even lighter. **Use patterns or colors** to distinguish multiple lines.
6. **Build a legend** if necessary.

Sample Line Graph

- • Make data lines heavy and distinct.
- • Make axis increments consistent.
- • Label units.
- • Start the axis at zero.
- • Use a legend if necessary.

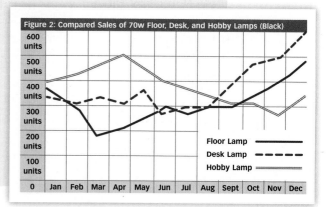

Figure 2: Compared Sales of 70w Floor, Desk, and Hobby Lamps (Black)

Problem:

I need to compare different amounts.

Listen for:

- "Which sells better?"

Solution:

Use bar graphs.

Create a bar graph to compare amounts using a series of vertical or horizontal bars. The height or length of each bar represents a quantity at a specific time or in a particular place. Here are the types.

- **Single-bar graphs** show quantity differences for one item.
- **Bilateral-bar graphs** show amounts both above and below a zero line.
- **Segmented-bar graphs** divide bars to show what parts make up their wholes.
- **Multiple-bar graphs** present groups of bars so that readers can (1) compare bars within each group and (2) compare one group to the next.

I don't know how to make a bar graph.

Follow these tips for making a bar graph.

1. **Develop bars that are accurate and informative.**
   - Choose a scale that doesn't exaggerate or minimize differences between bars.
   - Maintain a consistent bar width and spacing between bars.
   - Use two-dimensional bars; 3-D bars can blur differences and amounts.
2. **Design bar graphs that are easy to read.**
   - Label bars and axis units clearly.
   - Add a legend if necessary.
   - Use patterns or colors to distinguish between different bars or segments.
   - Present items in a logical order within a group or within single-bar segments (ascending order, descending order).

Multiple and Single Bar Graph

- Limit to five the number of bars in a group, or the number of segments in a single bar.
- Keep words and numbers horizontal.

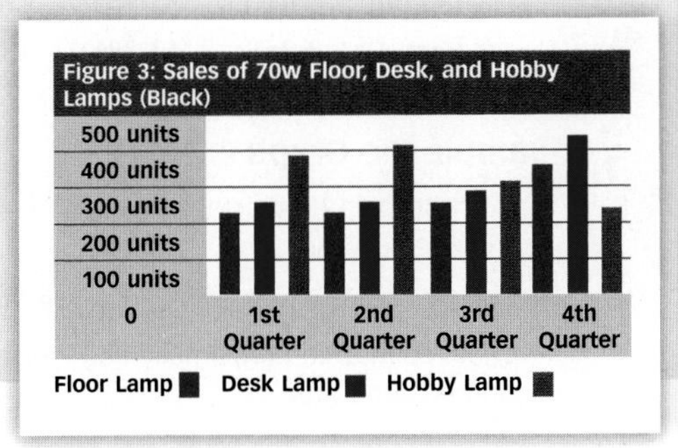

Figure 3: Sales of 70w Floor, Desk, and Hobby Lamps (Black)

	1st Quarter	2nd Quarter	3rd Quarter	4th Quarter
Floor Lamp ■	Desk Lamp ■	Hobby Lamp ■		

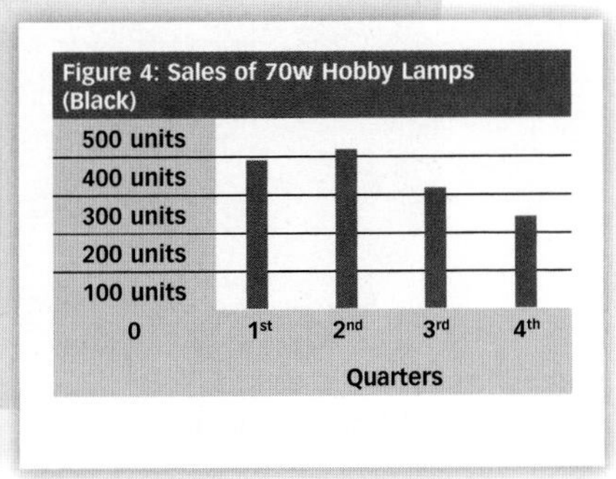

(500 units, 400 units, 300 units, 200 units, 100 units, 0)

Figure 4: Sales of 70w Hobby Lamps (Black)

(500 units, 400 units, 300 units, 200 units, 100 units, 0 — 1st, 2nd, 3rd, 4th Quarters)

Problem:

I need to compare parts of a whole.

Listen for:

- "Show a budget breakdown."
- "How do the parts compare?"

Solution:

Use a pie graph.

Create pie or circle graphs to divide a whole quantity into parts. These graphs show how individual parts relate to the whole and to each other. Use pie graphs to

- show proportions.
- give the big picture.
- add visual impact.

I don't know how to make a pie graph.

Use these tips to create a pie graph.

1. **Keep your graph simple.** Divide the circle into six slices or fewer. If necessary, combine smaller slices into a "miscellaneous" category, and explain its contents in a note or in the text.

2. **Make your graph clear and realistic.** Avoid confusion and distortion.
   - Use a moderate-sized circle and avoid 3-D effects.
   - Distinguish between slices with shading, patterns, or colors.
   - Use a legend if necessary.
   - Measure slices (number of degrees) to assure accuracy. Use graphics software or the formula below.

To Calculate Degrees for Each Slice:

Amount of part ÷ whole quantity x 100 = percentage x 3.6 = number of degrees

Slices	$1,936	100%	360 degrees
Part 1	$775	40%	144.1 degrees
Part 2	$484	25%	90.0 degrees
Part 3	$415	21.4%	77.2 degrees
Part 4	$262	13.5%	48.7 degrees

Figure 5: 2010 Office Expenditures

$262 Hardware Repairs

$415 Hardware Upgrades

$775 Paper Supplies

$484 Software Upgrades

Total Expenditures: $1,936

Sample Pie Graph

- Start at the 12:00 o'clock position with the largest slice and move clockwise.

- Follow with the next slices in descending order.

- Label each slice horizontally and indicate actual percentages and or/ amounts.

Problem:

I need to show data about different regions.

Listen for:

- "Show the breakdown by state."

I don't know how to create a map.

 To make a map, try an online resource such as the National Atlas <http://nationalatlas.gov.>.

Solution:

Use a map.

Create a map to present a wide range of useful information: communication and transportation data, distances, directions, regions and zones, natural and urban features, market segments, and so on.

Use these tips to create a map.

1. **Make the geographic area clear.** While your map need not be geographically accurate to be highly effective, it should clarify the area in question. Orient the reader by providing a directional arrow (usually north).

2. **Provide useful content.** Select details carefully, making sure that features, markings, and symbols are distinct and easy to understand. If necessary, use labels and a legend. Add a note or caption to help the reader interpret the map.

3. **Indicate differences for regions by**
   - coloring, shading, cross-hatching, or dotting.
   - creating bar or pie graphs in each area on the map.
   - labeling areas with actual numbers.

Sample Map

- Make the actual geographic area clear.

- Indicate differences by using color, shading, or a pattern.

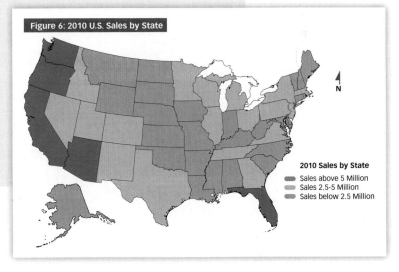

Figure 6: 2010 U.S. Sales by State

2010 Sales by State
- Sales above 5 Million
- Sales 2.5-5 Million
- Sales below 2.5 Million

Problem:

I need a really clear picture of an object.

Listen for:

▪ "Show me all the parts."

Solution:

Use a line drawing.

Create a line drawing to screen out unnecessary details and provide clear, simplified images of objects. Different types of line drawings focus on different key features.

▪ *Surface* drawings present objects as they appear externally.

▪ *Cutaway* drawings or cross sections show an object's inside parts.

▪ *Exploded* drawings "pull apart" an object, showing what individual parts look like and how they fit together.

I don't know how to create a line drawing.

Follow these tips for line drawings.

1. **Use the right tools.** Use drawing instruments or a CAD (computer-aided design) program. Get expert help if necessary.
2. **Select the viewpoint and angle** needed to show key details: surface, cutaway, or exploded; front, side, diagonal, back, top, or bottom.
3. **Pay attention to scale and proportion** to represent the object accurately.
4. **Include the right level of detail** (for the reader). Avoid clutter, and use colors to highlight and clarify information.
5. **Use labels,** or "callouts," to identify key parts of the object.

Sample Exploded Drawing

• Use labels or callouts.

• Represent proportions of objects accurately.

Figure 7: Front-Wheel Assembly

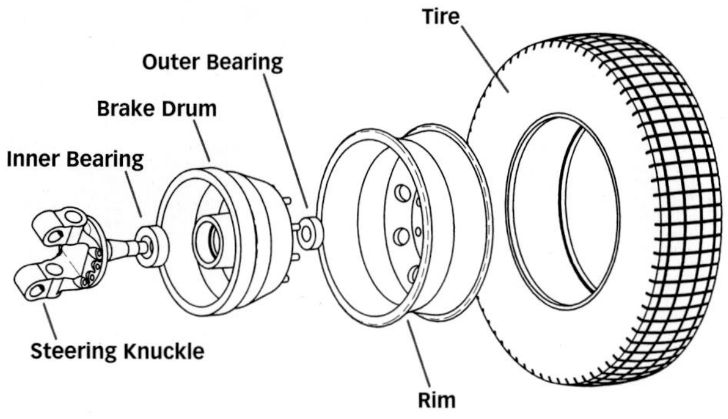

Tire

Outer Bearing

Brake Drum

Inner Bearing

Steering Knuckle

Rim

Problem:

I need to show how something really looks.

Listen for:

- "Let me see it."

I'm not great with using photos.

shutterstock.com

Solution:

Use a photograph.

Use photographs and other visual images to provide detail. Traditional photographs, black-and-white or color, show surface appearance of reality—from people to things to landscapes.

The very latest photographic technologies can be used to show external and internal images of a different nature: infrared pictures, x-rays, ultrasounds, CAT scans, 2-D and 3-D computer-generated images, and so on.

Follow these tips for using photos.

1. **Be creative and ethical.** Software such as Adobe Photoshop and Paint Shop Pro allows you to modify images, but make reasonable changes that do not distort or distract.
   - Removing blemishes and cropping images is standard practice.
   - Adding, subtracting, and distorting should be avoided or well documented.
2. **Take, develop, and print quality images.**
   - Use good equipment or seek expert help, if needed.
   - Select distances and angles to clarify size and details.
   - Enlarge and crop images to focus on key objects.
   - Place images on the page or import them digitally into documents.
3. **Obtain permission** to use any recognizable photo of a person or place.
4. **Clarify images.** Use labels, arrows, size references, and so on to help the reader get an accurate picture.

Sample Photographs

- Indicate a specific portion of an image with an arrow.
- Consider including a hand or ruler as a size reference.

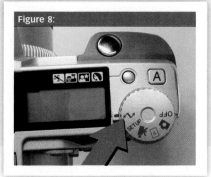

Figure 8:

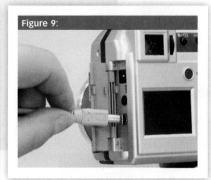

Figure 9:

Checklist Design

Your goal is to create a design that uses graphics to communicate your message in the clearest, most compelling way.

_____ **1.** Is my page layout balanced?

_____ **2.** Have I used headings to break up text?

_____ **3.** Do I use lists to help make points clear?

_____ **4.** Do I effectively use white space (margins, space between paragraphs)?

_____ **5.** Have I selected a readable typeface for the text?

_____ **6.** Have I selected an appropriate page design?

_____ **7.** Are graphics logically positioned?

_____ **8.** Have I followed good page-layout principles?

_____ **9.** Do I use tables to present raw data?

_____ **10.** Do I use line graphs to show changes over time?

_____ **11.** Do I use bar graphs to compare quantities over time?

_____ **12.** Do I use pie graphs to compare quantities at one time?

_____ **13.** Have I included appropriate maps?

_____ **14.** Have I included helpful line drawings?

_____ **15.** Have I provided photographs as needed?

Corbis

8
Using the Writing Process

A finished piece of writing is rarely created in a single attempt. It would be great if we effortlessly produced effective letters, memos, and reports, but we don't. Instead, effective documents grow from a process. That process begins with the writer's need to write. It continues with prewriting, drafting, revising, and refining, and concludes when the writer shares the document with readers.

This chapter explains the steps in the writing process. Whatever type of writing you're doing, these steps will carry you from start to finish. Use the explanations, techniques, and tips in this chapter to strengthen your writing process as a whole, or to refine a specific step you would like to improve.

The Process of Writing: An Overview

It's easy to feel overwhelmed about a writing project—especially if the form of writing is new to you, or the topic is complex. However, using the writing process will relieve some of that pressure by breaking down the task into manageable steps: **Prewriting, Drafting, Revising,** and **Refining.**

Fyi The diagram on this page shows how the writing process works. The diagram indicates the usual order of the steps in the process; the arrows show that writers commonly move back and forth between steps.

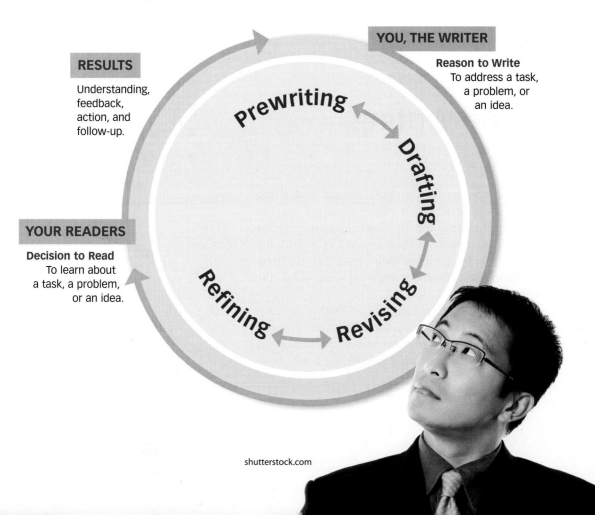

YOU, THE WRITER

Reason to Write
To address a task,
a problem, or
an idea.

RESULTS

Understanding,
feedback,
action, and
follow-up.

Prewriting

Drafting

YOUR READERS

Decision to Read
To learn about
a task, a problem,
or an idea.

Refining

Revising

shutterstock.com

Top 10 Tips for Business Writing

You can develop successful workplace documents if you make the writing process work for you. Follow the tips below.

1   **Be committed.** Care about your writing. It is a clear reflection of both you and your company.

2   **Be conversational.** Write as if you were speaking to your reader. Test your writing for effective tone by reading it out loud. (See pages 25-32.)

3   **Be considerate.** Know your reader and his or her needs in order to make recommendations or referrals.

4   **Be connected.** Understand your subject well by consulting customers, coworkers, and company records to gather information.

5   **Be consistent.** Make your point and stick to it. Keep your thoughts organized, and don't wander off the subject.

6   **Be clear.** First, be clear in your thinking. Then, write with common words, avoiding jargon or inflated language. (See pages 33-40.)

7   **Be concrete.** Always use specific names, numbers, and examples. (*Eight* is concrete; *some* is abstract.)

8   **Be concise.** Get to the point. You need not cover everything or try to include every detail.

9   **Be complete.** Tell the reader how to respond. Include all the names, dates, and numbers the reader might need.

10   **Be correct.** Check your facts for accuracy and your language for appropriateness. Always double-check names of people and companies for correct spelling.

The Process Up Close

Each of the steps in the writing process has a specific goal that can be achieved with a variety of activities.

■ Prewriting

Goal: Find your focus and prepare to draft.

Activities: Clarify your purpose, think about your reader, choose a format, and list the information you need to share. Then do any necessary research, review models, and develop an outline.

■ Drafting

Goal: Get your thoughts on paper.

Activities: Expand your outline with sentences and paragraphs that use a fitting tone.

■ Revising

Goal: Fix any content problems in the first draft.

Activities: Test the quality and clarity of the ideas, organization, and voice. Also check words and sentences. Add, cut, and clarify as needed.

■ Refining

Goal: Fine-tune the piece before sending it out.

Activities: Review format and design. Edit and proofread by checking grammar, punctuation, spelling, and mechanics.

"Good planning helps to make elusive dreams come true."

—Lester R. Bittel

Guidelines Prewriting

Your Goal ▶ Your goal is to zero in on the message you want to send, think about the reader and context, and gather and organize information.

1. Clarify your message.
- What is the subject of the message?
- What specific result do you want to see from the message?
- Is the desired goal or outcome realistic and measurable?
- Do you need to inform or persuade to achieve results?

  Informing tasks: state, clarify, outline, list, record, report, analyze, compare, describe, define, explain

  Persuading tasks: request, sell, recommend, convince, apologize, evaluate, complain, turn down, promote

2. Profile your reader.
- Is your reader within or outside your organization?
- How well do you know your reader?
- How much does your reader know about the topic?
- What are your reader's values, needs, and priorities? Is your message likely to be received positively or negatively?
- Will your reader be making a decision or doing something? What authority and responsibility does your reader have?
- Will there be a number of readers? If so, are they diverse in age, occupation, gender, education, culture, and language skills?

3. Know the context.
- What type of document are you writing? What are its design requirements? How will you create, send, and store this document?
- When must the document be finished and sent?
- What information do you have available? What additional information do you need to gather?
- What future contact or action might be needed by you, the reader, others?

Gathering and Organizing Information

You can identify key ideas, gather reliable material, and organize information by using a variety of prewriting techniques like those below and on the next two pages. Remember, you should not be overly concerned with grammar or mechanics at this stage in the process.

Using a Planner

Consider using a planner similar to the one below to help you clarify your message, reader, and context. Planners can be especially helpful for longer projects such as reports or proposals.

Prewriting Planner

1. What is the subject? _____
   _____

2. Why am I writing? _____
   _____

3. Who is the reader? _____
   _____

4. What do I want the reader to think or do? _____
   _____

5. What are her or his needs, biases, questions? _____
   _____

6. How can I get the desired results? _____
   _____

7. What information do I need? _____
   _____

8. Where can I find this information? _____
   _____

9. What form of writing should I use? _____
   _____

10. When and where do I need to send or submit this? _____
   _____

Fyi A prewriting planner similar to the one shown here can help you better understand the writing situation by focusing your attention on the 5W's and H: who, what, when, where, why, and how.

Freewriting

Writing whatever comes to mind on a particular topic is called *freewriting*. Freewriting is really brainstorming on paper (or on the computer). It helps you record, develop, and understand your thinking.

1 Write nonstop about your subject or project, *following* rather than *directing* your thoughts.

2 Resist the temptation to stop and judge or edit what you write.

3 If you get stuck, switch directions and follow a different line of thinking.

4 When you finish, reread your material and highlight passages you think might be useful.

Clustering

Clustering creates a web of connections between a general topic and specific subtopics. A cluster allows you to see the structure of your topic and plan your writing.

1 Write a key word or phrase in the middle of your page.

2 Record or "cluster" related words and phrases around this key word.

3 Circle each idea and link it to related ideas in your cluster.

4 Continue recording related ideas until you have covered the topic.

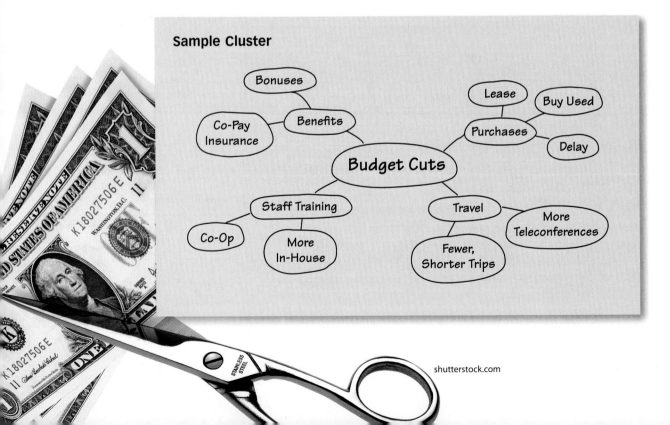

Sample Cluster

- Bonuses
- Co-Pay Insurance
- Benefits
- Lease
- Buy Used
- Purchases
- Delay
- Budget Cuts
- Staff Training
- Co-Op
- More In-House
- Travel
- More Teleconferences
- Fewer, Shorter Trips

shutterstock.com

Using a Diagram

Diagrams can be used to help you record and organize information graphically. The diagrams below are two of the most useful.

1 Use a Venn diagram. Use a Venn diagram to compare and contrast two things.

2 Use a problem/solution diagram. Use this diagram to help you understand a problem, break it into parts, specify its causes, list its effects, and develop solutions.

Using an Outline

One way to organize the information you've collected is to construct an outline or a detailed list. Follow the guidelines below to get started.

1 Find your focus. Clarify the main point or controlling idea of your writing project.

2 Develop your outline. A good outline provides a plan for developing your main point:
- Highlight the key ideas you'll want to use to develop your main point.
- Connect your supporting details to these key ideas. Add ideas and details as needed, and number them appropriately.
- Arrange your information into the best possible order. Consider your reader's likely response, and select a sequence that best advances your main point. You may use your own method of development or one of these approaches:

cause/effect	question/answer
chronological order	classification
compare/contrast	order of importance
partitioning	problem/solution

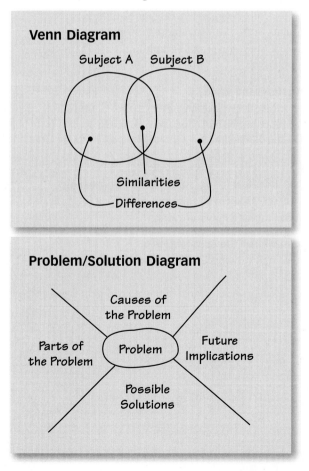

Venn Diagram

Subject A   Subject B

Similarities

Differences

Problem/Solution Diagram

Causes of the Problem

Parts of the Problem

Problem

Future Implications

Possible Solutions

Outline

I. Introduction
II. Body
  A. Main Point
    1. Supporting details
    2. Supporting details
  B. Main Point
    1. Supporting details
    2. Supporting details
III. Closing

Guidelines Drafting

Your Goal ▶ Your goal when drafting is to get your ideas on paper or in the computer, using your prewriting to guide you.

"Why do writers write? Because it isn't there."

—Thomas Berger

1. **Gather your materials.**
   - Make your writing area efficient and comfortable.
   - Set aside a block of uninterrupted time if possible.
   - Place your writing tools and prewriting material within easy reach.

2. **Use your prewriting material.**
   - Draw on your planning, clustering, freewriting, or outlining.
   - Review other documents related to your message.
   - Highlight statements, facts, examples, and graphics to include in your draft.

3. **Focus on ideas, organization, and voice.**
   - Expand and connect ideas, always keeping your purpose in mind.
   - Use your outline as a map, but remain open to new ideas.
   - Maintain a natural, polite, and professional voice or tone.

4. **Develop a logical flow.**
   - Common approaches include moving from overview to close-up, background to discussion, problem to solution, main idea to explanation, or familiar topic to new information.

5. **Use paragraphs to group similar thoughts together.**
   - Present the topic in a single sentence, and then support that topic in a single paragraph.
   - Consider possible closings or conclusions. Doing so can help focus and direct your drafting.

shutterstock.com

Drafting Openings

Your opening should quickly set a clear direction for your writing. Use the guidelines and models below to help you do that.

Fyi In many documents, the subject line opens your message. Write subject lines that clearly and succinctly state your subject.

An effective opening should

- indicate the document type (report, proposal, instructions).
- state your topic, your reason for writing, and your main point (if appropriate).
- get the reader's attention and interest.
- establish a tone or voice.
- provide background and context.
- preview the content.
- provide a summary (if appropriate).

Sample Openings

- *context*
- *main point*
- *positive tone*

Simple Opening (letter)

Thank you for requesting a credit account at Cottonwood Hills Greenhouse and Florist Supply. We are pleased to extend you $100,000 in credit based on Dale's Garden Center's strong financial condition. Congratulations!

- *writing form and topic*
- *subject line*
- *background*
- *objective tone*
- *preview of content*

Complex Opening (report, proposal)

Subject: Report on Investigation of Cockroach Infestation at 5690 Cherryhill

During the month of July 2010, 26 tenants from the 400-unit building at 5690 Cherryhill informed the building superintendent that they had found cockroaches in their units. On August 8, the Management-Tenant Committee authorized our group to investigate these questions:
1. How extensive is the cockroach infestation?
2. How can the cockroach population best be controlled?

We investigated this problem from August 9 to September 10, 2010. This report contains (1) a summary, (2) an overview of our research methods and findings, (3) conclusions, and (4) recommendations.

Drafting the Middle

In the middle part of your message, you need to develop strong, clear paragraphs that advance the main idea presented in your subject line and introduction. Follow your outline and tackle one paragraph at a time. If necessary, go back to your prewriting material or rework your outline.

An effective middle should

(1) link back to the opening through a clear transition,

(2) provide readers with necessary information, and

(3) include well-written paragraphs that have strong opening sentences.

To achieve the goals above, follow these guidelines:

- Develop each main point in a separate paragraph.
- Keep each paragraph fairly short, 3 to 8 lines in length.
- Use a topic sentence to signal each paragraph's direction.
- Expand and connect ideas, always keeping your reader in mind.
- Incorporate headings, lists, and graphics when appropriate.
- Maintain the tone established in the opening.
- Prepare readers for the closing.

> "The art of writing is the art of applying the seat of the pants to the seat of the chair."
>
> —Mary Heaton Vorse

shutterstock.com

Sample Middle Paragraphs (Letter)

- clear topic sentences
- helpful tone throughout
- prepare reader for closing

As you requested, I have enclosed a list of Home Builders' affiliates in Missouri. Each affiliate schedules and handles its own work groups. Call or write directly to any of them for more information about local offerings.

Because you are in college, I have also enclosed some information on Home Builders' Campus Chapters. The pamphlet explains how to join or start a Campus Chapter and discusses service learning for academic credit. Feel free to contact Ben Abramson, the Campus Outreach Coordinator for your area, at the address on the enclosed material.

Drafting Closings

Close your writing logically and naturally by recalling your goal and main point. Your closing should help the reader understand and act on the message.

An effective closing should

- restate your main point and offer conclusions.
- provide recommendations, propose the next step, or offer help.
- focus on appreciation, cooperation, and future contact.
- include all details needed for follow-up and action.
- end with energy by using clear, strong verbs.

Note: Avoid stating the obvious in your closing, or rambling on and on.

Fyi If appropriate, present possible outcomes or long-term implications of what has been discussed. In other words, what's the real bottom line?

Sample Closings

• focus on cooperation

• recommendation and follow-up

Simple Closing (memo, e-mail, letter)

With short-term solutions and long-term cooperation, together we will keep Premium Meats operating and prospering.

If you have any questions or suggestions, please speak to your immediate supervisor or a member of the Quality Task Force. (Task Force information is supplied in the attachment.)

• restatement of main point

• focus on outcomes

• recommendation

• action, future contact

Complex Closing (report, proposal)

Our proposal is to replace our internal-combustion forklifts with electric lifts. This change will involve a higher initial cost but will reap two important benefits: (1) CO levels will drop below OSHA's recommended 25 ppm, ensuring employee safety and product quality; (2) in the long run, the electric lifts will prove less costly to own and operate.

Therefore, I recommend that Rankin management approve this plan, to be phased in over the next four years as outlined above. Improved safety and product quality, combined with total operating costs over the long run, outweigh the plan's initial costs. If you wish to discuss this proposal, please call me at extension 1449.

Guidelines Revising

Your Goal ▶ Your goal when revising is to make major improvements to ideas, organization, voice, words, and sentences.

"Saint, noun. A dead sinner revised and edited."

—Ambrose Bierce

1. Set aside the draft.
- Let your draft sit for a few minutes if it's a simple e-mail.
- Let your draft sit for a day or two if it's a major report.

2. Print a hard copy.
- Assess the overall effectiveness of your writing and map out changes as you review the entire document.

3. Review your purpose.
- Check to see that your message stays focused.
- Make sure you address your reader's potential questions: Why did I receive this? What's the point? Why is it important?

4. Read the draft aloud.
- Identify problems in content and tone.

5. Check ideas, organization, and voice.
- Add comments in the margins about the focus, details, and overall flow of your draft.
- Try the cut-clarify-condense system: [Bracket] material that could be cut. Underline material that needs to be clarified. Put (parentheses) around material that needs to be condensed.
- Transfer changes to your electronic draft.

6. Check words and sentences.
- Use precise nouns, active verbs, and modifiers that clarify.
- Vary sentence beginnings, functions, and structures.

7. Get input from others.
- Get a fresh view of your writing from an objective perspective.

shutterstock.com

Revising for Ideas: Problems and Solutions

If your first draft lacks focus, substance, or clarity, you need to revise your ideas. (See also pages 9-16.)

Problem:	Solution:
The message is unfocused.	**Check the focus of the document and each paragraph.**
Listen for:	**Cut** material that does not support the main point. Make sure the main point clearly states the subject and purpose of the message. Check that the details in each paragraph support the topic sentence.
▪ "This just rambles."	
Look for:	
▪ Thursdays are generally light days for truck undercoating. However, during a routine inspection, I found an undercoater struggling to breathe under a truck. It was the same day that we got the oil filters.	*Revised Version:* During a routine inspection of work on Thursday, March 21, at 10:45 a.m., I found undercoater Bob Irving struggling to breathe underneath the truck he was working on.
The message isn't very informative.	**Expand explanations and offer examples.**
Listen for:	**Answer** the reader's main questions about the subject—who? what? where? when? why? and how? Provide concrete examples if needed.
▪ "It's not very specific."	
Look for:	
▪ Maintainer Corporation provides suits to protect undercoaters from this.	*Revised Version:* Maintainer Corporation provides oxygen suits to protect undercoaters' skin and oxygen supply from sealants that (a) produce noxious fumes, (b) cause choking if swallowed, and (c) injure skin upon contact.
The message is unclear	**Rework your main point and rewrite confusing parts.**
Listen for:	**Express** your main point clearly and specifically. Define any terms that may be unclear. Tell the reader specifically what outcome you seek.
▪ "I don't get it."	
Look for:	
▪ We should do something about the problem. The facts point toward an investment in new equipment and in undercoaters working together.	*Revised Version:* To further protect undercoaters from sealant hazards, I recommend the following actions: 1. Purchase oxygen suits and equipment that meet the 2010 OSHA oxygen-safety standards. In particular, air-hose locks should have emergency-release latches. 2. Raise trucks on a lift so that undercoaters may stand.

Revising for Organization: Problems and Solutions

If your draft has a weak opening, middle, or closing, revise for organization. (See also pages 17-24.)

Problem:

Solution:

The opening is weak.

Listen for:
- "I didn't finish reading."
- "What is this about?"

Look for:
- As you know, insurance is important when accidents happen. How are you doing with coverage?

Check your main point and background.

Make sure your main point clearly names your subject and your purpose for writing. Provide any background needed to understand the main point. Also, focus on the reader's needs to get his or her attention.

Revised Version: Periodically, insurance companies review the cost of offering their policies and then make changes where needed. When changes are made, it's my responsibility as an agent to inform my clients and help them make necessary adjustments.

The middle is disorganized.

Listen for:
- "It's all a jumble."

Look for:
- Hawkeye Casualty has chosen not to renew you. In order to keep their premiums low, some insurance companies will not cover high-risk drivers. In the past two years, you have had an at-fault accident and four moving violations. Your present coverage will cease January 31, 2010. A nonstandard company is willing to insure you.

Check your supporting points and order.

Make sure each paragraph has a topic sentence that supports the main point and that summarizes the point of the paragraph. Place these supporting points in the best order.

Revised Version: Last week Hawkeye Casualty, your auto insurance carrier, discontinued all policies for "high-risk" drivers. Your at-fault accident and four moving violations put you in that category. As a result, Hawkeye Casualty has cancelled your auto insurance policy effective January 31, 2010. However, I have found another company that will cover you. While the cost of the new policy is somewhat higher than your present policy, the coverage is comparable, and the company is reliable.

The closing is weak.

Listen for:
- "It just ends."

Look for:
- This coverage issue needs attention soon.

Restate the main point and give next steps.

Summarize the document and tell the reader specifically what should happen as a follow-up. Provide a call to action (a command statement) if appropriate.

Revised Version: Please call me at 555-0020 before the end of the month so that we can discuss the situation and decide how to proceed.

Revising for Voice: Problems and Solutions

If the voice does not fit the writing situation, you'll need to revise it. (See also pages 25-32.)

Problem:

Solution:

The voice sounds arrogant.

Listen for:

■ "It's off-putting."

Look for:

■ We at Birks Cleaners provide the best dry cleaning around. We're in our third generation. Our quality speaks for itself.

Focus on the message and receiver, not on yourself.

Create a "you attitude" by addressing the receiver's needs and interests.

Revised Version: At Birks Cleaners, you'll find services to meet all your dry cleaning needs. For three generations, our goal has been to treat your clothes as if they were our own.

The voice gets in the way of the message.

Listen for:

■ "It's too flowery."

Look for:

■ From the starting pistol of this pivotal project, Janice worked with super-human strength to maneuver the company ship through the turbulent waters of this transition.

Make the voice transparent.

Focus on the message instead of the words. Rewrite passages that say, "Look at these words."

Revised Version: From start to finish, Janice worked hard to help us manage during this often difficult transition.

The voice is inappropriate.

Listen for:

■ "Don't be flip."

Look for:

■ Even though your being inconvenienced wasn't entirely our fault, we're obviously sorry about it.

Use the right formality for the situation.

Match the seriousness of tone to the message, medium, receiver, and context.

Revised Version: We apologize that your confirmed room was unavailable last night, and we are sorry for the inconvenience this may have caused you.

Revising for Words: Problems and Solutions

If the message is wordy, unclear, or negative, you'll need to revise the word choice. (See also pages 33-40.)

Problem:	**Solution:**

The message is wordy.

Listen for:
- "Get to the point."

Look for:
- The committee has been organized and set up in order to provide leadership in our effort to improve our abilities to communicate in and between departmental structures.

Cut repetition and vague phrases.

Make your point in as few words as necessary. Replace wordy phrases with concise, specific nouns and verbs.

Revised Version: The committee's goal is to improve communication between all departments.

The words are unclear.

Listen for:
- "It's cliched."
- "What is this jargon?"

Look for:
- Pursuant to his request, I analyzed Bob's physiological constitution and determined that his physical state of being was unimpaired.

Use clear, direct words.

Cut jargon and cliches. Use clear, simple, specific words to get your point across.

Revised Version: I checked Bob for injuries and determined that he was unharmed.

The message is negative.

Listen for:
- "You sound angry."

Look for:
- I read your memo requesting that all sales reps be given a whole day off for training in Cincinnati. While that stuff is important, Oscar, the bottom line is no less important! So I have no choice but to say, "No."

Use neutral or positive words.

Focus on the positive instead of the negative. Avoid insensitive or derogatory phrasing.

Revised Version: I reviewed your request to send all the sales reps to the training seminar in Cincinnati. Oscar, I agree that this training would help your staff be more productive. However, our budget for . . .

Revising for Sentences: Problems and Solutions

If the sentences in the message sound choppy, tired, or rambling, revise them. (See also pages 41-50.)

Problem:	Solution:

The sentences sound choppy.

Listen for:

- "Smooth this out."

Look for:

- I am responding to your job advertisement. It appeared in the *Seattle Times*. The date was June 12, 2011. It's the Software-Trainer job.

Combine sentences and add transitions.

Connect related sentences using a comma and a coordinating conjunction or a subordinating conjunction. Add transition words and phrases to smooth the flow of thought.

Revised Version: In response to your advertisement in the *Seattle Times* on November 12, 2011, I am applying for the position of Software-Training Specialist.

The sentences sound tired.

Listen for:

- "This sounds sluggish."

Look for:

- Your getting back to me in a short time was greatly appreciated. Some people take a lot longer. Some of your other people may also want to meet me next Thursday.

Use active voice, and change negative to positive.

Find what is performing the action of the verb and make it the subject of the sentence. If a sentence states a negative (what is not going to happen), rewrite it to state a positive (what is going to happen).

Revised Version: Thank you for your quick response to my letter of application for the position of Software-Training Specialist. I look forward to meeting you and the staff at Evergreen Medical Center next Thursday.

The sentences ramble.

Listen for:

- "I got lost."

Look for:

- I enjoyed touring your facilities and meeting your office managers, and I would enjoy contributing to the work that you and other staff members do at Evergreen, and I believe that my hospital training would be an asset.

Divide rambling sentences into shorter units.

Separate ideas into smaller groups, perhaps made up of one, two, or three ideas (not more).

Revised Version: After touring your facilities and meeting your office managers, I am certain that I would enjoy working at Evergreen Medical Center. I believe that my hospital training would be an asset.

Guidelines Refining

Your Goal ▶ Your goal when refining is to check grammar, usage, and mechanics; check the format; and create an effective final design.

> "A synonym is a word you use when you can't spell the word you first thought of."
>
> —Burt Bacharach

1. Make sure you've finished revising for overall meaning.
- If possible, let the draft sit for a while.
- Get mentally prepared to check your draft word by word.

2. Gather your tools.
- Use the models and the "Proofreader's Guide" in this handbook.
- Keep a dictionary, thesaurus, and company style sheet handy.
- Utilize computer tools (spell check, online thesaurus, grammar check, templates, cut-and-paste, find-and-replace).

3. Decide how much time and effort to put into refining.
- Consider the overall importance of the document.
- The wider the distribution, the higher the reader's status, or the more complex the content—the more refining you should do.

4. Follow logical steps.
- First, edit for errors in grammar, usage, and mechanics.
- Next, check the document's format and design for correctness, readability, and consistency with similar documents.
- Finally, address details related to distributing the document.

5. Find an objective reader.
- Turn to a coworker with good editing skills.
- Share documents with managers, experts, and legal counsel as needed.

6. Use your computer wisely.
- Run a final grammar check and spell check to catch basic errors.
- Print out your document and proofread it carefully.

Editing for Correctness

In addition to spelling errors and typos, the issues listed below commonly plague business documents. When refining your writing, use this list to find and correct the problems. See pages 51-58 and consult your "Proofreader's Guide," pages 256-352.

- Pronoun-Antecedent Agreement (page 325)

  To help a new employee learn our day-to-day procedures, please take ~~them~~ *her or him* through the orientation program.

- Shift in Person (page 326)

  When new employees go through this orientation, ~~you~~ *they* learn ~~your job~~ *their jobs* more quickly.

- Subject-Verb Agreement (pages 323-324)

  The procedure, as well as the attached checklist of steps and items, ~~cover~~ *covers* key orientation topics.

- Dangling Modifier (page 327)

  After filling in the review form for the new employee, ~~the form should be sent~~ *you should send the form* to Human Resources.

- Unparallel Construction (page 326)

  The form describes issues at each stage in the evaluation process: after 1 day, *after* 1 week ~~later,~~ *after* ~~then~~ 2 weeks ~~after starting,~~ and *after* ~~when~~ 30 days.

- Sentence Fragment (page 328)

  The form will streamline orientation for new employees, *and shorten the* ~~Much less~~ time it takes them to learn their assignments.

- Comma Splice (page 48)

  The new checklist includes more information than the old one , therefore, the new one will take more time to complete.

- Comma Omission After Introductory Phrases and Clauses (page 258)

  After the final review, the supervisor and the employee will sign the form.

- Comma Omission Between Independent Clauses (page 258)

  Reviewers should use the form for 30 days, and then they should forward the form to Human Resources.

- Comma Omission Around Nonrestrictive Modifiers (page 260)

  For each new employee, Human Resources, which is responsible for the initial orientation, will prepare a checklist with the employee's name on it.

"A process cannot be understood by stopping it. Understanding must move with the flow of the process, must join it and flow with it."

—Frank Herbert

shutterstock.com

Checklist The Writing Process

Your goal is to develop important messages by using the writing process—prewriting, drafting, revising, and refining.

Prewriting

____ **Ideas:** Have I analyzed my purpose and audience, developed a measurable goal, and collected information?

____ **Organization:** Have I organized my thoughts by using graphic organizers and/or outlining?

Drafting

____ **Ideas:** Have I recorded all my key points and essential information?

____ **Organization:** Have I created an opening, a middle, and a closing?

____ **Voice:** Have I maintained a person-to-person tone from start to finish?

Revising

____ **Ideas:** Have I fixed problems with the draft's overall focus, clarity, and content? If appropriate, have I gotten feedback from a colleague?

____ **Organization:** Have I sharpened the opening to pull readers in, reworked the middle paragraphs to improve flow and coherence, and improved the closing to help readers take the next step?

____ **Voice:** Have I fixed any lapses in attitude, level, or energy so that the topic and reader are in the foreground and I am in the background?

____ **Words:** Have I eliminated cliches, jargon, and redundancy so that the wording is concise, clear, and positive?

____ **Sentences:** Have I removed choppy, tired, and rambling sentences by using combining, parallelism, transitions, active voice, and variety?

Refining

____ **Correctness:** Have I proofread for sentence, punctuation, mechanics, spelling, and usage errors (using but not relying solely on a grammar check and a spell check)? If appropriate, have I gotten editing help?

____ **Design:** Have I fine-tuned the format, page layout, and typography to make the document professional, inviting, and readable?

Section 2:
Writing Three Message Types

In this section

shutterstock.com

9
Writing Good or Neutral News

There's no news like good news. That's as true in the workplace as it is in the rest of life. Readers are happy to receive good-news e-mails, memos, and letters, and they usually respond, "It's good to know this!" or "It's my job to deal with this, so I'll take care of it."

This chapter will help you craft good- or neutral-news messages quickly and effectively, using the SEA organization formula (see page 21). The formula walks you through a process that delivers the news up front, and then follows up with supporting details that explain what the message means and why it's good. If your message requires the reader to respond, the formula also helps you shape that request.

Guidelines Good-News and Neutral Messages

Your Goal ▶ Your goal when writing a good-news or neutral letter, memo, or e-mail message is to present the news effectively and invite the reader's response.

> "Good words are worth much, and cost little."
>
> —George Herbert

1. **Prewrite:** (Ideas and Organization)
   - Ask yourself what you want your message to do.
   - Think about the person you are writing to, what he or she already knows, and what he or she needs to know.

   Prepare to draft.
   - Consider what your reader wants or expects.
   - Gather work-related reasons for your news.
   - If appropriate, explore other options for the reader.

2. **Draft:** (Ideas, Organization, and Voice)
   Remember SEA—Situation (main point), **Explanation, Action.** (See page 21.)
   Opening Identify the topic and explain why you are writing. Present your key point as either a statement, a question, or a request.
   Middle Support your main point with details that clarify the situation, news, and implications. If appropriate, focus on benefits.
   Closing Note any action the reader should take; include steps that may be taken; and add contact information. Indicate *who* should do *what*, *when*, *where*, *why*, and *how*. If action is unnecessary, simply end the message positively and politely.

3. **Revise:** (Ideas, Organization, Voice, Words, and Sentences)
   - ☐ Have you included accurate details—in the best order?
   - ☐ Have you used a businesslike tone with polite attention to the reader's needs and benefits?
   - ☐ Have you used clear, concise wording?
   - ☐ Do you have clear, concise sentences?

4. **Refine:** (Conventions and Design)
   - ☐ Have you checked grammar, punctuation, and spelling?
   - ☐ Have you checked the format (spacing, type size, fonts, and so on)?

shutterstock.com

Announcement or Notice

Subject line

State the subject.

Opening

State the main point up front.

Middle

Provide details to explain the main point.

Present information from the reader's point of view.

Closing

Explain what the reader should do. Close the message by inviting feedback.

Send | Attach | Fonts | Colors | Save As Draft

To: All Rankin Employees

▶ Main Point

Cc:

Subject: New Policy for Air-Travel Arrangements

Good morning:

Starting April 1, please make all your company-related flight arrangements through the Travel Center. This change will require some adjustments, but it will actually benefit both you and the company.

The business office is implementing the change because the Travel Center is now offering several options for its corporate customers. In checking out the options, we found an attractive reservation and payment plan. Here are some details:

- If you personally book a flight with the Travel Center, you will accumulate bonus miles in your name.
- If the company books the flight, as in the past, the company will receive the bonus miles.
- The company will have a more efficient way to track travel costs.

Please follow the procedure below for all future company flights:

1. Book flights through the Travel Center (262-555-8898 or travelcenter.com) and charge them to Rankin.
2. When Sherri Pomerenki forwards the invoice to you, specify the account to be charged, sign the invoice, and return it to her.

If you have any questions, please contact me by phone (ext. 9721) or e-mail (belias@rnkn.com).

Thanks,
Brittany Elias
Director, Human Resources

Update

| Send | Attach | Fonts | Colors | Save As Draft |

To: Randall Poole

Cc:

Subject line

State the subject.

Subject: Update on New-Employee Orientation Process

Attach: Orientation Checklist.docx

Opening

Announce your purpose and subject.

Hi, Randall:

Here's an update on the new-employee orientation program.

First, I developed a new checklist by combining two forms into one and by adding several items. The new form is attached, with additions highlighted.

Middle

Organize your points clearly, logically, and completely.

Present information in lists.

Second, I fine-tuned the orientation procedure to work with the new form. Here's an overview:

1. Human Resources will enclose this checklist in each new employee's orientation packet.

2. Rebecca will cover items one through six during her new-employee presentation.

3. The employee's supervisor will confirm that the employee understands items one through six, and then cover the remaining items.

4. The supervisor will fill out the performance reviews on the reverse side of the form following this schedule: after day one, at the end of week one, at the end of week two, and after 30 days.

5. After the final review, the supervisor and the new employee will sign the form, and the supervisor will return it to Human Resources.

Closing

Anticipate the next step.

Please look at the attached form and evaluate the procedure. With your approval, we will present this information to area supervisors at their next meeting.

Thanks,
Melissa St. James

Cover Message

Send | Attach | Fonts | Colors | Save As Draft

To: Department Heads

Cc:

Subject line

State the subject.

Subject: New-Employee Orientation Checklist Adopted

Attach: Orientation Checklist.docx

Good morning:

Opening

Announce the attachment and its purpose.

To help new employees become familiar with day-to-day procedures, Human Resources has revised the New-Employee Orientation Checklist (attached). The revised checklist should shorten the time it takes for new employees to learn their assignments, company policies, and department procedures.

Middle

Use a numbered list to provide details the reader needs to understand.

You will receive the checklist on the first day that a new employee starts work in your department. As before, please use the form for 30 days and then return it to Human Resources. Note the following details:

1. While the form does not cite all topics addressed during orientation, the form does list the key topics that need to be covered.

2. The form lists the topics Human Resources will address and the topics that department heads will need to cover.

3. The last section of the form covers how new employees are reviewed. The review process is broken into four time periods: after day one, at the end of week one, at the end of week two, and after 30 days.

Closing

Request feedback.

Because the updated checklist includes more information, it will take more time to complete. However, we believe this checklist will help all new employees learn their jobs more quickly. Please review the checklist. If you have questions about it, call me at extension 89, or e-mail me with any questions.

Thanks,
Melissa St. James

Credit Approval

If needed, insert a confirmation notation.

Cottonwood Hills
GREENHOUSE AND FLORIST SUPPLY

Rural Route 2 • Macon, GA 31220-2339
Phone 655-555-3321 • Fax 655-555-1440
www.cottonwoodhills.com

March 3, 2010

Confirmation of e-mail sent March 26, 2010.

Mr. Grant Bostwick, President
Dale's Garden Center
484 Leeward Avenue, SE
Tuscaloosa, AL 35406-3770

Dear Mr. Bostwick:

Opening

State the approval positively.

Thank you for requesting a credit account at Cottonwood Hills Greenhouse and Florist Supply. We are pleased to extend you $100,000 in credit based on Dale's Garden Center's strong financial condition. Congratulations!

Middle

To avoid future problems, spell out details or credit terms.

Here are some details concerning your account:
1. You will be billed the first day of the month.
2. The balance is due within 30 days, interest free.
3. Any balance owed beyond 30 days will be subject to a 15 percent annual finance charge.

I have enclosed a brochure describing our credit policies and procedures in more detail. Please call me (655-555-3321) if you have any questions.

Closing

Include sales material and anticipate a positive future.

Because you indicated that you plan to expand your sales of bedding plants and silk flowers, I have also enclosed our spring catalog with these sections flagged. Mr. Bostwick, we look forward to filling your orders and satisfying your customers. Count on us to help Dale's flourish!

Yours sincerely,

Salome Nguru

Salome Nguru
Sales Manager

Enclosures 2

Information Request

Wilson & Wilson *Attorneys-at-Law*

626 State Street, Halifax, NS B3J 3A5 ■ 613-555-7500 ■ wilsnandwilsn.com

February 22, 2010

Planning & Development Services
Halifax Regional Municipality
P.O. Box 1749
Halifax, NS B3J 3A5
CANADA

SUBJECT: ZONING INQUIRY FOR 219 WELLS ST., HALIFAX, NS

Opening

Put key details up front so that the request makes sense.

I represent the purchaser, Hector Coyote, in a transaction for the property noted above, presently owned by Diana Elbach. I'm writing to request information necessary for moving forward with the sale.

Middle

Make your requests politely.

List questions in logical order.

Please send me the following information:

1. According to the owner, the building on the property is being used as a residence with a second unit (an attic apartment). Does this use conform with the current zoning code?

2. Were building and occupancy permits issued for this property? If so, when was each issued? Were conditions attached? If so, what?

3. Does the property meet municipal standards for side- and front-yard clearance? (Please refer to the enclosed survey.)

Closing

Give clear, simple response directions and close politely.

Because of the purchase agreement between Ms. Elbach and Mr. Coyote, I need this information by March 1. Please feel free to fax (613-555-7501) or mail your answers on the enclosed form.

Thank you for your assistance.

David S. Wilson

DAVID S. WILSON

DSW/BBK
Enclosures 2

Invitation

R T Rankin Technologies

1595 Rosa Plaza SE ❖ Albuquerque, NM 87105-1029 ❖ Phone 507.555.9000 ❖ Fax 507.555.9002 ❖ www.rnkn.com

May 28, 2010

Ms. Lorraine Scott
Sales Representative
206 West Dundee Street
Chicago, IL 60614

Dear Lorraine:

Opening

State the invitation politely.

Welcome to the Sales Seminar! I hope that you will have a productive week. While you are here, please help us celebrate Rankin's 20th anniversary.

Middle

Provide the context.

Give all necessary details of the event.

This year, we have a lot to celebrate. Our office expansion is finished, and sales grew by 16 percent. On Wednesday, June 2, we would like you to be our guest at the following events:

- an open house from 8:30 a.m. to 4:00 p.m. with hourly tours of the new office, engineering, and manufacturing facilities.

- a ribbon-cutting ceremony at 4:00 p.m. on the west lawn, with refreshments served at 4:30 p.m.

Closing

Anticipate participation and offer help.

You are a big part of Rankin's success, Lorraine. I hope that you can take a break from your busy seminar schedule and join us. If you need directions, transportation, or other information, please speak with Rebecca Wright or call Matthew Nicolai at 555-1980, extension 4, or send him an e-mail at mnicolai@rnkn.com.

Sincerely,

Sharissa Hershey

Sharissa Hershey
Vice President of Sales

rh/svw

Positive Adjustment

1400 NW Academy Drive
Phone 412/555-0900

 AC Drives

Atlanta, GA 30425
Fax 412/555-0054

July 8, 2010

Confirmation of e-mail sent July 1, 2010.

Mr. Jamaal Ellison
Southeast Electric
1976 Boulder Road, Suite 1214
Charlotte, NC 28216-1203

Dear Mr. Ellison:

Opening

Provide necessary background, apologize, and offer solutions.

Thank you for your patience and understanding as we investigated the malfunction of the ATV16 drives that you had installed for American Linc Company. I apologize for the inconvenience caused to both your company and American Linc. Below is a description of the problem, along with our solution.

Middle

Explain causes and solutions clearly in neutral language.

Problem: Serial-link failure. In response to your report on the malfunction, AC Drives sent a technician to American Linc Company. He determined the cause of the failure to be a defective voltage regulator in the serial-link box.

Solution: Our technician replaced the voltage regulator and apologized to Jean Snow, plant manager. This morning I wrote an e-mail and a follow-up letter to Ms. Snow in which I acknowledged that the problem was ours (not yours), and I apologized for the inconvenience.

Closing

Express appreciation and focus on future business.

Thanks again for alerting us to the problem. With your help, it was resolved promptly. I look forward to future business with Southeast Electric.

Yours sincerely,

Elaine Hoffman

Elaine Hoffman
Product Manager

Positive Reply to an Inquiry

Aspen State Bank

4554 Ridgemount Boulevard, Aspen, CO 81225-0064, PHONE 459-555-0098, FAX 459-555-5886
contact@aspenstatebank.com

February 24, 2010

Christine and Dale Shepherd
1026 11th Avenue, NE
Aspen, CO 81212-3219

Dear Christine and Dale:

Opening

State the reason for your response and your appreciation for the inquiry.

Thank you for your inquiry yesterday about financing your resort project. I enjoyed discussing your project and appreciated your frankness about your current loan with Boulder National Bank.

Middle

Provide the reader with the desired information and stress its value.

Although you commented that you will seek an extension of your loan from Boulder National, I have enclosed Aspen State Bank's commitment letter, subject to the terms we discussed. Perhaps you will consider our package. Rates available are as follows:

15-year fixed rate	5.875%
20-year fixed rate	6.25%
30-year fixed rate	6.25%

In case you do not proceed with the Boulder loan, this commitment will be good for 60 business days from today (February 24). If lower rates are available at closing, you will receive the benefit of that reduction.

Closing

Anticipate and invite future contact.

Thank you for your interest. I hope that your project goes well. If we can't work together on this project, please keep us in mind for future credit needs.

Yours sincerely,

Cara Harrison

Cara Harrison
Loan Officer

Enclosure: Commitment Letter

Request or Proposal Acceptance

Juanita Guiverra, Computer Consultant

368 Palm Palace Boulevard
Miami, FL 33166-0064
Telephone: 313.555.0010
Fax: 313.555-0500
E-Mail: jguiverra@cnsult.com

March 22, 2010

Mr. Gavin Farnsworth
Miami Computer Enterprises
1202 South Benton
Miami, FL 33166-1217

Dear Mr. Farnsworth:

Opening

State your acceptance positively.

I have reviewed your letter of March 15. In response to your proposal, I am happy to offer my consulting services to Miami Computer customers.

Middle

Stress the benefits of the decision and cover details that need to be clarified or recorded.

This arrangement will benefit all parties involved. Together, we will be able to offer your clients "one-stop shopping" for all their computer needs—hardware, software, training, and support. And I will be able to work with your established customer base without having to generate my own.

Therefore, I accept your proposed rate of $45 per hour (minimum of 20 hours per week) as indicated in the amended agreement (outline enclosed). Please note that the bold items on the outline indicate additions to the original proposal. I simply added the items covered in your letter.

Closing

Explore the next step and anticipate a positive outcome.

Please let me know of any specific information or documentation that you need to see on my invoices. I look forward to a productive partnership in which we will serve each other and your clients.

Yours sincerely,

Juanita Guiverra

Juanita Guiverra

Enc.: Agreement Outline

Thank-You Message

Hope Services *Child Development Center*

2141 South Fifth Place, Seatle, WA 907761 • Telephone 436-555-1400
www.hopeserv.org

May 14, 2010

Mr. Donald Keebler
Keebler Electronics
466 Hanover Boulevard
Penticton, BC V2A 5S1
CANADA

Dear Mr. Keebler:

Opening

State your thanks directly.

On behalf of the entire staff at Hope Services, I want to thank you for helping us choose a sound system that fits both our needs and our budget. Thanks, too, for working around our schedule during installation.

Middle

Provide clear, specific details.

Be personal and professional in tone.

We have found that the system meets all our needs. Being able to adjust sound input and output for different uses in different rooms has been wonderful. The system helps staff in the family room with play-based assessment, and team members are tuning in to different conversations as if they were in the room themselves. As a result, children who might feel overwhelmed with too many people in the room can relax and play naturally.

In addition, parents also use the sound system to listen in on sessions in the therapy room as therapists model constructive one-on-one communication methods with children.

Closing

Use the reader's name and stress cooperation and future contact.

Thanks again, Donald, for your cooperation and excellent work. I would be happy to recommend your services to anyone needing sound equipment.

Yours sincerely,

Barbara Talbot

Barbara Talbot
Executive Director

Apology

MAGNOLIA GRAND

2580 Peach Tree Court
Memphis, TN 64301
901-555-5400 maggrand@hytp.com

July 7, 2010

Note: An apology puts the good news up front: an apology, expression of regret, and amends.

Opening

Be positive, and provide your main point (the apology). Indicate how you will make amends.

Middle

Explain what caused the problem, repeat the apology, and reiterate how you have addressed the situation.

Closing

Stress further assistance and continued satisfaction.

Ms. Joan Meyer
605 Appleton Avenue
Green Bay, WI 53401

Dear Ms. Meyer:

Thank you for choosing Magnolia Grand! We apologize that your confirmed room was unavailable last night. For your trouble, there will be no charge for last night's lodging, and we've upgraded your room at no expense to you.

We make every effort to accommodate guest requests, but when several guests did not depart as scheduled, we were forced to change your accommodations. We are sorry for any inconvenience this may have caused you, but hope the upgrade and free night make up for this change. As always, our goal is to offer you outstanding service and genuine hospitality.

Should you need any assistance, please call the front desk or contact me directly at extension 408. We hope you enjoy the remainder of your stay with us. Thank you for your patience, understanding, and patronage.

Yours sincerely,

Mary-Lee Preston

Mary-Lee Preston
Front Office Manager

MP/AM

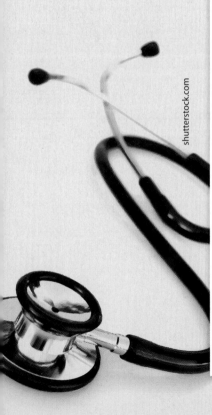

"For most folks, no news is good news; for the press, good news is not news."

—Gloria Borger

Checklist Good or Neutral News

Your goal when writing a good-news or neutral letter, memo, or e-mail message is to present the news effectively and invite the reader's response.

Ideas   9-16
____ has a main point, and all supporting points are clear, precise, and accurate.
____ supplies readers with all the necessary information.

Organization   17-24
____ has an opening that provides necessary background and presents the key point as either a statement, a question, or a request.
____ has a middle that expands the main point by adding supporting details while explaining benefits to the reader.
____ has a closing that calls for action, stresses continued contact, offers help, and/or focuses positively on the future by answering *who* should do *what, when, where, why,* and *how.*
____ follows the SEA organization pattern.

Voice   25-32
____ uses a businesslike and polite voice that is not rushed or abrupt.

Words   33-40
____ uses everyday language (plain English) as much as possible.
____ defines words unfamiliar to readers.

Sentences   41-50
____ states the main point in a clear sentence.
____ contains helpful transitions and reads well aloud.

Correctness   51-58
____ is free of errors in grammar, spelling, punctuation, and typing.

Design   59-70
____ uses correct format for a letter, a memo, or an e-mail message.
____ includes white space and easy-to-read type.
____ organizes ideas, points, and details using numbers, bullets, or graphics.

shutterstock.com

shutterstock.com

10
Writing Bad News

It used to be dangerous to be the bearer of bad news. In ancient times, people often killed the messenger if they disliked the message! Business today may be more civilized, but the fact remains that a bad-news message is one that your reader doesn't want to receive.

To deliver bad news, you have two choices: (1) state the bad news right away, or (2) soften it by leading up to it with an explanation. If the bad news is minor, or if your reader expects it, go ahead and be direct. But in most cases, the second approach is better.

Guidelines Bad-News Messages

Your Goal ▶ Your goal when sending bad news is to write a message that is clear, fair, and courteous.

> "Tact is the art of making a point without making an enemy."
> —Howard H. Newton

shutterstock.com

1. Prewrite: (Ideas and Organization)
- Aim to convince the reader that your news is necessary and fair.
- Strive to continue a good relationship with the reader.

Prepare to draft.
- Consider what your reader wants or expects.
- Gather work-related reasons for your news.
- If appropriate, explore other options for the reader.

2. Draft: (Ideas, Organization, and Voice)
Remember BEBE—**B**uffer, **E**xplanation, **B**ad news (main point), **E**xit. (See page 22.)
Opening Begin with a buffer: a neutral statement like thanking the reader for past business, agreeing on a point, or expressing understanding.
Middle Build up to the bad news.
- Be brief. One good reason is preferable to several weak ones.
- If helpful, explain company policy.
- State the bad news in the middle or at the end of a paragraph. If possible, follow with an alternative.

Closing Express regret (without apologizing) and end politely.

3. Revise: (Ideas, Organization, Voice, Words, and Sentences)
- ☐ Have you supplied a clear, sensitive explanation that helps the reader say, "I understand"?
- ☐ Have you used a sincere, gracious tone that avoids a "we" versus "you" attitude?
- ☐ Have you used neutral, exact, and sensitive wording?
- ☐ Do you have easy-to-read sentences with smooth transitions?

4. Refine: (Conventions and Design)
- ☐ Have you checked names, data, grammar, punctuation, and spelling?
- ☐ Have you checked format (spacing, type, and so on)?

Bid Rejection

EVERSON CITY PLANNING AND DEVELOPMENT COMMITTEE

Everson City Council • Everson, WA 98247-2311 • 306/555-2134 • www.eversonpdc.org

▶ Main Point

February 12, 2010

Mr. Felix Grove
Sea-to-Mountain Landscapers
8900 Coast Road
Seattle, WA 98134-6508

Dear Mr. Grove:

Opening

Buffer: Specify the bid and thank the bidder.

SUBJECT: Bid 4459 Everson City Park

Thank you for your bid to design and develop Everson's eight-acre city park adjacent to Kingston Elementary School and the Nooksack River.

Middle

Highlight the reader's strengths objectively, but specify why another bid won.

Your bid was competitive for several of the criteria outlined in our original Request for Proposals (RFP). Your cost estimates, experience, and references were as strong as those from other bidders. However, Earth-Scape Design's overall plan tipped the bid in their favor. By including a variety of native plant species, Earth-Scape's natural, sustainable landscape will require less long-term care and create less stress on the Nooksack watershed. Because their plan contained a variety of plants, it also offered added educational value.

Closing

If appropriate, encourage bidding on future projects.

The Planning and Development Committee appreciates the work that you put into your proposal. We look forward to your interest in future Everson projects.

Yours sincerely,

Alice Potter

Alice Potter
Development Committee Chair

Claim Denial

1400 NW Academy Drive
Phone 412/555-0900
www.acdrives.com

Atlanta, GA 30425
Fax 412/555-0054

June 16, 2010

Confirmation of e-mail sent on June 15, 2010.

Mr. Jamaal Ellison
Southeast Electric
1976 Boulder Road, Suite 1214
Charlotte, NC 28261-1203

Dear Mr. Ellison:

Opening

Buffer: Restate the problem and show concern.

We have finished investigating your concerns about the ATV16 drives that you installed for American Linc Company. We do understand that the drive and serial-link failures have inconvenienced both you and American Linc.

Middle

Use sound evidence and state the claim denial clearly.

Offer helpful alternatives.

After testing the drives you returned, our line engineer determined that they failed because the temperatures in the cabinet exceeded the maximum operating temperature of the drives, leading to electronic-component failure. As noted in the ATV16 manual, the drive may malfunction under such conditions. For this reason, we cannot repair the drives without charge. We would be happy, however, to consider the following solutions:

1. We could remove the drive's plastic cover and install a stirring fan in the enclosure to moderate the temperature.

2. We could replace the ATV16 drives with the ATV18 model, a model more suitable for the machine you are using. (If you choose this option, we would give you a 15 percent discount on the ATV18s.)

Closing

Focus on the next step and on future business.

Please let me know how you would like to proceed. I look forward to hearing from you and to continuing our partnership.

Yours sincerely,

Elaine Hoffman

Elaine Hoffman
Product Manager

**Complaint
(Basic)**

brunewald systems design 5690 Brantley Boulevard, P. O. Box 6094
Trenton, NJ 08561-4221
451.555.0900
www.brunewaldsystemsdesign.com

February 26, 2010

BHC Office Supply Company
39 Davis Street
Pittsburgh, PA 15209-1334

ATTENTION: Shipping Manager

Opening

Buffer: Establish
the claim's context.

I'm writing about a problem with the purchase order #07-1201. Copies of the original PO plus two invoices are enclosed.

Here is the sequence of events concerning PO 07-1201:

Dec. 16, 2009: I faxed the original purchase order.

Middle

Tactfully spell
out the facts.

Point out results of
the problem
in a neutral tone.

Specify the
adjustment that
you want.

Jan. 8, 2010: Because I hadn't heard from your office, I spoke with Kim in customer service. Then I re-sent the PO because she could not find the original in your system.

Jan. 15, 2010: I received a partial shipment, with the remaining items back-ordered (invoice 0151498).

Jan. 21, 2010: I then received a second shipment that was complete (invoice 0151511). Noting the duplication, I contacted Kim, and she cancelled the back-ordered items.

I am returning the partial order (duplicate items) by UPS. Please credit our account for the following: (1) the duplicate items listed on invoice 0151498 ($863.85), (2) the shipping costs of the partial order ($69.20), and (3) the UPS costs to return the duplicate items ($58.10). The total credit comes to $991.15.

Closing

Anticipate future
business.

I look forward to receiving an adjusted statement and to continued cooperation in the future.

Gary Sheridan

GARY SHERIDAN—OFFICE MANAGER

gs/mc
Enclosures 3

**Complaint
(Serious)**

R_T *Rankin Technologies*

1595 Rosa Plaza SE ❖ Albuquerque, NM 87105-1029 ❖ Phone 507.555.9000 ❖ Fax 507.555.9002 ❖ www.rnkn.com

January 15, 2010

Mr. Steven Grinnel
Director of Operations
Industrial Aggregate Equipment Company
4018 Tower Road
Albuquerque, NM 87105-3443

Dear Mr. Grinnel:

Opening

Buffer: Specify the
problem and the
reason for concern.

I am very concerned about the 40-foot Snorkel Lift that we contracted with
you to rebuild when we traded in our old Marklift. Continued delays in the
rebuilding schedule and subsequent problems with the lift itself leave me
uncertain about Industrial Aggregate's ability to provide Rankin Technologies
with continued service.

Middle

Provide a
detailed outline
of the problem and
its history.

Keep your
tone neutral.

Be specific
and factual.

Here is an overview of the problem:

1. We ordered the Snorkel Lift in April 2009, and you promised delivery in
   July. We did not receive the lift until September.

2. When the lift arrived, we noticed several key parts had not been replaced,
   and the boom did not operate correctly. Your project supervisor, Nick
   Luther, assured us that the parts would be fixed in a timely manner, and he
   provided a substitute lift for free.

3. Two months later, Mr. Luther called to say that everything was fixed.
   However, when we visited your facility on December 18, the gauges and
   tires on the lift had not been replaced, and the dual fuel unit had not been
   installed.

4. When we finally received the Snorkel Lift on December 22, several items
   we noticed on December 18 still had not been fixed. In fact, the lift still
   had these deficiencies:
   • several oil leaks
   • missing "on/off" switch in the basket
   • no dual fuel capabilities
   • boom vibration when retracted after full extension

Page 2
Steven Grinnel
January 15, 2010

Middle

Give needed
background and
attach relevant
support.

We have been extremely disappointed with the lift's condition and overall performance. Your original promise of a fully operational Snorkel Lift in "like new" condition by July 2009 (agreement copy enclosed) has not been met.

In the past, we have appreciated your service and assistance. From our experience of the past six months, however, we can only conclude that you are experiencing problems that make it difficult for you to provide the service Rankin Technologies needs.

Closing

State the
proposed
solution clearly and
firmly.

We want to resolve this issue. By February 16, 2010 please provide us with a lift that meets all the specifications agreed to and that has no operational deficiencies. If you are unable to provide the lift by that date, we will cancel our order and seek reimbursement for the used Marklift we traded in April 2009.

Sincerely,

Jane Ballentine

Jane Ballentine
Maintenance Project Engineer

JB/RD
Enc.: copy of agreement
cc: Andrew Longfellow
        President, Industrial Aggregate Equipment Company

Credit or Loan Application Denial

LONE STAR BANK

5550 North Adeline Road, Houston, TX 77022
Phone 547.555.0100, FAX 547.555.7024, E-Mail contact@loanestar.com

May 5, 2010

Ms. Mary-Lou Twain
780 East 41st Street, Apartment 712
Houston, TX 77022-1183

Dear Ms. Twain:

Opening

Buffer: Express appreciation for the application.

Thank you for meeting with loan officer Jean Olms last Friday and applying for a loan to open your gift shop.

Middle

Provide objective reasons for the rejection. Then state the rejection and offer suggestions.

When we review an application, one of the factors that we consider is the applicant's credit history. A good credit history shows a pattern of paying obligations. At this time, because you have not established a credit history, we cannot approve your request to borrow $200,000. However, you can establish a good credit history in one of two ways:

- Apply for, use, and make prompt payments on a credit card.
- Take out and repay a smaller loan at Lone Star Bank. Just a $5,000 loan successfully repaid would establish a positive financial record.

Closing

If appropriate, encourage applying when conditions change.

We hope that these suggestions will help you begin to establish a good credit history. Then you may reapply for the loan that you requested.

Sincerely,

Rodney Thayer

Rodney Thayer
President

RT/BJH

P.S. Please see the reverse side of this letter for information about your rights under the Federal Equal Credit Opportunity Act and other relevant laws.

Crisis Management

Subject line

Use a neutral subject line.

Opening

Buffer: State your reason for writing.

Middle

State the bad news factually and calmly.

Focus on solutions: what has been done and what needs to be done.

Closing

Stress a positive future, but be realistic. Ask for feedback, if appropriate.

| Send | Attach | Fonts | Colors | Save As Draft |

To: All Staff

Cc:

Subject: Recent FDA Plant Inspection Presents Challenges

Good Morning:

As you know, this past Monday, July 12, the FDA came to our plant for a spot inspection. I'm writing to share the inspection results and our response.

The good news is that the FDA inspectors did not find problems warranting a shutdown of Premium Meats. However, the bad news is that the inspectors cited us for three major violations resulting in a fine of $100,000.

The FDA is sending us a clear message. We must take immediate steps to protect our customers, our jobs, and our company. To that end, I have taken the following steps:

1. The Executive Committee met with me to review the FDA report and determine the problem areas in our production process.

2. I have directed the Production Management Team to review quality-control procedures and conduct two retraining sessions immediately.

3. I have appointed a Quality Task Force of both management and production staff to study the production process and make further recommendations.

4. I have briefed Sales and Public-Relations staff and directed them to contact customers and the media.

With short-term solutions and long-term cooperation, we will keep Premium Meats operating and prospering. If you have any suggestions or questions, please speak to your immediate supervisor or a member of the Quality Task Force.

Lawrence Durante

Negative Change Announcement

Wright Insurance Agency

3406 Capitol Boulevard, Suite 588
Washington, DC 20037-1124
Phone 612-555-0020
wright@insre.com

January 15, 2010

Policy 46759

Ms. Virginia Beloit
72 Elias Street
Washington, DC 20018-8262

Dear Ms. Beloit:

Opening

Buffer: Introduce the topic and its context.

Periodically, insurance companies review their policies, assess the cost of offering the policies, and make changes where needed. When that happens, it's my responsibility as an insurance agent to inform my clients and help them make necessary adjustments.

Middle

Give rationale for the change.

State the change. If possible, offer help.

Last week Hawkeye Casualty, the company with whom you have your auto insurance policy, discontinued all policies for drivers considered "high risk." Because you have had a traffic accident within the past 12 months and have received two speeding tickets during the same period, the company has relabeled your status as "high risk." As a result, Hawkeye Casualty has cancelled your auto-insurance policy effective January 31, 2010. However, I have found another company that will offer you auto insurance. While the cost of this new policy is somewhat higher than your present policy, the coverage is comparable, and the company is reliable.

Closing

Explain what the reader should do.

Please call me at 612-489-0020 within the next week so we can discuss the situation and decide how to proceed.

Sincerely,

Eric Wright

Eric Wright

EW/RN

Poor Results Explanation

Heading

Send a copy to the appropriate people.

Use a neutral subject line.

Opening

Buffer: Explain the context and give some good news.

Middle

Explain the problem, focusing on issues and solutions, not individuals.

Closing

Politely explain follow-up.

| Send | Attach | Fonts | Colors | Save As Draft |

To: `<laurie@vgouto.com> <julie@vgouto.com> <mark@vgouto.com>`

Cc: `<micah@vgouto.com> <rachel@wgauto.com>`

Subject: Van Gorp Automotive 2009 Sales Report and Customer Survey

Good morning, Laurie, Julie, and Mark:

Last week, Jesse Cam from marketing sent me the 2009 sales report, along with a summary of our customer survey (copies attached). As the report shows, we had another good year: annual receipts in our three stores increased 9 percent. In addition, the survey shows that customers' satisfaction with our Maintenance Departments continues to be high: 74 percent, Excellent; 18 percent, Good; 6 percent, Fair; and 2 percent, Poor. That's great news—and our employees deserve the credit!

However, the survey also shows that our sales personnel can improve. During your next meetings with them, please read through customers' comments listed in Jesse's summary. Note statements like those listed below, identify the problems, and discuss how we can improve:

1. "Nobody greeted me when I walked in."

2. "The sales guy talked to me and two other customers—all at the same time."

3. "Your salesman knew his stuff—but he seemed to push a sunroof, and I didn't want one."

4. "Leah was great, but she was your ONLY female salesperson!"

After reviewing the attachments and then meeting with your sales staffs, please write a report on your findings and send copies to Jim N., Jamie, and me.

Thanks,
Bernice Gardener

Proposal Rejection

Juanita Guiverra, Computer Consultant

368 Palm Palace Boulevard
Miami, FL 33166-0064
Telephone: 313.555.0010
Fax: 313.555-0500
E-Mail: jguiverra@cnsult.com

March 24, 2010

Mr. Gavin Farnsworth
Miami Computer Enterprises
Box 115
South Benton Mall
Miami, FL 33166-1217

Dear Gavin:

Opening

Buffer: Show appreciation.

Thank you for your proposal that I join your Customer Training Department. I appreciate your confidence in my ability to provide Miami Computer Enterprises' clients with instruction and technical support.

Middle

Give your reasons objectively, stress positives in the proposal, state the rejection tactfully, and explore other options.

While considering your proposal, I reflected on the reasons that I started my own computer-consulting service two years ago. One of the reasons was flexibility. As an independent consultant, I could regulate my work activities around family demands. Although your proposal was financially attractive, I must turn down your offer, at least for now.

In 17 months (August 2011), my youngest child will enter grade school. If you are still interested in me at that time, I would be happy to reconsider your proposal. Until then, I hope you will want me to continue doing contract projects for MCE, especially with your Spanish-speaking clients.

Closing

End positively.

Thanks again for your generous proposal. I wish MCE continued growth and success.

Yours sincerely,

Juanita Guiverra

Juanita Guiverra

Donation-Request Denial

*R*_{*T*} *Rankin Technologies*
401 Manheim Road ❖ Albany, NY 12236 ❖ Phone 708.555.1980 ❖ Fax 708.555.0056 ❖ www.rnkn.com

April 16, 2010

Ms. Marlis DeQuincey
Executive Director
Family First Center
468 Provis Way
Fairfield, NY 12377-2089

Dear Ms. DeQuincey:

Opening

Buffer: Express interest in the reader's cause.

I read with interest your letter about Family First Center's project. Your efforts to build a shelter for women and children victimized by domestic violence are certainly commendable.

Middle

Provide clear reasons for not participating.

State the refusal tactfully.

If possible, offer an alternative.

I am honored that you have invited Rankin Technologies to participate in your project. Rankin seeks to be a good corporate citizen and a positive force in the community. To that end, we have already committed ourselves to partnerships with nonprofit organizations that mesh with Rankin's interests in the environment, in urban renewal, and in Third-World development. For this reason, we cannot participate in your project at this time.

Rankin employees will, however, be encouraged to continue to support your work in the community campaign. In fact, I will distribute materials about your project to our employees so that individuals may choose to get involved.

Closing

Affirm the reader.

I wish you well, Ms. DeQuincey, in your important work of helping the victims of physical and emotional violence in this community.

Yours sincerely,

Barbara Reinholdt

Barbara Reinholdt
Office Manager

br/dn

Funding-Request Denial

| Send | Attach | Fonts | Colors | Save As Draft |

To: Oscar Nunez@rnkn.com

Cc:

Subject: Netware Training for Sales Staff

Dear Oscar:

I've reviewed your request to send all the sales reps to the Netware training seminar in Cincinnati. Oscar, I agree that this training would help your staff be more productive.

With your request in mind, I reviewed our training budget to see if we could afford the seminar. A large portion of our budget has already been used to upgrade design software for the engineering staff. In addition, we have some prior commitments for training office staff in August. Therefore, there is not enough money available to send all sales reps to Cincinnati.

Perhaps there's another way. If we sent two of your key staff to the seminar, they could then train others in your department. Or we could plan an extensive in-house training session for your entire group.

I'd be happy to explore these or other options with you. With a little creativity, I think that we could get your reps the training they need. Just call or e-mail me (ext. 3957).

Sincerely,
Jim

Opening

Buffer: Restate the request and offer a point of agreement.

Middle

State your reasons briefly, clearly, and objectively. If possible, explore alternatives.

Closing

End on a note of encouragement.

Avoid the following words and phrases when rejecting a request:

I am surprised	I question/take issue with
company policy prohibits	you apparently overlooked
are not able to	you obviously failed to
must refuse/reject	I cannot understand your
you claim/complain	contrary to what you say
has never happened before	unjustified
misinformed	I trust you will agree

Suggestion Rejection

| Send | Attach | Fonts | Colors | Save As Draft |

To: Duane Bolten@rnkn.com

Cc:

Subject: Offering Telecommuting to Employees

Hi, Duane:

Opening

Buffer. Restate the suggestion and show appreciation.

Thanks for suggesting that Rankin create work-at-home possibilities for staff. I've been intrigued with this work concept for some time.

Middle

Explain how you reviewed the suggestion and why it won't work. Explore other options.

I asked Melissa St. James in Human Resources about the costs and benefits of telecommuting. She said that her department conducted a feasibility study on telecommuting three years ago and concluded that it would not benefit the company for these reasons:

1. Employees could become isolated.

2. Few tasks could be efficiently performed away from the plant.

3. Home offices could prove too costly.

Perhaps the situation has changed since that study. Melissa said that she would be willing to discuss the idea with you.

Closing

Affirm the reader and invite further suggestions.

Please follow up on that offer, Duane. In addition, please continue to submit suggestions for improving operations here at Rankin. I appreciate your work!

Best wishes,
Art

> "Nothing travels faster than the speed of light with the possible exception of bad news, which obeys its own special laws."
>
> —Douglas Adams

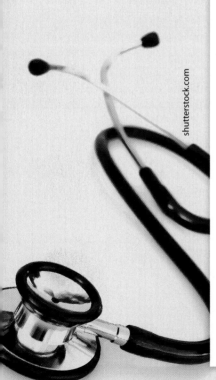

shutterstock.com

Checklist Bad-News Messages

Your goal when sending bad news is to write a message that is clear, fair, and courteous.

Ideas 9-16

____ is clear yet tactful.

____ presents all the facts accurately and focuses on solutions.

Organization 17-24

____ begins with a buffer statement that
  • explains the message's purpose.
  • establishes common ground.
  • builds sensitively (indirectly) to the bad-news statement.

____ develops a middle that
  • provides well-supported reasons without overexplaining.
  • states the bad news tactfully in the middle of a paragraph.
  • offers the reader a compromise or an alternative, if possible.

____ closes in a manner that
  • clarifies steps needed for an alternative solution.
  • looks forward to future work or contact, without sounding too upbeat.
  • follows the BEBE organization pattern.

Voice 25-32

____ uses an understanding yet firm voice that is not defensive or angry.

Words 33-40

____ conveys the bad news clearly but tactfully.

____ avoids the pronoun "you" if it sounds accusatory.

Sentences 41-50

____ reads well aloud; sentences aren't awkward or wordy.

____ uses passive voice to soften negative or difficult statements.

Correctness 51-58

____ is free of grammar, spelling, punctuation, and typing errors.

Design 59-70

____ features an attractive layout with ample white space.

____ organizes points and details with numbers, bullets, or graphics.

shutterstock.com

11
Writing to Persuade

All persuasive messages are sales pitches—whether you're selling an idea, a product, a service, or a special request. However, even though you may have a great idea, a dynamite product, or a noble cause, your readers won't necessarily see that. They may be indifferent or even resistant to your message.

So how, exactly, do you persuade readers to accept your point of view? How do you sell the value of your idea, product, service, or request? If you can speak to your readers' needs and focus on how they will benefit, then your letter, memo, or e-mail may produce the results you want.

Guidelines Persuasive Messages

Your Goal ▶ When writing persuasive messages, your goal is to convince the reader to do something (buy a product, pay a bill) by showing the value of the action.

"The best argument is that which sounds like merely an explanation."

—Dale Carnegie

1. Prewrite: (Ideas and Organization)
- What motivates your reader and what does she or he need?
- What benefits (publicity, contacts, or satisfaction) might the reader gain from supporting your cause?

Consider your purpose and clarify your cause.
- What outcome do you want or can you realistically expect?
- What exactly is your idea, cause, or product?
- What are the social or economic benefits of your cause?

2. Draft: (Ideas, Organization, and Voice)
Remember AIDA—Attention, **I**nterest and **D**esire, **A**ction (main point). (See page 23.)
Opening Get your reader's attention and present your idea, cause, or product.
Middle Explain its value and show how your reader will benefit.
- Use facts, quotations, and examples to help the reader understand and appreciate what you're promoting.
- Address obstacles and counter any objections if possible.

Closing Confidently ask for a reasonable action. Supply response cards, e-mail addresses, web sites, or other easy-response options.

3. Revise: (Ideas, Organization, Voice, Words, and Sentences)
- ☐ Have you provided a complete explanation that speaks to your reader's motivations?
- ☐ Have you used a sincere tone that avoids pressure tactics, flattery, and exaggeration?
- ☐ Does the message follow a clear, logical pattern?
- ☐ Do you have exact, fresh phrasing and easy-to-read sentences?

4. Refine: (Conventions and Design)
- ☐ Have you checked grammar, punctuation, spelling, and mechanics?
- ☐ Have you made sure headings, lists, and other format and design issues are consistent and effective?

shutterstock.com

**Collection
Letter (First
Notice)**

HANFORD BUILDING SUPPLY COMPANY, INC.
5821 North Fairheights Road, Milsap, CA 94218, Phone 567-555-1908
www.hanfordbuildingsupply.com

▶ Main Point

June 1, 2010

Account: 4879003

Mr. Robert Burnside, Controller
Circuit Electronics Company
4900 Gorham Road
Mountain View, CA 94040-1093

Dear Mr. Burnside:

Opening

State the account's
status.

This letter is a reminder that your account is past due (presently 60 days).

Middle

Review the
account's history.
Focus on keeping a
positive
relationship.

As of today, we have not yet received your payment of $1,806.00, originally
due March 31. A copy of the March 2 invoice #QR483928 is enclosed. It
refers to your January 8, 2010, order #S95832 for 3,000 mitered flanges that
we shipped January 28.

Hanford appreciates your business, Mr. Burnside. Please give this matter
your prompt attention so that Hanford Building Supply Company and Circuit
Electronics can continue their good relationship. Your check for $1,828.58
(past due amount, plus 1.25 percent interest) will keep your account in good
standing and avoid further interest charges and penalties. We have enclosed a
postage-paid envelope for your convenience.

Closing

Urge the reader to
contact you with
any problems.

If there are any problems, please call (567-555-1908, ext. 227) or e-mail me
(marta@hanford.com). As always, we look forward to serving you.

Sincerely,

Marta Ramones

Marta Ramones
Billing Department

Enclosures 2

HANFORD BUILDING SUPPLY COMPANY, INC.

5821 North Fairheights Road, Milsap, CA 94218, Phone 567-555-1908
www.hanfordbuildingsupply.com

July 2, 2010

Account: 4879003

Mr. Robert Burnside, Controller
Circuit Electronics Company
4900 Gorham Road
Mountain View, CA 94040-1093

Dear Mr. Burnside:

Opening

Express concern
about the
account.

Despite the reminder we sent on June 1, your account is now 90 days past due.

Middle

Review the
account's history.

Outline benefits of
good credit and
offer to help.

As of today, your payment of $1,828.58 has not arrived. A copy of your
March 2 invoice #QR483928 is enclosed. It refers to your January 8, 2010,
order #S95832 for 3,000 mitered flanges that we shipped January 28.

Because of your excellent credit rating, you have enjoyed substantial discounts,
convenient payment terms, and positive credit references from us. If you wish to
maintain your good credit rating, we need your payment.

Circuit Electronics has been one of Hanford's most valued customers for more
than five years. You have always paid your bills promptly. We are concerned
about this uncharacteristic tardiness. Is there a problem we can help solve?

Closing

Request payment
or contact; stress
cooperation.

Please send your payment of $1,851.44 today (includes 1.25 percent interest)
or contact me at 567-555-1908, ext. 227 so that we can resolve this matter.

Sincerely,

Marta Ramones

Marta Ramones
Billing Department

Enclosure 1

HANFORD BUILDING SUPPLY COMPANY, INC.

5821 North Fairheights Road, Milsap, CA 94218, Phone 567-555-1908
www.hanfordbuildingsupply.com

August 3, 2010

Account: 4879003

Mr. Robert Burnside, Controller
Circuit Electronics Company
4900 Gorham Road
Mountain View, CA 94040-1093

Dear Mr. Burnside:

Opening

Recap the facts.

On January 28, 2010, we shipped you the 3,000 mitered flanges you ordered (#S95832) on January 8, 2010. On March 2, we sent you the invoice for $1,806.00 (#QR483928). Copies of your purchase order and our invoice are enclosed.

Middle

Outline the steps taken. State the next step in clear, neutral terms.

Each month since then, Hanford has sent Circuit Electronics a reminder urging payment and asking you to contact us. We have not heard from you, and your account is now 120 days past due with a balance of $1,874.58 (includes 1.25 percent interest per month). Consequently, we must begin collection proceedings.

Closing

Offer one final way to cooperate by a specific date.

However, you can still resolve this matter, Mr. Burnside. Either call me now to discuss this problem (ext. 240 at the number above), or send a check by August 14 for the balance owed. By choosing either option, you can prevent this account from being turned over to a collection agency.

Sincerely,

Floyd Kovic

Floyd Kovic
Vice President
Finance Division

Enclosures 2

**Credit
Application**

**Dale's
Garden Center**

484 Leeward Avenue, SE, Tuscaloosa, AL 35406-3770
Phone 908/555-8900 FAX 908/555-1600
Email grant@garden.com

January 1, 2010

Ms. Salome Nguru, Manager
Cottonwood Hills Greenhouse and Florist Supply
R.R. 2
Macon, GA 31220-2339

Dear Ms. Nguru:

Opening

Stress positive
aspects of the
current
relationship.

For the past nine months, Dale's has been ordering fresh, dried, and silk
flowers from Cottonwood Hills. We have been impressed with the quality of
your products, most recently with those we sold for the Christmas holidays.

Middle

Explain the need
for credit.

Stress benefits for
the reader.

Establish your
credit record.

We are now planning to expand our product offerings, particularly of silk
flowers and bedding plants. For this reason, we expect to make larger orders
more frequently. However, before we can submit the orders, we need
Cottonwood Hills to set up an account for us with a $100,000 line of credit.

Dale's Garden Center has been in business for almost a year and is on solid
financial footing. The attached references and financial statements show that
we are strong and growing.

Closing

Ask for reasonable
action and suggest
further benefits.

By January 22, we hope that you will be able to check our statements and
references, send information about your credit terms, and confirm a credit line
of $100,000. Dale's will then submit an order for spring plants.

Thank you for considering our request.

Yours sincerely,

Grant Bostwick

Grant Bostwick
President

Enclosures 4

Fund-Raising Message

NATIONAL CAMPAIGN FOR LITERACY
1516 West Elizabeth Terrace, Wadsworth, IL 60421
Phone 431-555-900, Fax 431-555-1066, Web Site ncl.org

November 12, 2010

Mr. Cecil Featherstone
Words, Words, Words, Inc.
541 West 34th Street
New York, NY 10001-7352

Dear Mr. Featherstone:

Opening

Use attention-getting facts.

More than 20 percent of adults in this country cannot read at a third-grade level. Each year, more than a million students leave high school functionally illiterate (some with diplomas).

Middle

Sell your cause with key details.

Create a sense of urgency.

Request a donation politely.

List benefits for both giver and receiver.

As you know, the National Campaign for Literacy has spent 14 years helping millions of citizens learn to read. We work with more than 300 schools, neighborhood groups, and government agencies to combat illiteracy. Yet, illiteracy remains an enormous problem. To address this need, we plan to fund 29 new programs this year, as well as to expand existing ones.

We appreciate your past generosity and hope we can count on your continued support. In addition, to enable us to help more people, we are asking that you please consider raising your donation level.

Of course, your gift will bring you recognition, including a personal acknowledgment of your generosity in more than 100,000 promotional brochures. However, the greatest benefit comes as you help millions of people get better jobs and earn personal dignity.

Closing

Make donating simple.

Please continue supporting our effort to promote adult reading. You may make out your check to National Campaign for Literacy and return it to me, or you may call me at 431-555-9000, ext. 0786.

Sincerely,

Gail Goldstein

Gail Goldstein
Associate Director

Request for Assistance

| Send | Attach | Fonts | Colors | Save As Draft |

To: Felton Engineering Staff

Cc:

Subject line

State the subject.

Subject: Please Send Ideas for Open House Displays

Dear Colleagues:

Opening

Create a sense of shared purpose.

As you know, we will be moving to our new location on August 18, and we have scheduled an open house for September 1. To help visitors at that event learn what Felton Engineering does, I plan to set up displays showing samples of your unique heater designs and interesting product applications.

Middle

Give any needed background information.

Ask for specific help.

As you pack for the move, please help me by doing the following: (1) identify products that would interest visitors, and (2) look for blueprints, sketches, or small models that illustrate those products. (Remember that visitors may understand commercial applications more easily than technical military or aerospace designs.)

Then, list (1) your name, (2) the name of the product, (3) the product number, and (4) the type of display materials that you have.

Closing

Set a deadline, make cooperation simple, and be positive.

Please reply to this e-mail no later than August 20. I will pick up your materials, set up the displays, and return the materials to you after the open house. I look forward to turning your ideas and samples into great displays!

Thanks,
Jiliane Seaforth

**Sales Letter
(First Contact)**

Juanita Guiverra, Computer Consultant

368 Palm Palace Boulevard
Miami, FL 33166-0064
Telephone: 313.555.0010
Fax: 313.555-0500
Email: jguiverra@cnsult.com

November 19, 2010

Mr. Alexander Bennitez
Nova Advertising
664 Helene Boulevard, Suite 200
Miami, FL 33135-0493

Dear Mr. Bennitez:

Opening

Show that you
understand the
reader's situation.

Do you have numerous projects on hold because your staff is too busy?
Consider getting your important projects back on schedule by outsourcing.

Middle

Create interest by
relating your
services to the
reader's needs.

Sell your credibility.

My areas of expertise include the following:
- writing, editing, and keyboarding documents.
- processing mailings from start to finish.
- developing spreadsheets or flyers.

Outsourcing with me offers the following advantages:
- no long-term employment commitment.
- satisfaction guaranteed (most reworking at no charge).
- confidentiality.

You can put my 10 years of experience in the advertising business to work for
you. The enclosed pamphlet describes my services, equipment, and rates. I
have also enclosed samples of my work.

Closing

Call for action.

Mr. Bennitez, I can help Nova Advertising complete its projects in a timely
and professional manner. I would be available for an interview at your
convenience.

Sincerely,

Juanita Guiverra

Juanita Guiverra

Enclosures 4

Postscript

Offer an incentive.

P.S. As a new client, your first in-office consultation would be free.

Sales Letter (Following a Contact)

Rankin Technologies
401 Manheim Road ❖ Albany, NY 12236 ❖ Phone 708.555.1980 ❖ Fax 708.555.0056 ❖ www.rnkn.com

April 28, 2010

Mr. Henry Danburn
Construction Manager
Titan Industrial Construction, Inc.
P.O. Box 2112
Phoenix, AZ 85009-3887

Dear Mr. Danburn:

Opening

Mention previous positive contact.

Thank you for meeting with me last week at the national convention in Las Vegas. I want to follow up on our discussion of ways that Rankin Technologies could work with Titan Industrial Construction.

Middle

Provide details the reader needs.

Build credibility.

Enclosed is the information that you requested: Rankin's corporate brochure, past and current job lists, recommendation letters, and more. I believe this material demonstrates that Rankin Technologies would be a solid match for your projects in western Illinois.

You mentioned that you will be the construction manager for the Arrow Mills renovation project in California. Rankin did the electrical installation on that project initially, and we would be very interested in working with you on the renovation. Someone who is familiar with our work at Arrow Mills is Mitch Knowlan, Plant Manager. He can be reached at 606-555-6328 or atmknowlan@arrowmills.com.

Closing

Stress cooperation and the key selling point.

Henry, here at Rankin, we're excited about the possibility of working with you on any future project, and the Arrow Mills project, in particular. Please call me with any questions (507-555-9011).

Sincerely,

James Gabriel

James Gabriel
Vice President

Enclosures 5

Sales Letter (Following a Sale)

Dale's Garden Center

484 Leeward Avenue, SE, Tuscaloosa, AL 35406-3770
Phone 908/555-8900 FAX 908/555-1600
Email grant@garden.com

December 6, 2010

Ms. Taryn Dionne
93 Claremont Crescent
Tuscaloosa, AL 35401-1553

Dear Ms. Dionne:

Opening

Thank the reader for previous business.

Thank you for your recent order of a Southern Charm Bouquet. We hope you were pleased with the arrangement.

Middle

Introduce other products without high-pressure tactics. Stress value and benefits.

Because this was your first order with Dale's, we're sending you the enclosed *2011 Occasions Diary* as a gift. The diary will help you remember important events in the lives of people you care about. You'll find room for birthdays, anniversaries, graduations, and more.

Flowers are a thoughtful gift for any occasion. That's why we've listed appropriate arrangements at the back of your diary. On the first page of each month, you'll also notice our monthly specials at the low price of $29.95 (plus delivery and tax).

Closing

Invite action.

So keep your *2011 Occasions Diary* handy throughout the year. Then just call our toll-free number on the inside front cover (or visit our Web site), and we'll gladly make all the arrangements!

Best wishes,

Bryce Calahan

Bryce Calahan
Customer-Service Manager

Postscript

Emphasize a special offer.

P.S. I've also enclosed a *2011 Christmas Floral Selection Guide* filled with gift-giving ideas for friends and family.

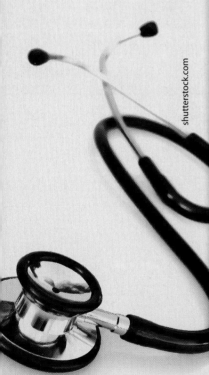

"If you would persuade, you must appeal to interest rather than intellect."

—Benjamin Franklin

Checklist Persuasive Messages

When writing persuasive messages, your goal is to convince the reader to do something (buy a product, pay a bill) by showing the value of the action.

Ideas 9-16
____ states the main point clearly and convincingly.
____ uses accurate and persuasive details.
____ connects with the reader's needs and concerns.

Organization 17-24
____ uses an opening that
- gains the reader's attention.
- identifies a benefit to the reader and supplies the necessary context.

____ offers a strong argument in the middle that
- establishes a need and shows how to meet it.
- uses clear, convincing evidence to "sell" the idea or product.
- anticipates and answers objections.

____ ends with a closing that
- asks the reader to take a specific, realistic next step.
- encourages a prompt response with an appropriate incentive.
- follows the AIDA organizational pattern.

Voice 25-32
____ uses a polite and personal voice, not hesitant, apologetic, or aggressive.
____ demonstrates, sensitivity to the reader's needs and concerns.

Words 33-40
____ avoids cliches, jargon, flowery phrases, and "business English."
____ uses precise nouns, vivid modifiers, and energetic verbs.

Sentences 41-50
____ uses transitions to tie ideas together and reads well out loud.

Correctness 51-58
____ is free of grammar, spelling, punctuation, and typing errors.

Design 59-70
____ uses page layout, white space, and type for accessibility.
____ organizes points and details with headings, lists, and graphics.

Section 3:
Workplace Writing and Communicating

In this section

shutterstock.com

12
Communication Options

Imagine you need to make an important change to a project or procedure. How would you get your point across? Would you write a note, send an e-mail, fill out a request? Would you deliver the information in person or on the phone? Now, imagine you need to lay someone off. Would you deliver the information in the same way?

Each communication situation calls for a specific medium of communication. These days, businesspeople have hundreds of options: phone calls, e-mails, instant messages, blog posts, social-media pages, forum posts, webinars, letters, memos, reports, and so on. Each medium has its own strengths and weaknesses—and its best uses. It's important to choose a medium that matches the communication situation.

This chapter provides guidelines to help you select a medium of communication that will best get your message across.

Analyzing the Situation

The communication situation includes five elements:

Communication Situation

1. Sender
- What is your **role** in the situation?
- How do you want to be **perceived**?

2. Message
- What is the **main point**?
- What **outcome** is desired?
- How **serious** is the message?

3. Medium
- What **medium** best suits the situation?
- What issues of **speed, distribution,** or **privacy** apply?

4. Receiver
- Who needs to receive the message?
- What does the receiver **know** or **need to know**?
- What does the receiver **want**?

5. Context
- What is the **history** and **current climate** of the situation?
- What **benefactors** and **barriers** does the message have?
- What **time window** exists for delivering the message and receiving responses.

 Fyi When choosing a medium, you have many communication options. The medium should match your needs and those of the message, receiver, and context. The chart on the next page can help you choose the best medium.

shutterstock.com

Understanding the Medium

The options for communicating lie along a continuum from quick, informal types to deliberate and formal types. The following chart shows these differences.

The Continuum of Communication

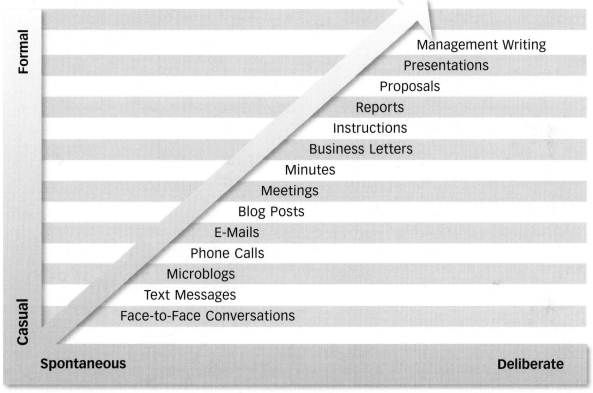

Choose a Medium

To select an appropriate medium for your message, do the following:

1. Put your finger down on the medium that you think might be most appropriate.
2. Consider the options just above your finger and just below it.
3. Move down and to the left if you need a faster, more casual medium.
4. Move up and to the right if you need a more deliberate and formal medium.

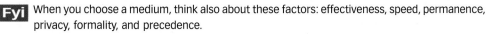

Fyi When you choose a medium, think also about these factors: effectiveness, speed, permanence, privacy, formality, and precedence.

Considering Pros and Cons

As you select a medium of communication, keep the following pros and cons in mind.

Casual, Spontaneous Options (Face-to-Face Conversations, Text Messages, Microblogs, Phone Calls)

PRO

These options are fast and convenient, and they allow a quick exchange of information back and forth. They are interactive and work well for brainstorming and decision making. For example, phoning someone to meet for lunch may be better than e-mailing the person.

CON

These options are in the moment, which means you do not have time to think carefully about issues. For that reason, these options work best for minor or everyday subjects. Also these options may not preserve a permanent record of what was said.

Semiformal, Moderate Options (E-Mail, Blog Posts, Meetings, Minutes, Business Letters)

PRO

These options are common, day-to-day types of communication suitable for most business applications.

CON

Though these options may seem casual, they do leave permanent records (for example, meeting minutes). So, they require a bit more time and care.

Formal, Deliberate Options (Management Writing, Presentations, Proposals, Reports, Instructions)

PRO

These options show your best thinking. Because you have taken care as you create these types of writing, they carry the most weight. They are also most likely to be published, read by a wide audience, and preserved.

CON

These options take work. They require focus and commitment, and they are judged most strongly because they are expected to be very well created.

shutterstock.com

13
Forms

Forms may not be particularly glamorous, but they do an important job: collecting standard information needed about people, jobs, orders, requests, and many other aspects of business. For many years, paper forms dominated business, and now, with online transactions, forms seem to be taking over the world.

This chapter focuses on common workplace forms. The guidelines at the beginning of the chapter give tips for completing forms accurately. Many models afterward show typical forms and how they should be completed. For each paper form shown in this chapter, an electronic version also exists, to be filled out the same way.

"I've worked in several large companies. . . . You couldn't get anything done without filling out a form. There was even a form that you had to fill out when there wasn't any regular form available."

—Mark Schneider

shutterstock.com

Guidelines Completing Forms

Your Goal ▶ When filling out a form, your goal is to provide complete, correct information.

1. Prewrite: (Ideas and Organization)
- Think about who needs this information and why.
- Don't be intimidated: Keep your mind on what the form will accomplish for you.

Review the form.
- Carefully read the instructions.
- Gather the information you need.

2. Draft: (Ideas, Organization, and Voice)
- Follow the directions.
- Complete each required field.

3. Revise: (Ideas, Organization, Voice, Words, and Sentences)
- ☐ Are all required fields completed?
- ☐ Is the correct information entered in every field?
- ☐ For handwritten forms, did you double-check the readability?

4. Refine: (Conventions and Design)
- ☐ Have you checked spelling, especially of names?
- ☐ Have you checked all numbers to make sure they were copied correctly?

Phone Memo

Provide key information.

Write a note that answers the 5Ws.

PHONE MEMO

Date: Feb. 1, 2011   Time: 9:30 a.m.

To: Greg Phillips

From: Amika Layton

Phone: 762-555-6912   Fax: 762-555-6800

Message: Mr. Layton called to remind you about the meeting at Elmwood Bank on Friday, Feb. 11. Please call him today to discuss a new item on the agenda.

PHONED ☒   CALL BACK ☒   RETURNED CALL ☐   WANTS TO SEE YOU ☐   WILL CALL AGAIN ☐   WAS IN ☐   URGENT ☐

Job-Completion Form

Provide key details.

Clearly indicate what was done.

JOB COMPLETION FORM

Client: Oneida School District   Date: August 24, 2011

Project: Copier service call

Description: I disassembled the copier in the main office at Elmwood Middle School. After cleaning, oiling, and replacing toner, I left the copier in good working condition.

Comments: This machine is showing the usual wear for its age, and maintenance will begin to involve replacement parts within a year.

Please review the work that has been completed before signing this document. After the review is complete and if all changes are satisfactory, sign this document and fax or mail it to the service provider.

By signing below, I certify that the job was done to my satisfaction.

Reviewed by:_____   Date: _____

Accident-Report Form

Provide key details.

Write a clear, complete description of what occurred.

Include hospital information if needed.

ACCIDENT/INCIDENT REPORT FORM

Date of incident: March 3, 2011   Time: 2:25   AM ___ ✓ PM ___

Name of injured person: Carlos LaMachia, EMT

Address: 5621 Evergreen Ct./Rockview, IL 61233

Phone number(s): (630) 555-4455, cell

Age: 33   Male ✓ Female ___

Type of injury: grade 1 sprained right ankle

Details of incident: During emergency call #783B06, I slipped on the steps of the caller's front porch, twisting my right ankle. I kept walking on the foot to complete the initial patient interview and checks. But I had to call a backup (John Baumgard) to assist with the safe transfer of the patient. After delivery to hospital was complete, I had my ankle checked and x-rayed.

Did the injury require a physician/hospital visit? Yes ✓ No ___

Name of physician/hospital: St. Mary's Prompt Care

Physician/hospital phone number: (708) 238-3222

Signature of injured party: Carlos LaMachia

Date: March 5, 2011

---

*Sign below if no medical attention was desired and/or required.

Signature of injured party: _____

Date: _____

Order Form

Date: 2/15/10

PF Whaler Automotive

8290 East Grade Blvd.
Deerfield, MI 48126
Phone (269) 555-9235
Fax (269) 555-9246

shutterstock.com

ORDER FORM

ITEM NUMBER	DESCRIPTION	UNIT PRICE	QUANTITY	TOTAL (Multiply unit price by quantity ordered)
JB140	Super Swamper Tire (Mfr. # SM06)	95.99	12	1,151.88
PX 26	Accu-Pressure Safety Cap 4pk.	17.99	4	71.96
PX 28	Accu-Pressure Safety Cap 2pk.	10.99	4	43.96
KL 5	Tire Pressure Monitor System	349.99	1	349.99
			Subtotal	
			Tax	1,617.79
			Shipping	
			Total	

List items, identifying numbers, quantities, and prices.

TO PROCESS YOUR ORDER, ALL INFORMATION MUST BE PROVIDED BELOW. PLEASE PRINT CLEARLY.

Record contact information.

Name: Michael Farrity

Organization: Mike's Tire and Service

Address: 4200 Drake Street

City/State/County: Canton, MI   Postal Code: 46321

Phone: (320) 555-1923   Fax: (320) 555-1933

PAYMENT INFORMATION

Provide billing information.

✓ Bill my institution or business. An authorized purchase order number must be provided. (U.S. orders only) P.O. Number 89376

Cash $ _____   Check #_____

Credit card: ___ American Express ___ VISA ___ MasterCard ___ EuroCard

Credit Card Number: _____   Exp. Date: _____

Signature: _____

Service Invoice

HOME SAFE, INC.
2900 Bering Place
Oak Woods, IA 50652
Phone (640) 555-9182
Fax (640) 555-8122

SERVICE INVOICE

BILL TO: Mr. Louis Moratto
822 Romayne Avenue
Oak Woods, IA 50652

INVOICE # 823831
INVOICE DATE: February 1, 2011
DUE DATE: February 15, 2011
PROJECT: In-home care (MTW)
P.O. NUMBER:

Provide contact information.

Describe services, hours, rates, and amounts.

DESCRIPTION	HOURS/ QUANTITY	RATE	AMOUNT
December (2010) care	56 hrs.	$19.00	$1,064.00
January (2011) care Morning Visits - Wash up/dressing - Breakfast/meds - Light housework	26 hrs.	$19.50	$507.00
Evening visits - Snack/meds - Undressing/wash up - Transfer to bed - Kitchen cleanup - Secure home	26 hrs.	$19.50	$507.00

Make totals and note payment and balance due, if any.

Thank you. It has been a pleasure working with you!

TOTAL	$2,078.00
PAYMENTS/CREDITS Client ck. # 8235	$900.00
BALANCE DUE	$1,178.00

**Fax Cover
Sheet**

Bayfield Health Clinic
6027 North Avenue
Bayfield, ME 04659
Phone (207) 555-2146
Fax (207) 555-1122

FAX COVER SHEET

Provide contact
information.

Date: March 4, 2011

To: Shannon Pflug, MRI Technician

Company: Advanced Imaging Center

Fax Number: (207) 830-6798

From: Robert Allwright, CMA

Fax Number: (207) 555-1122

List pages included.

Total number of pages: 2

Write a clear
message that
answers the 5 W's.

Message: Dr. Alexander has ordered an MRI for Alexis Kitterling,
who has requested your center's services. Please see the attached
order and note the insurance coverage. The patient will be calling
to set up the appointment.

Job Application

Provide contact information.

Detail education.

List work experience.

APPLICATION FOR EMPLOYMENT

Name: Rachel Guardiola

Present address: 3724 Thurston Avenue/Marsh Plains, WI 53078

Telephone: 612-555-5672

Social security number: 123-45-6789

Position applied for: Certified Medical Assistant   Salary desired: $28,000

Education

Type of School	Name of School	Location	Years Completed	Major & Degree
High School	Marsh Plains High School	Marsh Plains, WI	4 years (2005-2009)	Diploma
Business or Trade School	Central Technical College	Freestone, WI	1 year (2009-2010)	Certified Medical Assistant
College				

Work Experience

Please list your work experience for the **past five years** beginning with your most recent job held. If you are or were self-employed, give firm name. **Attach additional sheets if necessary.**

Name of present or most recent employer: Southwood Health Center

Location: Marsh Plains, WI   Telephone: 612-555-8333

Name of last supervisor: Marlene Keller, R.N.

Employment dates: Aug. 2009-present

Pay or salary (Start/Final) $9.50 hr./$11.00 hr.

Reason for leaving (be specific) I decided over a year ago to further my health career by going to CTC for my CMA diploma. I am now eager to put that training to good use.

Page 2

List the jobs you held, duties performed, skills used or learned, and advancements or promotions while you worked at this company.

I work as a CNA evenings and some weekends, taking care of our

residents' basic needs (bathing, grooming, dressing, feeding).

I also check vital signs as needed and work with the activity director.

May we contact your present employer? _____ No ___✔ Yes

Name of previous employer: Green's Drug Store

Location: Marsh Plains, WI   Telephone: 612-555-7526

Name of last supervisor: Douglas Paton, Pharm.D

Employment dates: May 2008-Aug. 2009

Pay or salary (Start/Final) $8.00 hr./$9.00 hr.

Reason for leaving (be specific)

I knew I wanted to get into a health-care career, but I needed

more hands-on experience. Moving on to a CNA job made sense.

List the jobs you held, duties performed, skills used or learned, and advancements or promotions while you worked at this company.

Trained on the job, I worked as a pharmacy cashier and processed

customers' payments for their prescriptions.

Do you have a driver's license? ___ No ✔ Yes Number: G732-5002-0823-08
State: WI Expiration: 08-17-13

Please list one or two references other than relatives or previous employers.

Mark Savich (612-555-8316), guidance counselor at Marsh Plains High

School; Pam Tuka (523-555-5213), instructor at Central Technical College

Use the space below to summarize any additional information necessary to describe your full qualifications for the specific position for which you are applying. Consider volunteer experiences, hobbies, and other interests.

I recently graduated from CTC with a GPA of 3.50, so I'm qualified. I'm

also very interested in wellness. I want to be part of a group that helps

people stay well but knows what to do when they get sick.

Provide references.

Give additional information.

**Electronic
Form**

Provide shipping
information.

Include billing
information.

Include a payment
method.

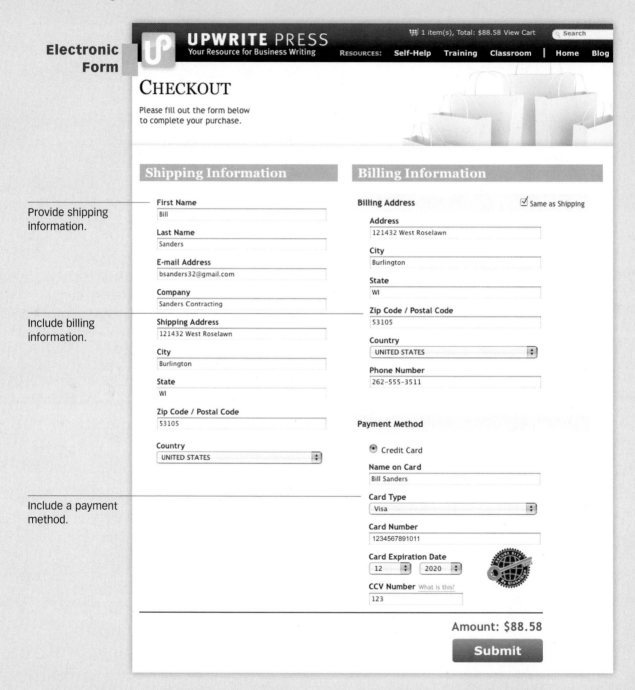

UPWRITE PRESS
Your Resource for Business Writing

1 item(s), Total: $88.58 View Cart

Search

RESOURCES: Self-Help   Training   Classroom | Home   Blog

CHECKOUT

Please fill out the form below
to complete your purchase.

Shipping Information

First Name
Bill

Last Name
Sanders

E-mail Address
bsanders32@gmail.com

Company
Sanders Contracting

Shipping Address
121432 West Roselawn

City
Burlington

State
WI

Zip Code / Postal Code
53105

Country
UNITED STATES

Billing Information

☑ Same as Shipping

Billing Address

Address
121432 West Roselawn

City
Burlington

State
WI

Zip Code / Postal Code
53105

Country
UNITED STATES

Phone Number
262-555-3511

Payment Method

● Credit Card

Name on Card
Bill Sanders

Card Type
Visa

Card Number
1234567891011

Card Expiration Date
12   2020

CCV Number What is this?
123

Amount: $88.58

Submit

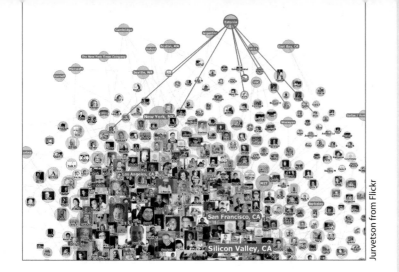

14
Social Media

It's no secret that the Internet has changed the way people connect. The image above uses a mapping algorithm to show the connections and cliques of one person's Facebook contacts—centering around Silicon Valley. It's a snapshot of a complex online community, one that the creator then uploaded to a file-sharing site to share with the world.

That's the power of social media. Private individuals are discovering its ability to create new connections, and businesses are increasingly using these tools to participate in that new, exciting connectivity.

This chapter provides an overview of social media, defining some of the basic ways that people connect and share. Then it offers some general advice for businesses to successfully use these ever-evolving tools.

Understanding Social Media

Social media are simply online programs that connect people. Much if not most of the content on social media is generated by people instead of by businesses. In that way, social media are the electronic equivalent of sitting around a fire trading jokes and gossip, singing songs, showing pictures—in other words, being social. But social media also help businesspeople track trends and get the word out. Here are some of the most common forms of social media.

Chat

Chat features such as Instant Messenger allow users to communicate in real time to one or more others through typed messages. Chat features may be stand-alone programs or may be integrated into other social networking programs.

Microblogging

Microblogging applications such as Twitter allow users to send out brief messages (140 or fewer characters). Users can send messages

- to everyone who follows them,
- to one particular person but viewable by all, and
- to one specific person and viewable only by that person.

The messages can contain links to videos, blog posts, articles, or any other assets available on the Web. They also can be tagged so that people can find messages more easily. Programs that aggregate feeds help users create groups of people and sift the messages they want to see.

UpWrite
9:55am, Mar 09 from **HootSuite**

RT@GrammarGirl RT @funnyordie: Celebrating #grammarday on Twitter is trying to hold an AA meeting in the middle of Mardi Gras. ^CE

Social Networking

Social networking applications such as LinkedIn and Ning allow users to set up profiles, connect to contacts, post files, send messages, join groups, and communicate. Social networking programs allow users to determine how much or how little they share, and with whom. Different social networking sites focus on connecting people for different purposes: friendship, business, romance, fandom, art, music, and so on.

Blogging

Blogging applications such as WordPress allow users to create Web logs. The central part of most blogs (Web logs) are periodic posts that usually include text, photos, or videos. Most blog posts allow for readers to post replies. Blog sites also often contain other pages with information about the person or organization, lists of products or services, reviews, and other information. The main point of a blog is to be topical.

File Sharing

File sharing sites such as Youtube (videos) and Flickr (photos) allow people to upload content they have created or found, search for and view content others have created or found, rate it, and comment on it. File sharing sites exist for all types of content, including audio, video, photos, and humor.

Message Boards

Message boards and forums provide a location for people with common interests to ask questions and get answers. Often, topics are posted by users, but moderators also propose topics for discussion.

Wikis

Wikis allow users to work collaboratively on projects, discussing and revising each other's work. Some wikis have millions of contributors, while others have only a handful of people. Wikis focus on "crowdsourcing"—or creating content through the involvement of many individuals.

RSS Readers/Social Bookmarking

RSS readers and bookmarking features such as Google Reader and Digg allow users to find articles recommended by others with similar interest. RSS readers and bookmarking cover topics from sports to fashion to science to politics.

Fyi New social media are appearing every day, and social media are constantly evolving. The best way to learn about what is currently available in social media is to engage and experiment.

Getting the Most Out of Social Media

Whether blogging, microblogging, networking, or writing for the Web, the key is to keep the writing *social* in nature. Business is all about making connections—the people you know and trust, and the people who know and trust you. Companies and businesspeople who use social media in this way succeed with it.

Here are a few specific tips to help you connect with others:

- **Project a personality.** The personality may belong to your brand, or it may belong to the people behind the brand—or some combination. For other users to want to interact with you, they need to know who you are. For them to trust you, they definitely must know who you are.

- **Offer value.** Most of the posting you do on social media should help the reader. Provide a reason for people to "follow, fan, or friend"—and the reason can't be just to hear sales pitches.

- **Connect with others.** Don't just point to yourself. Follow, fan, and friend others, linking to them and passing along the value that they provide. By doing so, you become a trusted and active part of an online community.

- **Connect technologies.** Join your microblog to your blog, and link your blog to a video posted on a hosting service. The more media you use, the more engaging your presence will be.

- **Invite people in.** Engage others by asking questions, inviting responses, running contests, having giveaways, providing quizzes, asking for ratings, and soliciting feedback. Give up a little control so that users have room to enter the conversation.

- **Do a little every day, not a lot all at once.** Maintaining a presence on social media requires continual small-scale contributions, which keep you in front of others in your community. Set up a broadcast schedule to keep yourself on track.

- **Revise and edit your work.** Though social media may feel fast and loose, misspellings, grammatical errors, and other such problems create a negative and untrustworthy image. Make sure that what you post is correct.

shutterstock.com

15
E-Mail

E-mail has become the major workhorse of business communication. It is fast and official, accessible on many different devices. Here are just a few of the uses of e-mail in business:

- To provide day-to-day communication and updates
- To carry newsletters to customers and clients
- To link to important Internet pages
- To carry documents, pictures, or photos
- To track the use of social media
- To provide official, date-stamped communications

This chapter focuses on the basics of e-mail communication, with guidelines for writing e-mail and help with e-mail etiquette.

Guidelines E-Mail

Your Goal ▶ In writing an e-mail message, your goal is to provide clear, concise information in a fast, efficient manner.

> "I try to leave out the parts that people skip."
> —Elmore Leonard

1. **Prewrite:** (Ideas and Organization)
   - Clarify what you want your e-mail message to accomplish.
   - Think about your reader's position and possible reaction.
   - Gather necessary information and arrange your points.

   Write with the computer screen in mind.
   - Complete the routing information required by your program.
   - Give an informative subject line. Don't leave it blank.
   - Limit the length of your message to one screen if possible.
   - Send longer messages as attachments, pointing to them in the e-mail.

2. **Draft:** (Ideas, Organization, and Voice)
   Opening Use a greeting to personalize the message. Then state your reason for writing the message.
   Middle Provide details that answer readers' questions: What is this message about? What does it mean to me? Why is it important? (Try to restrict each e-mail message to a single topic.)
   Closing Indicate any follow-up needed. Who will be responsible for what? Then close politely.

3. **Revise:** (Ideas, Organization, Voice, Words, and Sentences)
   - ☐ Have you supplied a clear, sensitive explanation that helps the reader say, "I understand"?
   - ☐ Have you used a sincere, gracious tone that avoids a "we" versus "you" attitude?
   - ☐ Have you used neutral, exact, and sensitive wording?
   - ☐ Do you have easy-to-read sentences with smooth transitions?

4. **Refine:** (Conventions and Design)
   - ☐ Have you checked names, data, grammar, punctuation, and spelling?
   - ☐ Have you checked format (spacing, type, and so on)?

shutterstock.com

| Send | Attach | Fonts | Colors | Save As Draft |

**Basic
E-Mail**

To: personnelcom@glothru.com

Cc: pburns@glothru.com, lmoor@glothru.com, kjans@glothru.com

Subject: Agenda for Personnel Committee Meeting on November 10

Opening

Greet readers and introduce the topic.

Middle

Present your message in a simple format that your reader's e-mail program will accept.

Closing

Focus on action and conclude politely.

Personnel Committee Members:

Next Monday, November 10, we'll meet in Conference Room 16 L at 4:30 p.m. to continue our discussion of Shawn Greer's dismissal.

We will discuss the following topics:

1. Shawn Greer's job description (copy attached)

2. Shawn's last two evaluations, dated January 29, 2010, and August 2, 2010

3. Shawn's letter of dismissal, dated October 8, 2010

Please bring the documents listed above to the meeting and be ready to discuss how our committee and association should proceed.

Thank you,

Joyce Pool

Format Tips
- Use short paragraphs and double-space between them.
- Create lists with numbers, bullets, or asterisks.
- Begin with an appropriate greeting and conclude with a fitting closing.
- In the subject line, clarify the nature of your message and use labels when appropriate (FOR ACTION, FYI, URGENT).

E-Mail Tips

When should you choose e-mail over a phone call, letter, or memo? Check the tips below to help you decide.

Strong Points

Simplicity and Speed ▪ An e-mail message is composed on-screen through simple key strokes and travels instantly to the reader.

Flexibility and Power ▪ With e-mail, you can send, receive, and store messages easily, communicating with both on-site coworkers and far-off customers. In addition, you can embed Web address hyperlinks for reader convenience.

Clarity ▪ E-mail replies can include the original correspondence, establishing a clear electronic trail.

Economy ▪ Once an e-mail system is set up, maintenance costs are minimal—no postage, no paper.

Weak Points

Quality and Reliability ▪ Because e-mail is easy to use, writers may overload readers with poorly written messages. Also, e-mail systems occasionally malfunction.

Accessibility and Respect ▪ Reading e-mail on a computer screen is harder than reading print. Some readers may look at e-mail as lightweight correspondence—easy to delete or ignore.

Confidentiality ▪ E-mail can sometimes end up in the wrong place, so confidentiality cannot be guaranteed. In addition, your message may be forwarded, so think twice before sending sensitive information by e-mail.

Global Issues ▪ Because e-mail can travel around the globe to diverse readers, be sensitive to cultural differences. Avoid slang and colloquialisms.

Special Features

- **Address book** allows easy access to your e-mail addresses.

- **Mailing lists** allow you to distribute e-mail to groups of users.

- **Copy** allows you to send your message to more than your primary readers. *Blind copy* allows you to send your message to someone without the original reader's knowledge.

- **Reply** allows you to respond to an e-mail on screen—with the option of including the original message. Don't automatically reply to "all" instead of the writer.

- **Forward** allows you to distribute to others a message you have received.

- **Signature file** allows you to automatically attach contact info to your messages. Include your name, organization, department, and so on, stacked vertically.

- **Search** allows you to do a search of saved e-mail messages.

- **Folders** allow you to save, order, and group messages.

- **Attach** allows you to send digital files with your message.

E-Mail Etiquette and Shorthand

How should you behave in the digital world of e-mail? It's simple: Follow the rules of etiquette and use initialisms and emoticons only in informal communications, not official business.

Etiquette

Appropriate Use ▪ Use e-mail for group projects, bulletins, routine messages, and immediate follow-up. Generally, avoid e-mail for sensitive issues, serious topics, or bad news. As always, follow your company's policies about e-mail use.

Formality Level ▪ Use language appropriate for your reader, whether a coworker or a client. Distinguish between in-house e-mail and messages to people outside your organization.

Message Checking ▪ Check your e-mail several times a day. If you can't respond immediately, send a short message to indicate that you received the message and that you will reply by a specific time.

Distribution ▪ Instead of distributing e-mail messages too widely, send them only to those who need them. Otherwise readers may routinely delete your messages.

Flaming ▪ Use of anger or sarcasm, called *flaming* (it is often signaled with uppercase), is never appropriate. Cool off and avoid sending an angry message.

Spamming ▪ Avoid sending unsolicited ads by e-mail, a practice called *spamming*.

Forwarding ▪ Think carefully before forwarding messages. When in doubt, get permission from the original sender.

Ethics ▪ Because companies are legally responsible for their computer network activity, e-mail is company property. In addition, networks typically store messages for years. So only write messages you would not mind seeing in the company newsletter.

Emoticons

You make emoticons, often called *smileys,* with simple keyboard strokes. To get the picture, turn your head to the left.

:) or :-)	a smile
:D	a big smile
:-(	a frown, unhappy
:-O	shocked or amazed
:-P	tongue sticking out
:-/	skeptical or puzzled
:-*	oops!

Initialisms

Initialisms are abbreviations written in all capital letters with no periods.

LOL	Laugh Out Loud
OTOH	On The Other Hand
F2F	Face To Face
BTW	By The Way
FYI	For Your Information
IMHO	In My Humble Opinion
TIA	Thanks In Advance
IOW	In Other Words
FWIW	For What It's Worth

"I don't believe in e-mail. I'm an old-fashioned girl. I prefer calling and hanging up."

—Sarah Jessica Parker

Checklist E-Mail

In writing an e-mail message, your goal is to provide clear, concise information in a fast, efficient manner.

Ideas 9-16

____ is strong, clear, and accurate.

____ has answered the reader's questions: Why are you writing me? What needs to be done?

Organization 17-24

____ is appropriately direct or indirect, based on the reader's likely response.

____ contains an informative subject line.

____ follows a fitting opening, middle, closing structure.

Voice 25-32

____ is courteous throughout.

____ uses an appropriate voice and focuses on the reader's needs.

Words 33-40

____ uses plain English—precise, clear, and simple words.

____ uses and defines technical terms carefully.

____ uses names and personal pronouns, especially "you," effectively.

Sentences 41-50

____ has short- to medium-length sentences that pass the "read aloud" test.

____ uses transition words to link ideas.

Correctness 51-58

____ follows all punctuation and capitalization rules for memos and letters.

____ uses correct abbreviations, titles, and spelling throughout.

____ contains no grammar or typing errors.

Design 59-70

____ follows all the rules of the format.

____ contains short paragraphs.

____ uses headings and bulleted or numbered lists wherever helpful.

____ has a polished look—white space, clean typography, and good stationery.

shutterstock.com

shutterstock.com

16
Letters and Memos

Good communication is good business. This has been true throughout history. Well-written letters and memos help your business serve its clients well—to everyone's benefit.

When sending letters or distributing memos, your goal is for your reader to understand and respond to your message as planned. You also want to initiate or maintain a good working relationship. In other words, you want results. If you write messages that are clear, complete, and focused on your reader, you will get results.

Guidelines Letters

Your Goal ▶ In a letter, your goal is to communicate your message and give a positive impression of yourself and your organization.

"Be yourself when you write. You will stand out as a real person among robots."

—William Zinsser

1. Prewrite: (Ideas and Organization)
- Ask yourself what you want the letter to accomplish.
- Consider the reader's concerns about, knowledge of, and history with your organization.

Gather information.
- Gather files and other necessary resources.
- Jot down your main points in a logical order.
- Use the letter format (full-block, semiblock, or simplified) that your company prefers.

2. Draft: (Ideas, Organization, and Voice)
Opening State the situation (reason for writing, background).
Middle Give the full explanation, supporting points, and details. If your message is good or neutral news, make your key point early. For a bad-news or persuasive message, build up to the main point.
Closing End with a call to action (who should do what, when), and, if appropriate, mention future contact.

3. Revise: (Ideas, Organization, Voice, Words, and Sentences)
- ☐ Are all names, dates, and details accurate?
- ☐ Is information presented in a logical order?
- ☐ Do you use a conversational but professional tone?
- ☐ Do you emphasize the reader's perspective?
- ☐ Have you used precise wording?
- ☐ Have you used personal pronouns in a positive way?
- ☐ Do you have smooth sentences that pass the "read aloud" test?

4. Refine: (Conventions and Design)
- ☐ Have you checked spelling (especially double-checked names)?
- ☐ Have you checked grammar, punctuation, and mechanics?
- ☐ Have you checked format and design?

shutterstock.com

Professional Appearance of Letters

Before your readers catch a word of your message, they've already read your letter's overall appearance. What does it say to them? Use the guidelines on this page to ensure a good impression.

First Impressions

Choose your look. ■ Do you want your letter to look traditional and conservative or friendly and contemporary? (See "Letter Formats," pages 168-169.)

Frame your letter in white space. ■ Make your margins 1 to 1.5 inches left and right, top and bottom. Create a balanced, open look by centering the message vertically and adjusting the space between the parts of the letter.

Make reading easy. ■ Use sensible type sizes and styles.
- Keep type size at 10-12 points.
- Choose a user-friendly font. Serif type has fine lines finishing off the main strokes of the letter. (This is serif type.) Sans serif type has a block-letter look. (This is sans serif type.) Serif typefaces are easier to read and understand; sans serif typefaces work well for headings.
- Avoid flashy and frequent type changes, as well as overuse of italics or boldface.

Print for quality. ■ Use a quality printer and avoid any handwritten editing changes. Always print a clean final copy.

Letter Perfect

Use 20- to 24-pound bond paper. ■ The 20- to 24-pound bond paper folds cleanly, takes ink crisply, and works well in most printers.

Use 8.5- by 11-inch paper. ■ It's standard and files easily. Other sizes may be used for personal correspondence, executive letters, or mass mailings.

Use white or off-white paper. ■ Be careful with other colors. Light, subtle colors mean business. Bold colors scream, "I'm an ad!"

Match, don't mix. ■ Letterhead pages, continuation sheets, and envelopes should match in paper weight, size, color, and design.

Letterhead Design

If you are asked to design or redesign your company's letterhead stationery—or if you want to design a letterhead specific to your position—be sure to include the following:
- the company's complete legal name;
- the company logo or slogan;
- complete contact information—full address, phone number (including area code), a fax number, a Web-site address; and
- names of key people (perhaps in the left-margin sidebar).

Note: Make sure your design reflects your company's mission and character.

Parts of a Basic Letter

All letters should include a clear message and information about the writer and the reader. Details for basic and expanded formats follow.

Basic Letter Tips

- Do not indent paragraphs.
- Single-space within paragraphs.
- Double-space between paragraphs.
- Leave the right margin ragged (uneven).
- Set margins from 1 to 1.5 inches.

1 The **heading** provides the reader a return address. Type the address (minus the writer's name) at the top of the letter. Spell out words like *Road, Street, West.* Omit the address if you are using a letterhead.

2 The **date** shows when the letter was drafted or dictated. Write the date as *month, day, year* for U.S. correspondence (August 5, 2010); write *day, month, year* for international or military correspondence (5 August 2010).

3 The **inside address** gives the reader's name and complete mailing address. Type it flush left and include as many details as necessary, in this order:
- reader's courtesy title, name, and job title (if the job title is one word)
- reader's job title (if two or more words)
- office or department
- organization name
- street address/p.o. box/suite/room (comma precedes *NE, SE,* etc.)
- city, state, zip code (or city, country, postal code)

4 The **salutation** personalizes the message. Capitalize all first letters and place a colon after the name. (See "Forms of Address," pages 174-177.)

5 The **body** contains the message, usually organized into three parts:
- an opening that states why you are writing,
- a middle that gives readers the details they need, and
- a closing that focuses on what should happen next.

6 The **complimentary closing** provides a polite word or phrase to end the message. Capitalize the first word only and add a comma after the closing.

7 The **signature block** makes the letter official. Align the writer's name with the complimentary closing. Place a one-word job title on the same line as the typed name or below the name; place a longer title below the typed name.

8 Use an **enclosure note** whenever you enclose something. Type *Enclosure(s)* or *Enc(s).* and the number of enclosures. To list enclosures by name, type *Enclosure(s)* or *Enc(s).,* a colon, and the names stacked vertically. (See an alternate format of a vertical list on page 203.)

9 A **postscript** contains a personal or final note. Type *P.S.* (with periods but no colon) followed by the message. (Shown on page 114.)

**Basic
Letter**

1 R & J Law Office
105 East Bay Road
Bar Harbor, ME 04609-6327

2 August 5, 2010

Two to Eight Spaces

3 Ms. Abigail Bruins, Manager
Rena's Restaurant
3706 Chamberlain Avenue, SE
Bar Harbor, ME 04609-3427

Double Space

4 Dear Ms. Bruins:

Double Space

Opening **5** Early last week, we received your letter, along with a drawing of the deck that you want to add to the east side of your restaurant. In that letter, you described your building plan and asked that one of our attorneys advise you on how to proceed.

Middle I studied the plan and found it attractive. However, the drawing shows that the east edge of the proposed deck would extend within six feet of your side property line, thereby violating Article X in the city's building code. That article requires ten feet between a building and a side property line. (I have enclosed a copy of Article X.)

Closing Given this restriction, you could proceed with your building plan in one of two ways: (1) present your plan to the Planning and Zoning Commission and ask for a variance to Article X, or (2) adapt the plan so that it conforms to the code. Please call me at 555-0654 to discuss this matter.

Double Space

6 Yours sincerely,

Sydney George **Four Spaces**

7 Sydney George
Attorney-at-Law

Double Space

8 Enclosures:
1. Drawing
2. Article

Parts of an Expanded Letter

Adding Information

When you, your reader, a typist, a filing clerk, or future readers need additional information, include one or more of the items from this list.

1 A **method of transmission note** indicates how a letter should be or has been sent: via facsimile, via registered mail, via overnight courier.

2 A **reference line** begins with a guide word and a colon (*Reference:, In reply to:*) followed by a file, an account, an invoice, or a database number.

3 When appropriate, use a **confidential notation** on both the letter and the envelope. CAPITALIZE or underline the word *confidential* for emphasis.

4 In the **inside address,** stack names by alphabet or position for two or more readers. For two readers at separate addresses, stack the addresses (including names) with a line between.

5 The **attention line** designates a reader or department but encourages others to read the letter. Place it two lines below the inside address, flush left or centered. CAPITALIZE or underline for emphasis. (See page 111 for a model.)

6 The **subject line** announces the topic and is placed flush left two lines below the salutation. CAPITALIZE or underline for emphasis.

7 The **signature block** may include the writer's courtesy title typed in front of the name to clarify his or her gender or a preferred form of address. If two people must sign the letter, place the second name beside the first starting at the center of the page—or place it four spaces below the first name.

8 In the **identification line,** type the writer's initials in capitals and the typist's in lowercase, separated by a slash (but no spaces).

9 Use the **copies notation** by typing *c* or *cc*, followed by a colon and a vertical list of people (with job titles in parentheses). To send a copy to someone else without the reader knowing it, type *bc* or *bcc* (blind copy), but only on the copy sent to the person listed.

10 **Continuation pages** follow a letter's first page. On blank stationery, carry over at least two lines and use a heading in one of the formats below:

Page 2
Abigail Bruins
Paul Meyer
August 5, 2010

Abigail Bruins	Page 2	August 5, 2010
Paul Meyer		

Expanded Letter

R&J Law Office
105 East Bay Road, Bar Harbor, ME 04609-6327 • 207-555-0645 • rjlawoffice.com

August 5, 2010

Two to Eight Spaces

1 Via facsimile

Double Space

2 Reference: Article X

Double Space

3 CONFIDENTIAL

Double Space

4 Ms. Abigail Bruins
Mr. Paul Meyer
Rena's Restaurant
3706 Chamberlain Avenue, SE
Bar Harbor, ME 04609-3427

Double Space

Dear Ms. Bruins and Mr. Meyer:

Double Space

6 BUILDING PERMIT

Double Space

Early last week we received your letter, along with a drawing of the deck that you want to add to the east side of your restaurant. I studied the plan and found it attractive. However, the drawing shows that the proposed deck would extend within six feet of your property line, thereby violating Article X in the city's building code. That article requires ten feet between a building and a side property line.

Given this restriction, you could proceed with your building plan in one of two ways: (1) present your plan to the Planning and Zoning Commission and ask for a variance to Article X, or (2) adapt the plan so that it conforms to the code. Please call me at 555-0654 to discuss this matter.

Yours sincerely,

Double Space

7 *Sydney George*

Four Spaces

Ms. Sydney George
Attorney-at-Law

Double Space

8 SG/MB
Enclosures 2
9 cc: Leah Theodore (Senior Partner)

Special Note: Item 5 from page 166 is not shown in this model. See page 111 to see an attention line.

Letter Formats

You can arrange a letter in a full-block, semiblock, or simplified format. Choose the letter format that best fits the situation and your organization's guidelines. ***Note:*** For quick formatting, use the letter templates in your word-processing program.

Full-Block Format

Rules:	• All parts flush left
Character:	• Professional, clean, contemporary
Plus:	• Easy to set up and follow
Minus:	• May appear unbalanced to the left of the page
Best Uses:	• Routine letters, not social and executive letters
Note:	• More traditional and international readers may not prefer this format.

Semiblock Format

Rules:	• Date line, method of transmission line, reference line, complimentary close, and signature block align with a vertical line at the center of the page; all other parts of the letter are flush left.
Character:	• Professional, traditional
Plus:	• Balanced appearance on the page
Minus:	• More difficult setup than full block or simplified
Best Uses:	• International and traditional letters, as well as executive and social letters
Note:	• You may indent the subject line and all paragraphs to further soften the form. In addition, you may drop the space between paragraphs.

Simplified Format

Rules:	• All parts flush left
	• No salutation or complimentary close
	• Subject line and writer's name in caps; dash between the writer's name and title
Character:	• Bare-bones, functional
Plus:	• Easy setup
Minus:	• Impersonal format due to lack of courtesy elements
Best Uses:	• Routine letters—regular reminders, notices, bulletins, orders, mass mailings
	• Not appropriate for high-level or persuasive letters
Note:	• You may drop courtesy titles from the inside address.

Full Block

R & J Law Office
105 East Bay Road, Bar Harbor, ME 04609-6327
207-555-0654   rjlawoffice.com

August 5, 2010

Ref. A. Bruins #2

CONFIDENTIAL

Ms. Abigail Bruins
Mr. Paul Meyer
Rena's Restaurant
Box 248
Bar Harbor, ME 04609-3427

Dear Ms. Bruins and Mr. Meyer:

BUILDING PERMIT

Early last week, we received your letter, along with drawings of the deck that you want to add to the east side of your restaurant. In that letter, you described your building plan and asked that one of our attorneys advise you on how to proceed.

I studied the plan and found it attractive. However, the drawings show that the east edge of the proposed deck would extend within six feet of your side property line, thereby violating Article X in the city's building code. That article requires ten feet between a building and a side property line.

Given this restriction, you could proceed with your building plan in one of two ways: (1) present your plan to the Planning and Zoning Commission and ask for a variance to Article X, or (2) adapt the plan so that it conforms to the code.

Please call me at 555-0654 to discuss this matter.

Yours sincerely,

Sydney George

Ms. Sydney George
Attorney-at-Law

SG/MBB
Enc.: Article X
cc: Leah Theodore

Semiblock

R & J Law Office
105 East Bay Road, Bar Harbor, ME 04609-6327
207-555-0654   rjlawoffice.com

August 5, 2010

Ref. A. Bruins #2

CONFIDENTIAL

Ms. Abigail Bruins
Mr. Paul Meyer
Rena's Restaurant
Box 248
Bar Harbor, ME 04609-3427

Dear Ms. Bruins and Mr. Meyer:

BUILDING PERMIT

Early last week, we received your letter, along with drawings of the deck that you want to add to the east side of your restaurant. In that letter, you described your building plan and asked that one of our attorneys advise you on how to proceed.

I studied the plan and found it attractive. However, the drawings show that the east edge of the proposed deck would extend within six feet of your side property line, thereby violating Article X in the city's building code. That article requires ten feet between a building and a side property line.

Given this restriction, you could proceed with your building plan in one of two ways: (1) present your plan to the Planning and Zoning Commission and ask for a variance to Article X, or (2) adapt the plan so that it conforms to the code.

Please call me at 555-0654 to discuss this matter.

Yours sincerely,

Sydney George

Ms. Sydney George
Attorney-at-Law

SG/MBB
Enc.: Article X
cc: Leah Theodore

Simplified

R & J Law Office
105 East Bay Road, Bar Harbor, ME 04609-6327
207-555-0665   rjlawoffice.com

August 5, 2010

Ref. A. Bruins #2

CONFIDENTIAL

Abigail Bruins
Paul Meyer
Rena's Restaurant
Box 248
Bar Harbor, ME 04609-3427

BUILDING PERMIT

Early last week, we received your letter, along with drawings of the deck that you want to add to the east side of your restaurant. In that letter, you described your building plan and asked that one of our attorneys advise you on how to proceed.

I studied the plan and found it attractive. However, the drawings show that the east edge of the proposed deck would extend within six feet of your side property line, thereby violating Article X in the city's building code. That article requires ten feet between a building and a side property line.

Given this restriction, you could proceed with your building plan in one of two ways: (1) present your plan to the Planning and Zoning Commission and ask for a variance to Article X, or (2) adapt the plan so that it conforms to the code.

Please call me at 555-0654 to discuss this matter.

Sydney George

MS. SYDNEY GEORGE—ATTORNEY-AT-LAW

SG/MBB
Enc.: Article X
cc: Leah Theodore

Letters and Envelopes

Folding Letters

A Standard Fold: To put a letter in its matching envelope, place the letter face-up and follow these steps:

1. Fold the bottom edge up so that the paper is divided into thirds. Use your thumbnail to create a clean crease.

2. Fold the top third down over the bottom third, leaving 1/4 inch for easy unfolding, and crease firmly.

3. Insert the letter (with the open end at the top) into the envelope.

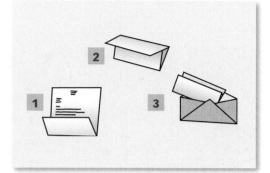

A Large Sheet in a Small Envelope: If you must place a letter in a small envelope, follow these steps:

1. Fold the bottom edge up so that the paper is divided in half, and create a clean crease.

2. Fold the right side to the left so that the sheet is divided into thirds; crease firmly.

3. Fold the left third over the right third and crease firmly.

4. Turn the letter sideways and insert it (with the open end at the top) into the envelope.

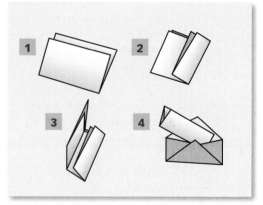

A Window Envelope: Position the inside address on the letter so that it will show through the window. Then place the letter face up and fold it as follows:

1. Fold the bottom edge up so that the paper is divided into thirds, and create a clean crease.

2. Turn the letter face-down with the top edge toward you and fold the top third of the letter back.

3. Insert the letter in the envelope and make sure that the whole address shows through the window.

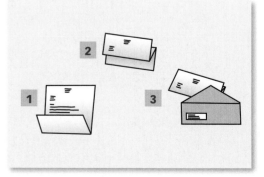

U.S. Postal Service (USPS) Envelope Guidelines

To be sure that your letters are delivered quickly and correctly, follow all United States Postal Service(USPS) guidelines when you address an envelope. See the envelope and helpful guidelines below.

```
MS ABIGAIL BRUINS
RENAS RESTAURANT
BOX 248
BAR HARBOR ME 04609-3427

CONFIDENTIAL        2 3/8" maximum from bottom

        MS ELIZABETH MOIZE
        ASSOCIATE EDITOR                    1" minimum
        NATIONAL GEOGRAPHIC SOCIETY          left and right
        1145 17TH ST NW RM 14
        WASHINGTON DC 20036-4701

        5/8" minimum from bottom
```

1. Type the receiver's name and address in black ink on a light-colored envelope. Use an all-cap style for everything in the address. Make sure all lines are horizontal and lined up flush left. Leave out all punctuation except the hyphen in the zip code.

2. Type the receiver's address—including the type of street (ST, AVE), compass points (NE, SW), and full ZIP code—in the order pictured. Place the suite, room, or apartment number on the address line, after the street address.

3. Use USPS abbreviations for states and other words in the address. Use numerals rather than words for numbered streets (9TH AVE). Add ZIP+4 codes. (Go to **www.usps.com** to get the ZIP code for any street address in the country.)

Tips for International Mail

When sending international mail, print the country name alone on the last line. As long as the country, city, and state or province are in English, the name and address may be in the language of the country listed.

Pattern: Name of Receiver
Street Address or PO Box
City, State/Province, Code
Country (Caps, English)

Examples:

MR BRUCE WARNER	MS TAMARA BEALS
2431 EDEN WAY	56 METCALFE CRES
LONDON W1P 4HQ	MONTREAL QC J7V 8P2
ENGLAND	CANADA

Standard Postal Abbreviations

States, Provinces, and Territories

U.S. States							Canadian Provinces, Territories	
Alabama	AL	Kansas	KS	Ohio	OH			
Alaska	AK	Kentucky	KY	Oklahoma	OK			
Arizona	AZ	Louisiana	LA	Oregon	OR			
Arkansas	AR	Maine	ME	Pennsylvania	PA		Alberta	AB
California	CA	Maryland	MD	Puerto Rico	PR		British Columbia	BC
Colorado	CO	Massachusetts	MA	Rhode Island	RI		Manitoba	MB
Connecticut	CT	Michigan	MI	South Carolina	SC		New Brunswick	NB
Delaware	DE	Minnesota	MN	South Dakota	SD		Newfoundland	
District of		Mississippi	MS	Tennessee	TN		and Labrador	NL
Columbia	DC	Missouri	MO	Texas	TX		Northwest	
Florida	FL	Montana	MT	Utah	UT		Territories	NT
Georgia	GA	Nebraska	NE	Vermont	VT		Nova Scotia	NS
Guam	GU	Nevada	NV	Virginia	VA		Nunavut	NU
Hawaii	HI	New Hampshire	NH	Virgin Islands	VI		Ontario	ON
Idaho	ID	New Jersey	NJ	Washington	WA		Prince Edward	
Illinois	IL	New Mexico	NM	West Virginia	WV		Island	PE
Indiana	IN	New York	NY	Wisconsin	WI		Quebec	QC
Iowa	IA	North Carolina	NC	Wyoming	WY		Saskatchewan	SK
		North Dakota	ND				Yukon Territory	YT

Abbreviations for Use on Envelopes

Fyi For mass mailings, check the Postal Service's bar-coding and mailing-list services for speed and savings. Go to **www.usps.com.**

Annex	ANX	Lake	LK	Route	RTE
Apartment	APT	Lakes	LKS	Rural	R
Avenue	AVE	Lane	LN	Rural Route	RR
Boulevard	BLVD	Meadows	MDWS	Shore	SH
Building	BLDG	North	N	South	S
Causeway	CSWY	Northeast	NE	Southeast	SE
Circle	CIR	Northwest	NW	Southwest	SW
Court	CT	Office	OFC	Square	SQ
Drive	DR	Palms	PLMS	Station	STA
East	E	Park	PARK	Street	ST
Expressway	EXPY	Parkway	PKWY	Suite	STE
Floor	FL	Place	PL	Terrace	TER
Fort	FT	Plaza	PLZ	Throughway	TRWY
Freeway	FWY	Port	PRT	Turnpike	TPKE
Harbor	HBR	Post Office Box	PO BOX	Union	UN
Heights	HTS	Ridge	RDG	Viaduct	VIA
Highway	HWY	River	RIV	View	VW
Hospital	HOSP	Road	RD	Village	VLG
Junction	JCT	Room	RM	West	W

	Titles in Address	Salutations
One Woman (avoid showing marital status)		
Preferred	Ms. Barbara Jordan	Dear Ms. Jordan:
Married or Widowed	Mrs. Lorene Frost	Dear Mrs. Frost:
Single	Ms. Adriana Langille	Dear Ms. Langille:
Two or More Women (alphabetical)		
Standard	Ms. Bethany Jergens Ms. Shavonn Mitchell	Dear Ms. Jergens and Ms. Mitchell:
Formal	Mmes. Bethany Jergens and Shavonn Mitchell	Dear Mmes. Jergens and Mitchell:
One Man		
Standard	Mr. Hugh Knight	Dear Mr. Knight:
With Jr., Sr., or Roman Numeral	Mr. Brian Boswell, Jr. Mr. Brian Boswell III	Dear Mr. Boswell:
Two or More Men (alphabetical)		
Standard	Mr. Alex Fernandez Mr. Nate Shaw	Dear Mr. Fernandez and Mr. Shaw:
Formal	Messrs. Alex Fernandez and Nate Shaw	Dear Messrs. Fernandez and Shaw:
One Man and One Woman (alphabetical)		
	Ms. Paula Trunhope Mr. Joe Williams	Dear Ms. Trunhope and Mr. Williams:
Married Couple		
Same Last Name	Mr. William and Mrs. Susan Lui	Dear Mr. and Mrs. Lui:
Different Last Names	Mr. William Bentley Ms. Sinead Sweeney	Dear Mr. Bentley and Ms. Sweeney:
One Reader (gender unknown)		
	M. Robin Leeds Robin Leeds	Dear M. Leeds: Dear Robin Leeds:
Mixed Group		
Company, Department, Job Title, or Unknown Reader	Acme Corporation Human Resources Dept.	Formal **Dear Sir or Madam:** Informal **Dear Manager:**

Courtesy Titles

- Choose "standard" or "formal" titles and salutations based on your relationship with the reader and the seriousness of the message.
- Abbreviate all courtesy titles: **Mr., Ms., Mrs.**
- Never guess your reader's gender (*Robin, Pat, Chris*).
- Use a woman's preferred courtesy title: Ms., Miss, or Mrs.
- Use a woman's preferred name: original, married, or combined (Smith-Olsen).

Government Officials and Representatives

To properly address government officials (national, state, local, judicial, and so on), follow this pattern:

Title in Inside Address:	The Honorable *(full name)* *(full title on second line)*
Formal Salutation:	**Dear Sir/Madam:** or **Dear Mr./Madam** *(position):*
Informal Salutation:	**Dear Mr./Ms.** *(last name):* or **Dear** *(position) (last name):*

	Titles in Address	Salutations
National		
President	The President	Dear Mr./Madam President:
Vice President	The Vice President	Dear Mr. Vice President:
Speaker of the House	The Honorable Steven Kudo	Dear Mr. Speaker:
Cabinet Members, Undersecretaries, etc.	The Honorable Jane Doe	Dear Madam:
		Dear Attorney General Doe:
Senators (U.S. or State)	The Honorable Bill Johnson	Dear Senator Johnson:
Representatives (U.S. or State)	The Honorable Joan Walker	Dear Ms. Walker:
		Dear Representative Walker:
Heads of Offices and Agencies	The Honorable John Hillman Postmaster General	Dear Mr. Postmaster General:
		Dear Mr. Hillman:
Chief Justice (U.S. or State)	The Honorable Shelby Woo Chief Justice of California	Dear Madam Chief Justice:
U.S. Ambassador	The Honorable Francis del Verda	Dear Madam Ambassador:
		Dear Ambassador del Verda:
State/Local		
Governor	The Honorable Mary Lee	Dear Governor Lee:
Mayor	The Honorable Mark Barne	Dear Mayor Barne:
Council Member	The Honorable Corey Springs	Dear Mr. Springs:
Judge	The Honorable Grace Kim	Dear Judge Kim:
Military		
General	Major General Karl P. Bastion, USAF	Sir: (formal) Dear General Bastion:
Lieutenant	Lieutenant Jane Evans, USMC	Dear Ms. Evans:

Official Titles

- Use a formal title (**Senator, General**) rather than a standard courtesy title (*Mr., Ms.*).
- Avoid outdated courtesy forms (*Gentlemen, To Whom It May Concern*).

Religious Titles

To address religious leaders from any faith with titles that fit their positions, follow these guidelines.

	Titles in Address	Salutations
Roman Catholic Clergy		
Cardinal	His Eminence, Edward Cardinal Romero	Your Eminence:
		Dear Cardinal Romero:
Archbishop and Bishop	The Most Reverend Henri Crétien	Your Excellency:
		Dear Bishop/Archbishop Crétien:
Priest	The Reverend Morris Franklin	Reverend Sir:
		Dear Father Franklin:
Nun	Sister Mary Jennsen	Dear Sister Mary:
		Dear Sister Jennsen:
Monk	Brother Atticus Bartholemew	Dear Brother Atticus:
		Dear Brother Bartholemew:
Protestant Clergy		
Bishop (Anglican, Episcopal, Methodist)	The Right Reverend Samuel Wolfe	Right Reverend Sir:
		Reverend Sir:
		Dear Bishop Wolfe:
Dean (Head of Cathedral or Seminary)	The Very Reverend Nicholas Cameron	Very Reverend Sir:
		Dear Dean Cameron:
Minister or Priest	The Reverend Susan Edwards	Dear Reverend Edwards:
	Pastor Edwards	Dear Pastor Edwards:
Chaplain	Chaplain Adam Carp Captain, USMC	Dear Chaplain Carp:
Jewish Clergy		
Rabbi	Rabbi Joshua Gould	Dear Rabbi Gould:
Rabbi with Doctor of Divinity Degree	Rabbi Joshua Gould, D.D.	Dear Dr. Gould:

Religious Titles

- The use of *The* before *Reverend* differs from church to church. Follow the organization's preference.
- In some religious orders, the title in the salutation is followed by the reader's first name. Other orders prefer the last name.
- If the person has a Doctor of Divinity degree, add a comma and *D.D.* after his or her name in the address (not the salutation).

Guidelines Memos

Your Goal ▶ Your goal is to make your point quickly, clearly, and effectively. If possible, keep your memo to a single page.

> "I have received memos so swollen with managerial babble that they struck me as the literary equivalent of assault with a deadly weapon."
>
> —Peter Baida

shutterstock.com

1. **Prewrite:** (Ideas and Organization)
   - Ask yourself why you are writing. What outcome do you want?
   - Consider your readers. Who needs this memo? Why? How should the memo be sent?

   Prepare to draft. Gather necessary facts, figures, and attachments. Brainstorm for more details and make a list of your main points.

2. **Draft:** (Ideas, Organization, and Voice)
   Opening Type "memo" or "memorandum" at the top of the page and complete the memo heading (name only one subject on the subject line).
   Middle Provide details that answer readers' questions: What is this memo about? What does it mean to me? Why is it important?
   Closing Clarify any action needed, especially who is responsible for what.
   Note: For good or neutral news, put your key point in the subject line and introduction. For bad-news or persuasive memos, use a neutral subject line and then build to your main point.

3. **Revise:** (Ideas, Organization, Voice, Words, and Sentences)
   - ☐ Have you given clear, accurate information?
   - ☐ Have you arranged your points logically?
   - ☐ Have you used a team attitude, focusing on company goals?
   - ☐ Have you used a polite, professional voice?
   - ☐ Have you used precise word choice, smooth sentences, and effective transitions?

4. **Refine:** (Conventions and Design)
   - ☐ Have you checked punctuation, capitalization, usage, and grammar?
   - ☐ Have you checked for a reader-friendly format and design that uses lists, headings, tables, boxes, and white space effectively?

Basic Memo

Center "Memorandum," or company name.

Complete and align all four items in the heading. Initial or sign paper memos.

Type "Subject" or "Re" and state your subject as a summary of your message.

Opening

Expand on the subject line.

Middle

Where appropriate, use lists for easy reading.

Double-space between paragraphs and items in a list.

Closing

Focus on action.

Memo

Date: August 9, 2010

To: Josie James

Single- or double-space the heading.

From: Ike Harris *ΙΉ*

Subject: Promotion of Mona Veal to Full-Time Graphic Artist

Triple Space

For the past 18 months, Mona Veal has done outstanding work as a part-time graphic artist in our Marketing Department. I recommend that she be promoted to full-time status and be given the necessary $5.50 per hour wage increase and full benefits.

Double Space

The promotion is warranted for two reasons:

1. Throughout the past 18 months, Mona has demonstrated those traits that Slenk Manufacturing most values in its graphic artists: creativity, dependability, and the ability to work well with others.

2. Presently we have four full-time and two part-time graphic artists. While this group was able to complete its projects on time last year, Allison Christian in Accounting tells me that the full-time employees averaged 3.5 hours of overtime per week throughout the year. Given that fact, our new contract with LEE-MAR Industries will soon put a strain on both the group and our budget.

Please let me know by August 16 whether you approve this promotion. I'd like Mona to begin full-time work on September 1.

Use 1" to 1.5" margins and a block style.

Parts of an Expanded Memo

While each memo includes the basic elements shown on page 179, sometimes you may need to add more elements. The guidelines below, which are numbered and modeled on the next page, show your options.

Heading

1 You can type "Memo," "Memorandum," or the company name at the top, but do not include the company's address or phone number.

2 For sensitive messages, label your memo **CONFIDENTIAL** and seal it in an envelope that is also marked **CONFIDENTIAL**.

3 Complete your heading with job titles, phone numbers, e-mail addresses, or a checklist showing the memo's purpose. In a paper memo, handwrite your initials after your name in the heading or after your job title, if one is used. If you have more than one reader, use one of these options:

- List the names after *To:* and highlight a different one on each copy of the memo.
- Put *See distribution* after *To:* and list all the readers at the end of the memo.
- Type a department's name after *To:*

Closing

4 Use quick-response options such as checklists, fill-in-the-blanks, or boxes.

5 Add an identification line showing the writer's initials (in caps) and the typist's initials (in lowercase) separated by a slash.

6 If you're sending documents with the memo, type *Attachment(s)* or *Enclosure(s)*, followed by either (a) the number of documents or (b) a colon and the document titles listed vertically.

7 If you want to send copies to secondary readers, type *c* (copy) or *cc* (courtesy copy) and a colon; then list the names and job titles stacked vertically (when job titles are included). To send a copy to someone without the main reader knowing it, add *bc* (blind copy) ONLY on the copy sent to the person listed after the *bc* notation.

| Ike Harris | Page 2 | 9 August 2010 |

Page 2
Ike Harris
9 August 2010

Fyi If your memo is longer than one page, carry over at least two lines of the message onto a plain sheet of stationery. Use one of the heading formats shown on the left.

Expanded Memo

1

Slenk Manufacturing

2 C O N F I D E N T I A L

Date: August 9, 2010

3 **To:**   Josie James, Director of Personnel
          Rebecca Tash, LAHW Representative

From: Ike Harris, Graphic Arts Director

Subject: Promotion of Mona Veal to Full-Time Graphic Artist

For the past 18 months, Mona Veal has done outstanding work as a part-time graphic artist in our Marketing Department. I recommend that she be promoted to full-time status. The promotion is warranted for two reasons:

1. Throughout the past 18 months, Mona has demonstrated those traits that Slenk Manufacturing most values in its graphic artists: creativity, dependability, and the ability to work well with others.

2. Presently we have four full-time and two part-time graphic artists. While this group was able to complete its projects on time last year, Allison Christian in Accounting tells me that the full-time employees averaged 3.5 hours of overtime per week throughout the year. Given that fact, our new contract with LEE-MAR Industries will soon put a strain on both the group and our budget.

If you approve the promotion, please initial below and return this memo.

4 Yes, proceed with Mona Veal's promotion to full-time graphic artist. ____

5 IH/gm
6 Attachment: Evaluation report of Mona Veal
7 c: Elizabeth Henry
     Mark Zoe

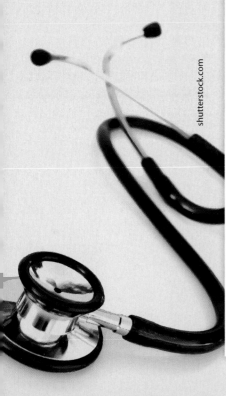

"I have made this [letter] longer, because I have not had the time to make it shorter."

—Blaise Pascal

shutterstock.com

Checklist Letters, Faxes, Memos

Your goal is to create a letter, fax, or memo that clearly communicates your message.

Ideas 9-16
____ is strong, clear, and accurate.
____ has answered the reader's questions: Why are you writing me? What needs to be done?

Organization 17-24
____ is appropriately direct or indirect, based on the reader's likely response.
____ memo contains an informative subject line
____ follows a fitting opening, middle, closing structure.

Voice 25-32
____ is courteous throughout, from salutation to complimentary closing.
____ uses an appropriate voice and focuses on the reader's needs.

Words 33-40
____ uses plain English—precise, clear, and simple words.
____ uses names and personal pronouns, especially "you," effectively.

Sentences 41-50
____ has short- to medium-length sentences that pass the "read aloud" test.
____ uses transition words to link ideas.

Correctness 51-58
____ follows all punctuation and capitalization rules for memos and letters.
____ uses correct abbreviations, titles, and spelling throughout.
____ contains no grammar or typing errors.

Design 59-70
____ follows all the rules of the format—spacing, margins, alignment, and so on.
____ contains short paragraphs.
____ uses headings and bulleted or numbered lists wherever helpful.
____ has a polished look—white space, clean typography, and good stationery.
____ includes initials, signatures, and attachments, if appropriate.

shutterstock.com

17
Reports

Good reports deliver. They deliver information and ideas that people need in order to complete projects, understand developments, evaluate outcomes, and advance the company's goals.

Specifically, reports can

- answer questions about what's happening in the company so that readers can check results, monitor progress, keep work on track, evaluate options, and make decisions.
- get to the point quickly with a factual, no-nonsense style.
- range from two pages to hundreds of pages.
- be presented as memos, letters, filled-out forms, online documents, or bound documents.

Guidelines Reports

Your Goal ▶ Your goal is to provide clear, accurate information and analysis about an incident, a time period, a project, a trip, or another business activity.

"This report, by its very length, defends itself against the risk of being read."

—Winston Churchill

1. **Prewrite: (Ideas and Organization)**
   - Know your purpose: Is it to supply information only, or to share conclusions as well? What outcome do you want?
   - Know your readers: What are their needs? What is their knowledge of the topic and expected use of the report? What will be their likely response? Do different readers have different needs?
   - Consider the big picture: Why is the report important? What effects might it have within and beyond your organization?

   Prepare to draft.
   - Carefully study the topic and gather accurate data.
   - Review previous reports or related documents. Consult with colleagues and experts as needed.
   - Outline your report using an appropriate method of organization.

2. **Draft: (Ideas, Organization, and Voice)**
   Opening Introduce the topic and provide a context. To be direct, summarize key points; to be indirect, exclude the summary and simply give appropriate background information.
   Middle Supply, organize, and explain your findings, including all essential details.
   Closing Offer conclusions and, if expected, recommendations.

3. **Revise: (Ideas, Organization, Voice, Words, and Sentences)**
   ☐ Have you supplied the facts objectively?
   ☐ Have you used effective transitions and summaries?
   ☐ Is your tone businesslike, but not stuffy or impersonal?
   ☐ Do you have a natural, condensed style: clear words and smooth sentences.

4. **Refine: (Conventions and Design)**
   ☐ Have you checked grammar, punctuation, spelling, and mechanics?
   ☐ Have you checked headings, lists, and numbering?
   ☐ Have you checked use of graphics, white space, boldface type, and color?

shutterstock.com

Organizing Reports

Organized reports deliver information in manageable pieces. You can organize your reports by following the three-part structure outlined below.

Opening

- **Label** the report with a title, your name, your reader's name, the date, a subject line indicating the topic, and any identifying information such as a reference number.
- **Introduce** the report's purpose, provide background information, and preview topics covered.
- **Summarize** your main points, conclusions, and recommendations if you want to be direct.

Middle

Organize findings according to one or more of these patterns:
- **Time**—in a step-by-step sequence.
- **Space location**—from top to bottom, left to right, near to far.
- **Order of importance**—from most to least, or least to most.
- **Categories**—by similarities and differences.
- **Alphabetical order**—by key terms.
- **Cause-effect**—by examining the forces that brought about a result or examining the results growing out of a specific force.
- **Compare-contrast**—by weighing and balancing alternatives against each other.
- **Hypothesis testing**—by suggesting possible conclusions, testing each, and selecting the best one.

Note: Present your data with the help of headings, lists, tables, spreadsheets, and other graphics.

Closing

- For an informative report, summarize the main points.
- For an analytical report, supply conclusions.
- For a persuasive report, include recommendations.

Maintainer Corporation of New Mexico

Date: March 19, 2010

To: Alice Jenkins, General Manager
          Roger Smythe, Safety Committee Chair

From: Gwen Vos, Supervisor
          Truck Finishing Department

Subject: Undercoating Safety Incident on March 18, 2010

Opening

Identify the type of incident.

Preview the report.

This report details a recent event in the undercoating bay. You will find (A) a description of the incident, (B) conclusions about the causes, and (C) recommendations for fixing the problem.

Middle

Divide the report into logical sections with clear headings.

Provide context, describe the incident, and explain what followed.

List and number the events in the order they happened.

A. The Incident: Tangled Air Hose

During a routine inspection of work on Thursday, March 18, 2010 at 10:45 a.m., I found undercoater Bob Irving struggling to breathe underneath the truck he was working on. While spraying liquid-rubber sealant on the undercarriage, he had rolled his dolly over his air hose, cutting off the air supply. I immediately pulled him out, untangled him, and took the following steps:

1. I checked Bob for injuries and determined that he was unharmed.
2. I asked him what had happened. He explained that he couldn't free himself because (a) he became tangled in the spray-gun cords, (b) his air hose was locked into his oxygen suit, and (c) he was lying down in a cramped space.
3. I discussed the incident with the undercoating crew. They confirmed that similar problems had developed before, but they hadn't filed reports because no one had actually been injured.
4. I inspected thoroughly all undercoating equipment.
5. As a short-term solution, I bought air horn alarms to attach to the undercoaters' dollies.

Middle

Develop clear cause-effect thinking.

Use strong transitional words.

Be precise and objective.

B. Conclusions: Probable Causes

Presently, undercoaters maneuver under trucks and spray liquid-rubber sealant on the undercarriage while lying on their backs. Maintainer provides oxygen suits to protect their skin and oxygen supply from this sealant that (a) produces noxious fumes, (b) causes choking if swallowed, and (c) injures skin upon contact. However, this incident shows that our safeguards are inadequate:

- Ten-year-old oxygen-suit meters and air tubes frequently malfunction. Masks and hoses are beginning to crack.
- The practice of lying on a dolly while spraying can cause undercoaters to get tangled in cords and hoses or roll over their air hoses.
- Spraying from a prone position allows liquid rubber to drip onto undercoaters' masks. This dripping obscures vision and makes it more likely that workers will get entangled and more difficult for them to get untangled.

Closing

Suggest solutions that clearly match the problem.

Be realistic.

Stress benefits of action.

C. Recommendations: New Safety Measures

To further protect undercoaters from these hazards, I recommend the following actions:

1. Replace oxygen suits and equipment to meet the 2008 OSHA oxygen-safety standards (air-hose locks with emergency-release latches).
2. Put trucks on lifts so that undercoaters can work standing up.
3. Have two undercoaters work together on the same truck in order to monitor each other.
4. Purchase No-Drip Sealant Applicators to eliminate dripping liquid rubber.

With these measures, undercoating incidents such as the one with Bob Irving should not happen again. Please contact me with any questions and with your response to these recommendations. My phone number is 555-1222, and my e-mail address is <GwenVos@maintainer.com>.

Periodic Report

STEWART PLASTICS, INC.
JOLIET ANNUAL REPORT

Date Submitted: November 14, 2010
Period Covered: November 1, 2009, to October 31, 2010
Prepared By: Denzel Irving
Prepared For: Senior Management

The following report reviews 2009–2010 activities at Stewart Plastics' Joliet facility. Topics covered include manufacturing, safety, and quality. Based on this review, the report projects sales and production needs for 2010–2011.

Summary

Major projects involved plastite screws for Fimco, spray-on graphics for Newland, Kelch steel clamps on EcoLab molds, and soda blasting to clean molds. Safety remained a priority through consultation with Liberty Mutual. First-Time Quality improved from 96.8 to 97.5 percent. Anticipated sales should be $6.4 million. To reach maximum output of $6.8 million, purchase a 5-Axis Router and hire a Process Engineer.

Year-End Operations Report

Manufacturing and Process Engineering
- Evaluated using thread-forming plastite screws to replace aluminum T-inserts on standard spot tank. Submitted samples to Fimco for testing.
- Completed testing of spray-on graphics and submitted samples to Newland. Though test parts looked good, the masking process proved time-consuming and costly. Alternate technology (Mark-It Company's post-molding graphic application) looked promising.
- Tested stainless steel clamps from Kelch on EcoLab molds. Clamps reduced maintenance downtime 50 percent.

Opening

Identify the report, the time period, the writer, and the reader.

State the purpose of the report and what it covers.

Provide main points in a summary. (The summary may be placed at the end.)

Middle

Divide information into logical categories with clear headings.

Use a "telegraphic" style (short clauses).

Safety and Maintenance

Use short lists and parallel structure.

- Tessa Swann, Loss Prevention Consultant from Liberty Mutual, continued to identify safety issues and to implement solutions.
- Safety Committee facilitated improvements.
- Crews completed annual maintenance on all machines.

Quality

- Thermo King Quality System assessment gave us a 53.7 rating.
- Awarded Newland Quality Award in June 2010.
- First-Time Quality for 2009 was 97.5 percent, up from 96.8 percent.

2010–2011 Goals

Sales Overview

Middle

Shift from looking back to looking forward.

Anticipated production output is $6.4 million, based on the following:

- Newland: anticipate sales to go from $1.4 to $1.6 million.
- Fermont: release of 5,10,15,30,and 60KW parts for production should mean $850,000 increase in sales.
- Fimco: anticipate sales to go from $1.1 million to $1.8 million.

Manufacturing Goals and Production Needs

- Combine the 800 and 160 work areas into a cell and analyze the effects on through-put and overall machine efficiencies.
- Consider purchasing a 5-Axis Router for custom-job applications requiring exact-trim procedures.
- Hire a Process Engineer by March 2011: crucial to success of custom-job applications and implementing 5-Axis Router technology.

Conclusions and Recommendations

Closing

Summarize the report and the suggested follow-up.

The Joliet Plant is capable of $6.8 million in sales. Roadblocks include the lack of a 5-Axis Router for custom-trimmed products and training for the use of this router. Therefore, I recommend the following:

1. Purchase a 5-Axis Router.
2. Hire a Process Engineer who can use the 5-Axis Router and conduct training.

Progress Report

Hope Services *Child Development Center*

2141 South Fifth Place, Seatle, WA 907761 • Telephone 436-555-1400
www.hopeserv.org

July 16, 2010

Mr. Anthony Jenson
Contract Compliance Officer
Community Planning and Development
473 Maple Street
Reading, PA 19608-3361

Dear Anthony:

Opening

Give a title and a reference number if appropriate.

Clarify the period and preview the report.

Subject: Hope Services Annual Progress Report (CDBG 2368-08)

Please accept this Annual Progress Report concerning Hope Services' work with minorities for fiscal year July 1, 2009, through June 30, 2010.

I have included these statistics: (1) total number of minority persons assisted, (2) the number of households and their ethnic origin, and (3) their status as low- or moderate-income households. In addition, I have included a narrative describing highlights of culturally specific services for the past fiscal year.

Middle

Provide precise project data.

Client Numbers (July 1, 2009–June 30, 2010)

The following is client information for the minority households served by the Hope Services' staff through the Cultural Diversity Program at the shelter:

1. 178 minorities served, including 102 children.
2. 76 households served, 100 percent female-headed (36 African American, 10 Asian, 23 Hispanic, 7 Native American).
3. 96 percent of households served had incomes below the poverty level, while the remaining 4 percent of households were at low-income levels.

2 of 2

Middle

Explain key developments.

Use lists where appropriate.

Outreach Highlights of the Cultural Diversity Program

In addition to the previous statistics, here are two illustrations of our progress on cultural-diversity issues:

- In January, Jasmine Michaels joined Hope Services to develop the Cultural Diversity Program, including (a) services for victims of sexual or domestic assault, and (b) community outreach to minority populations.
- In April, representatives from the following organizations formed Project SART (Sexual Abuse Response Team): Hope Services, Reading Hospital, Berks County Attorney's Office, Reading Police Department, and Penn State University.

Closing

Summarize the project's status, and look forward to the next stages.

Conclusions and Projections

As shown above, Hope Services (HS) continues to improve its services to minority clients and communities in Reading.

- Numbers indicate that HS is helping its target clientele (low-income minority households headed by women).
- Hiring a Cultural Diversity Specialist has given HS a strong presence in the community.
- In the coming year, HS will focus on strengthening its outreach to minority communities and increasing its training of staff and volunteers in cultural-diversity issues.

Anticipate further contact.

Thank you for supporting our work with minorities through Hope Services. If you need additional information, please contact me. My phone number is 555-66577; my e-mail address is <mdrummond@hopeservicesdevcenter. com>

Yours sincerely,

Melissa S. Drummond

Melissa S. Drummond
Resource Development Director

Trip Report

PACIFIC PIPELINE CORPORATION
REPAIR REPORT

Date: February 3, 2010

To: Ralph Arnoldson
           Pasco District Supervisor

From: Chris Waterford, Crew Chief

Opening

Identify the job.

Repair: Leak Clamp Installation
Location: Camas Eugene Lateral near the city of Mollala, Oregon
Date: February 2, 2010
Crew: #3 (Brad Drenton, Lena Harold, John Baldritch,
           Laura Postit, Jill Reynaldo, Chris Waterford)

Provide trip background.

Crew #3 and I (Chris Waterford, Crew Chief) responded to a call from the Eugene District crew asking for help on repairing a leak. Based on their request, we took the emergency trailer and a 24-inch Plidco clamp. Our response time was 6.5 hours (2 hours loading, 4.5 hours driving). We arrived about 2:30 p.m.

Middle

Divide trip activities into logical categories.

Use headings, subheadings, and lists.

Assessment of Problem
The Eugene crew had exposed the leak area on the pipe. Then Crew #3 and I assessed damage and conditions:
- Mud covered the work area and the ramps in the ditch.
- Water in the ditch came up to the bottom of the pipe.
- Rain was falling.
- The leak came from two quarter-inch cracks on a seam (at 10 o'clock looking south).
- A power generator was on site.
- Three bolt-on leak clamps and one hydraulic leak clamp were on hand.
- Space for a hydro crane and an emergency trailer was limited.

Middle

Condense key trip and events and issues.

Highlight decisions and developments.

Repair Plan and Decisions

With conditions in mind, we considered three issues: the possibility of more leaks, clamp selection, and safety precautions.

More Leaks? Eugene crew members probed three-foot sections of pipe on each side of the two quarter-inch cracks and found no more leaks.

Best Clamp? Laura indicated that the clamp would not need to be welded, so we decided to use the 24-inch bolt-on clamp.

Safety Precautions? We decided not to use the air systems for these reasons:
- The gas leak was minor (detectable only with a detecting agent).
- Safer installation of the clamp in daylight would be delayed by using air systems.
- Suits and breathing systems limit visibility, add weight, and create fatigue that could cause errors and injuries.

Based on these considerations, we installed the 24-inch bolt-on clamp in 1.5 hours. The Eugene crew took responsibility for site cleanup. We packed up, returned home in 4.5 hours, and unloaded in 1 hour.

Closing

Summarize work done.

Stress costs and benefits.

Summary

The February 2, 2010, repair trip for Crew #3 aimed to help the Eugene District crew repair two leaks on the Camas Eugene Lateral near Mollala. Based on the small leak size, the muddy site, and the poor weather (rain), we decided to repair the leak without using protective air systems while installing a 24-inch bolt-on clamp. As a result, we completed the repair with these benefits:
- A less-expensive clamp was used.
- A time savings of approximately two hours was realized.

Total time spent on this repair was 13.5 hours, including travel, repair, loading, and unloading.

"The report
of my death
was an
exaggeration."

—Mark Twain

Checklist Reports

Your goal is to provide clear, accurate information and analysis about an incident, a time period, a project, a trip, or another business activity.

Ideas   9-16

____ has a clear purpose.

____ spells out its purpose.

____ provides complete, accurate data.

____ offers conclusions and recommendations.

____ uses tables, charts (lists, graphics) to communicate information clearly.

Organization   17-24

____ is organized logically into three parts: (1) introduction, (2) findings, and (3) conclusions and recommendations.

____ presents a summary up front if the news is good or neutral; presents conclusions at the end in bad-news or persuasive situations.

____ arranges findings in a pattern: order of importance, time or space, cause-effect, problem-solution, comparison-contrast, and so on.

____ has informative, parallel headings that divide the report.

Voice   25-32

____ has a matter-of-fact but positive tone.

Words   33-40

____ uses words that fit the reader: the right formality and complexity.

Sentences   41-50

____ uses brief, parallel phrases or sentences in lists.

Correctness   51-58

____ uses correct grammar, punctuation, spelling, and mechanics.

____ is free of typing errors.

Design   59-70

____ has a format and presentation that follow company guidelines.

____ uses white space, boldface type, and graphics effectively.

shutterstock.com

shutterstock.com

18
Proposals

A proposal can be as simple as a suggestion-box memo or as complex as a book-length bid. Either way, a proposal identifies a need or a problem and lays out a convincing plan for meeting that need or solving that problem. A proposal can tackle issues like these:

- fixing inefficient operating practices;
- winning contracts and selling products or services;
- developing new markets, products, or services;
- improving current products or services; and
- meeting legal and ethical requirements.

A well-written proposal, whether it is designed to sell a service, fix a problem, or justify an expansion, is a force for positive change.

Guidelines Proposals

Your Goal ▶ Your goal is to persuade others that you have a workable solution or plan that solves a problem or meets a need.

"It is the duty of the president to propose, and it is the privilege of the congress to dispose."

—Franklin Delano Roosevelt

1. **Prewrite**: **(Ideas and Organization)**
   - To whom are you making this proposal? What are your reader's needs, attitudes, and concerns in relation to the issue?
   - Exactly what are you proposing? Why?
   - What outcome do you want?

   Study the need or problem and possible solutions.
   - Research the problem's background and history.
   - Break the problem into parts, noting causes and effects.
   - Review any solutions attempted in the past, noting their successes and failures.
   - Identify other solutions and choose the best one.

2. **Draft**: **(Ideas, Organization, and Voice)**
   Opening Provide context, as well as a summary, if appropriate.
   Middle Present the problem or need and your solution.
   - Explain what the problem is and why it should be corrected.
   - Map out the solution and stress its value.
   Closing Summarize your conclusions and recommendations.

3. **Revise**: **(Ideas, Organization, Voice, Words, and Sentences)**
   - ☐ Have you provided all the details that your readers need?
   - ☐ Does the proposal address alternatives, stress benefits, consider ripple effects (who will be affected and how), and show your ability to implement the solution?
   - ☐ Is your tone confident and positive, but not aggressive?
   - ☐ Have you used precise words, easy-to-read sentences, and strong transitions?

4. **Refine**: **(Conventions and Design)**
   - ☐ Have you checked grammar, punctuation, and spelling?
   - ☐ Have you checked document design?

Organizing Proposals

Opening

- **Label** your proposal with the following: a title or a subject line that promises productive change, your name, your reader's name, the date, and any reference numbers.
- **Introduce** your proposal by providing background and establishing the theme—the need to be met, the problem to be solved, and the benefits to be gained.
- **Summarize** your proposal if you want to be direct. To be indirect, do not include the summary.

Middle

- **Define** the problem or need. Explain its importance, limits, causes, effects, history, and connection with larger issues. Review any past attempts to solve the problem, noting their successes and failures. *Note:* If the reader is aware of the need or problem, be brief and informative. If the reader is unaware or resistant, build a persuasive case about the problem or need and its importance.
- **List** criteria for a solution. What should a solution accomplish?
- **Compare** alternative solutions. Then promote the best one.
- **Prove** the solution's workability by highlighting the following:
  - outcomes of the solution.
  - requirements (facilities, equipment, material, personnel, and so on).
  - schedules for start-up, stages, finishing dates, and follow-up.
  - cost breakdowns (services, equipment, materials, travel, and so on).
  - methods of monitoring costs and quality.
  - your qualifications for undertaking the task.

Closing

- **Summarize** the problem or need and alternative solutions.
- **Provide conclusions** about the best solution—results and benefits.
- **Review your recommendations** for implementing the solution.

Sales Proposal (Bid Form)

Opening

Provide details to identify the bid.

Middle

Outline the products and services to be provided.

State prices and delivery schedules.

Closing

Summarize the bid and its conditions.

Sign the bid and indicate a place for customer's signature.

ASPHALT SPECIALISTS

605 CHERRY STREET   SIOUX FALLS, SOUTH DAKOTA 57103   (605) 555-2402
www.asphaltspecialists.com

PROPOSAL

PROPOSAL SUBMITTED TO: Agnes Lead, Superintendent
Clark Elementary School
1206 Missouri Avenue South
Vermillion, SD 57701

PHONE: (605) 555-0800
FAX: (605) 555-0848
DATE: April 3, 2010
E-MAIL: alead@clarkelementary.edu

JOB DESCRIPTION:
South Parking Lot
1. Clean existing asphalt.
2. Overlay existing asphalt using SS-1 tack oil.
3. Apply two inches of hot-mix asphalt.
4. Compact asphalt with steel-wheel vibratory roller.
5. Re-stripe entire lot.
6. Clean up work area and dispose of all debris.

COST:
252,100 square feet @ $.85 per SF = $214,285.00

SCHEDULE:
Work will begin July 12, 2010, and be completed by July 16, 2010.

TERMS:
We shall furnish material and labor as specified above for the sum of $214,285.00.
Payment is due 30 days after the date shown on the invoice.

All material is guaranteed to be as specified. All work is to be completed in a professional manner according to standard practices. Any changes to the specifications and estimates listed above will be executed only after receiving your written agreement. All agreements are contingent upon strikes, accidents, or delays beyond our control.

AUTHORIZED SIGNATURE   James Dolan

Note: This proposal may be withdrawn by us if not accepted within 30 days.

ACCEPTANCE OF PROPOSAL
We accept the prices, specifications, and conditions listed above.

Signature _____

**Sales
Proposal
(Letter)**

BONIFACE SANITATION, INC.
846 Watson Way Tallahassee, FL 32308
302-555-2356 www.bonif.com

February 26, 2010

Ms. Agnes Grey
Millwood Pharmaceuticals
2211 Green Valley Road
Tallahassee, FL 32303-5122

Dear Ms. Grey:

Opening

Be positive
and polite.

Thank you for the opportunity to bid on Millwood's waste removal and
recycling needs.

Middle

Provide a precise
bid with the
necessary details.

Promote your
company.

Based on the bid requirements, we are submitting the following proposal:
• One eight-cubic-yard container for regular refuse, serviced twice a week.
• One eight-cubic-yard container for cardboard, serviced once a week.
• Total cost per month: $240.00.
• Extra pick-ups:$55.00 per trip.

As Tallahassee's leading waste collector, Boniface serves more than 300
organizations. References and brochures are enclosed for your review.

Closing

Anticipate a
positive reply.

Ms. Grey, I look forward to your response. Please call me if you have
questions.

Sincerely,

Robert Estavez

Robert Estavez
Sales Representative

Enclosures 3

Major Sales Proposal or Bid

A major bid is usually a response to an RFP (Request for Proposals) published by a company or a government agency. While the bid must follow the RFP specifications, a common pattern is outlined below:

Opening

- **Include** some or all of the following "front matter":
  — a title page with the title, writer, reader, and submission date
  — a cover letter that introduces the proposal, sells its strengths, notes the key players, and thanks the reader
  — a copy of the RFP or the letter of authorization
  — a table of contents and a list of illustrations
  — an executive summary in nontechnical language

Middle

- **Review** the reader's need as indicated in the RFP.
- **Explain** the solution—your product or service.
- **Describe** implementation, focusing on the following:
  — products and services to be delivered
  — methods of delivery and a schedule of delivery
  — costs, fees, budget breakdowns
  — evaluation plans for checking progress and results
  — personnel requirements
  — a statement of responsibilities (yours and the company's)
- **Outline** the bid's benefits for the client (results, efficiency, reliability, value, and so on).

Closing

- **Describe** your company and its resources; list relevant past and current jobs; and provide references, testimonial letters, and résumés of key personnel.
- **Summarize** your proposal, focusing on the reader's need, your solution, the results you can deliver, and the advantages.

**Trouble-
shooting
Proposal**

Rankin Manufacturing
PROPOSAL

Date: April 20, 2010

To: John Cameron

From: Nick Jeffries

Opening

State the account's
status.

Subject: Reducing Carbon Monoxide Levels

As you requested, I have investigated the high levels of carbon monoxide in
the main warehouse. The following proposal (A) explains the source of the
problem, (B) proposes a solution, and (C) details an implementation plan.

Middle

Review the
account's history.
Focus on keeping a
positive
relationship.

Be objective.

A. Problem: Emissions from Lift Trucks

From November 2009 through March 2010, Rankin has been registering high
carbon monoxide (CO) levels in Area 3 of the warehouse. General CO levels
in the area have exceeded 35 ppm, and many office spaces show levels of
40-80 ppm (OSHA recommends 25 ppm).

These CO levels are a concern for three reasons:
1. High CO levels cause sickness and lower productivity.
2. Using summer exhaust fans in winter to reduce CO results in low
   humidity that shrinks wood used for manufacturing.
3. High CO levels can result in a substantial OSHA fine.

To determine the cause of the high CO levels, I investigated all sources of
combustion in the warehouse. I concluded that the excess CO was caused by
lift trucks operating in Area 3.

Show clear
understanding of
the causes.

I then checked all lift trucks. They were in good working condition and were
being properly used and maintained.

Middle

List solution
criteria.

B. Proposal: Phase Out Internal-Combustion Lifts

In order to correct the CO emissions problem, the ideal solution should accomplish the following in a timely and cost-effective manner:

1. Bring CO levels within OSHA limits.

2. Maintain relative humidity to ensure product quality.

Show that you
considered
alternatives.

To do this, Rankin could continue using the exhaust fans and install humidifying equipment at a cost of $62,000. (See attached estimate.) Or Rankin could replace all internal-combustion lift trucks in Area 3 with electric lift trucks for $295,000.

Offer your solution
and provide a clear
rationale.

Instead, I propose gradual replacement of the internal-combustion lifts in shipping with electric lift trucks, for these reasons:

- Shipping (Area 3) has 14 lift trucks that operate almost 24 hours per day.

- The shipping area is well-suited for electric lift trucks (no long-distance travel or use of ramps is required).

- While electric lifts cost more initially, they have lower operating and maintenance costs. A five-year cost analysis shows that the cost of operating the two types of lift trucks is similar. (See attachment.) In fact, after five years, electric lift trucks save money.

C. Implementation: Phase In Electric Lifts

Show that
the solution
will work.

Because Rankin buys an average of four lift trucks annually, the plans below will complete the changeover in the shipping area within the next four years.

1. When an area requests replacement of an existing lift truck, management approves purchase of a new electric lift truck.

2. The new electric lift truck goes to the Shipping Department.

3. The newest internal-combustion lift truck in Shipping is transferred to the area that requested a new lift truck.

By beginning this plan in January 2011, we could replace all internal-combustion lift trucks in Shipping by December 31, 2014.

Closing

Restate your solution and its benefits.

Conclusion

Gradual replacement of internal-combustion lift trucks in Shipping with electric lift trucks will involve a higher initial cost but will reap two important benefits: (1) CO levels will fall below OSHA's 25 ppm, enhancing the safety of Rankin employees and guarding product quality; (2) the electric lift trucks will prove less costly to own and operate in the long run.

Therefore, I recommend that Rankin management approve this plan, and phase it in over the next four years as outlined. Improved safety, increased product quality, and lower total long-term operating costs outweigh higher initial costs.

If you wish to discuss this proposal, please call me at extension 1449, or write me at <Nick_Jeffries@rankin.com>.

Cite attachments.

Attachments: Renovation Estimate
                      Five-Year Cost Analysis

Continental Lift Truck Inc. from Flickr

Justification Proposal

Bayford Community Theater

Date: March 15, 2010

To: Sarah Helter, President
          Terry Petersen, Treasurer
          Don Wassal, Treasurer

From: Amanda Smith, Vice President

Subject: New Seating for the Theater

Opening

Present your idea and stress its benefits.

I'm writing to recommend that the Bayford Community Theater replace the seating in our auditorium. New seating will (1) make patrons more comfortable during performances, (2) beautify the theater, and (3) help us compete with other entertainment options.

Middle

Give the reason for your proposal.

Review the present situation in detail.

Current Seating

Our current seating is more than twenty years old and was secondhand when we acquired it. The seating poses a number of problems:

1. The hard plastic construction makes the seats uncomfortable for shows.
2. Some of the seats are damaged, requiring use of folding chairs.
3. The seats are not attached to the floor, making them shift as patrons move about.
4. The metal bases may damage the new flooring installed last year.
5. Some of the seats are stained, adding to the overall unsightly appearance.

Options

We have discussed a number of measures to address this problem.

1. **Buy plastic-covered stadium seat pads:** At $8 per pad (printed with the BCT logo), a hundred pads would cost $800 and would make seats more comfortable. However, they would be awkward to distribute and collect, and patrons would still be sitting on plastic.
2. **Create cloth cushion covers for chairs:** This solution would be more comfortable and less awkward than foam pads, though the expense in cloth and foam and the many hours of sewing involved would be prohibitive.
3. **Replace seating with comfortable chairs:** This solution would provide comfort and a more attractive appearance, but the slanted floor means that patrons would feel that they are tipped forward.

Middle

Justify an expenditure by stressing benefits.

Detail costs.

Recommendation

I recommend that we replace the existing seating with new theater seating, fastened to the floor. I have checked with four companies that offer theater seating and have attached their catalogues for your consideration.

In my opinion, the best option is the Turino style of seat offered by Custom Seating Specialists, with the following specifics:

1. **Dimensions:** Back heights 36"—37-1/2"; chair widths: 20-1/8"—23-1/8"
2. **Cushions:** Cold-molded polyurethane padding with ergonomic design
3. **Inner back:** Ribbed injection-molded polypropylene plastic, featuring lumbar curves for back support
4. **Outer back:** Injection-molded high impact resistant, textured, linear polypropylene plastic
5. **Frame structure:** Rectangular steel tube frame, stress-tested to meet the demands of heavy use
6. **Fabric:** Turino polyolefin with fire retardant and Scotch Guard; available in blue, red, gray, or tan
7. **Paint:** Powder-coat finish baked at 200 Celsius

See pages 36-37 in the Custom Seating Specialists catalog for more details. For an order of 100 seats, this seating would cost $365 per seat, installed, for a total cost of $36,500.

Financing

To pay for these seats, we can use a number of revenue sources:

1. **Building endowment:** We have $5,000 available per year for facility upgrades.
2. **Buy-a-seat program:** Supporters can "buy" a seat—and perhaps platinum supporters will buy whole rows.
3. **Recycling:** We can dismantle the current seats and sell the plastic and metal to a recycling plant.
4. **Auction:** We can earmark the proceeds from the pre-show auction to seat replacement. (We might even paint one of the old seats and auction it off.)
5. **50-50 raffle:** We can earmark the proceeds from the 50-50 raffle for seat replacements.

Closing

State recommendations clearly and positively.

Summarize the benefits.

Anticipate a positive reply.

Cite attachments.

New seating will improve the comfort, look, and image of our facility, not just now but for years to come. The seating drive will also bring the community into the theater.

If you need more information or wish to discuss this proposal, please call me at 555-3612 or e-mail me at asmith2631@gmail.com.

Attachments: 4 seating catalogs

> "Controversial
> proposals,
> once accepted,
> soon become
> hallowed."
>
> —Dean Acheson

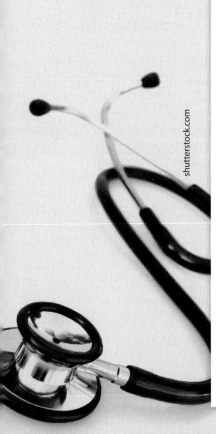

shutterstock.com

Checklist Proposals

Your goal is to persuade others that you have a workable solution or plan that solves a problem or meets a need.

Ideas 9-16

____ shows a thorough understanding of the problem, alternative solutions, the reader's needs, and your own resources.

____ where possible, supports its claim by citing the company's mission, goals, plans, or policies.

____ offers a clear, persuasive line of thinking from beginning to end.

____ contains accurate and realistic details, figures, and estimates.

____ includes supporting graphics such as tables and charts.

Organization 17-24

____ explains the problem (nature, importance, history, and so on).

____ states the solution, stresses benefits, and shows how this solution addresses the problem better than the alternatives do.

____ presents an implementation plan in terms of time, money, and personnel.

____ includes measures for checking progress and testing the outcome.

Voice 25-32

____ has a positive and confident but objective tone.

____ shows "you attitude"—careful attention to the reader's perspective.

Words 33-40

____ uses language at an appropriate level of formality.

____ uses technical terms carefully, defining any unfamiliar terms.

Sentences 41-50

____ passes the "read-aloud" test for smoothness and logical transitions.

____ states main points, conclusions, and recommendations in clear sentences.

Correctness 51-58

____ contains no errors in grammar, punctuation, usage, and spelling.

Design 59-70

____ follows the format expected by the company.

____ uses consistent, parallel, informative headings.

____ uses white space, underlining, boldface, and other layout features.

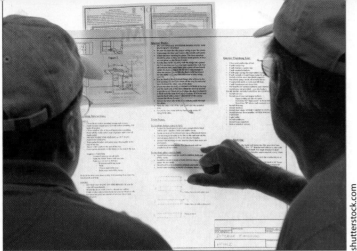

19
Instructions

Organizations need instructions that help employees produce goods and services efficiently and safely, and customers often need instructions in order to use those goods and services. When these important how-to documents are well written, they help organizations run smoothly and successfully. On the other hand, poorly written instructions can lead to frustrated customers, expensive errors, personal injuries, and lawsuits.

This chapter will help you write effective instructions. Guidelines and models will show you how to use tools such as lists, numbered steps, and photographs or drawings to get your message across. At the end of the chapter, a checklist will identify areas for special attention and suggest ways to refine your document.

In this chapter

Guidelines Instructions

Your Goal ▶ Your goal is to break down a task into logical steps and describe those steps so clearly that a reader can do the task.

> "Nothing is particularly hard if you divide it into small jobs."
> —Henry Ford

shutterstock.com

1. **Prewrite:** (Ideas and Organization)
   Make sure that you know your subject well: the materials needed to do the task, the number of people required to complete the task, starting and finishing times, and the steps in the process.

   Think about your reader.
   Is she or he familiar with the setting, the process, the equipment, the personnel needed, technical terminology, and the English language?

2. **Draft:** (Ideas, Organization, and Voice)
   Opening Introduce the process by
   - describing it briefly, explaining its importance, and stating its goal.
   - listing materials, equipment, and tools needed to get the job done.

   Middle Tell the reader what to do by
   - giving numbered, step-by-step instructions that use command verbs, short sentences, and precise terms for materials, tools, and measurements.
   - stating clear *warnings* (potential for danger or injury), *cautions* (possible error or damage to equipment), and *notes* (tips or clarification on how to do the task).
   - including clear, well-placed photos, drawings, or diagrams.

   Closing State the desired outcome and any final reminders.

3. **Revise:** (Ideas, Organization, Voice, Words, and Sentences)
   ☐ Make sure you've used numbered steps to help the reader move back and forth easily between the task and the instructions.
   ☐ Check that specific, closely related actions are grouped together.
   ☐ Test the instructions by reading them to a listener who completes the task. Check the clarity of any pronouns used.

4. **Refine:** (Conventions and Design)
   ☐ Are *WARNINGS* in boldface and caps and *cautions* in boldface?
   ☐ Are spelling, labels, numbers, and terms accurate?
   ☐ Do graphics, photos, and drawings enhance the message?

Instructions
with a List
of Materials

Instructions for Closing Off the Cash Register

Opening

Identify the task by
using a clear title.

List materials and/
or tools.

Follow the steps below in order to (1) close off the cash register and (2) account for the day's receipts.

Materials needed: Daily Account Form, deposit bag, adding machine, pen, and paper

Middle

Present steps in a
chronological order.

Use short
sentences with
command verbs.

Use few (if any)
pronouns.

Place **WARNINGS**
in boldface and
caps; place
cautions in
boldface only.

Steps:

1. **MAKE SURE THE STORE'S DOORS ARE LOCKED.** Then take the cash tray out of the register drawer and place the tray on the counter. (Leave the empty drawer open to deter thieves.)

2. Turn the cash-register key to the X setting and press the X key. The machine will print the X reading: the total amount of receipts for the day.

3. Turn the key to the Z setting and press the Z key. The machine will print the Z reading: itemized, department-by-department subtotals.

4. Count out $200.00 and place the bills in the envelope marked "FLOAT"; currency amounts are shown on the envelope. (The float is the $200.00 of cash placed in each cash register when the store opens.) The remaining cash, checks, and credit-card slips make up the day's receipts.
   Do not place the float back in the drawer.

5. Total the day's receipts using an adding machine, and check the total against the X reading. If the totals differ, count the receipts a second time and a third time if necessary. Write a note indicating any difference and attach the note to the receipts.

6. Fill out the Daily Account Form by entering the X reading total and the Z reading total and then the totals of the day's receipts. Place the day's receipts in the deposit bag.

Put closely related
actions
in a single step.

7. Lock the following in the safe: (1) the deposit bag, (2) the Daily Account Form, (3) the X and Z printouts, and (4) the envelope marked "FLOAT."

Closing

Review a key point.

DOUBLE-CHECK THE SAFE DOOR TO MAKE SURE IT'S LOCKED.

Instructions for a Procedure

Opening

Identify the task.

Explain when to do the procedure and how to prepare to do it.

Middle

List steps in chronological order.

State **WARNINGS** in boldface and in caps.

State **cautions** in boldface without full caps.

State notes in regular type.

Closing

End with a final point.

Regis City Hospital
HAND-WASHING PROCEDURE

Perform this procedure whenever you report for duty and before and after providing care for a patient. Also use this procedure after bathroom use, eating, coughing, or sneezing, and before and after using sterile gloves, gowns, and masks. **Whenever in doubt, wash your hands.**

Caution: Rings and other jewelry harbor bacteria and are difficult to clean. Before reporting for work, remove all jewelry.

Steps in the Procedure:

1. Remove the first paper towel, and place that towel in the wastebasket.

2. Take the next paper towel and use it to turn the water on to a comfortable temperature. **DO NOT TOUCH THE CONTROLS WITH YOUR HANDS.**

3. Put your hands and wrists under the running water, keeping your fingertips pointed downward. Allow the water to flow gently.

4. Once your hands and wrists are completely wet, apply antiseptic solution.

5. Bring your hands together and create a heavy lather. Wash at least three inches above the wrists, and get soap under your fingernails and between your fingers. **Wash well for one full minute.**

6. With the fingertips of your opposite hand, circle each finger on the other hand with a rotary motion from base to tip. Pay careful attention to the area between your fingers, around nail beds, and under your fingernails.

7. Rinse your hands well under running water. **Hold your hands down** so that the direction of the water flow is from the wrist to your fingertips.

8. Pat your hands dry with a clean paper towel, and turn off the water with the towel. Discard the paper towel into the waste basket.

Note: If your hands touch the sink, faucet, or spout, repeat the entire procedure.

Instructions for a Policy Procedure

Opening

Identify the topic.

State and summarize the policy.

Middle

Use clear headings throughout.

Note: The passive voice may be used to emphasize key points.

List steps clearly, including which documents to complete and submit.

Closing

Close with a fitting summary or restatement.

**Family and Children's Coalition
Confidentiality Procedures**

The Family and Children's Coalition Confidentiality Policy states that all clients have the right to confidentiality. Conduct your work in keeping with this policy by following the procedures below.

Client Intakes:

During the client intake, the Coalition counselor should discuss the conditions of confidentiality with the client. These conditions include the following:

1. Information will never be shared unless the client has given written permission using the Consent to Release Form.

2. Confidentiality may be limited or canceled if Coalition staff have serious concerns about child abuse or neglect, or if the client is a danger to herself or himself, or to others.

Outside Requests for Information:

Coalition counselors will handle outside requests for client information.

1. No client information will be shared without the client's written permission.

2. Clients will be notified of any outside requests for information. If the client gives permission, he or she must sign the Consent to Release Form and specifically indicate what information may be released and to whom. A Coalition counselor must also sign the release form.

Breaches of Confidentiality:

If a client believes that Coalition staff have not observed the confidentiality policy and procedures, the client should be directed to follow the Client-Grievance Process.

By carefully following the procedures above, the Coalition staff can help their clients while also respecting the clients' rights to confidentiality.

**Instructions
Containing
Photographs**

Opening

Use a descriptive title. Note or list materials needed.

Middle

Give steps and photos in chronological order.

Add graphics (such as the arrow) to create a quick visual cue.

To show an object's size, use a reference (such as the fingers).

Boldface words that need special attention.

Use only well-focused photographs.

Closing

Note common problems that are easily solved.

Downloading Photographs from the MC-150 Digital Camera

Note: MC-150 software must be loaded on your computer to download photographs from the camera.

1. Turn your computer on.

2. Plug the camera's USB cable into your computer.

3. Turn the camera's mode dial to the **data transfer setting** (Figure 1).

4. Open the camera's flash-card door and plug the other end of the USB cable into the **camera port** (Figure 2).

5. Select USB transfer from the camera screen menu. The MC-150 software will then launch onto your computer.

6. Follow the instructions on the computer screen to download all of your photos or specific photos.

7. When your download is complete, turn the camera off and unplug the USB cable from the camera and the computer.

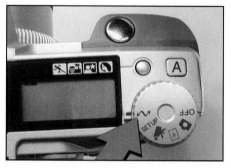
Figure 1: Data Transfer Setting

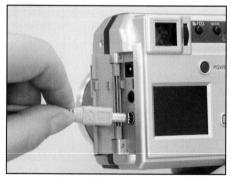
Figure 2: Camera Port

Note: If MC-150 software doesn't launch, disconnect the camera (step 7), and then restart the computer and continue on from step 2.

Instructions with Drawings

Opening

Identify topic.

List the parts needed in a table format. If helpful, add illustrations.

Middle

Indicate danger with a **WARNING** message in caps and in bold print. Use an icon, if helpful.

Give steps in chronological order.

Use the same terms in the steps as were used in the parts list.

Place the illustration next to the steps.

Closing

Use **cautions** (boldface without caps) to warn of damage.

Instructions for Replacing Auger Bearing on Bale-Press 64-D

Use the instructions below to replace the right, rear auger bearing on the Bale-Press 64-D.

Parts Needed:

Item No.	Quantity	Part No.	Description
1	1	RRAB20024	right, rear auger bearing
2	1	RRASP20007	right, rear auger-support post
3	2	BLT5/8X3.5HX	5/8" x 3 1/2" hex bolt
4	2	NUT5/8HX	5/8" hex nut
5	2	CP1/8X2	1/8" x 2" cotter pin

WARNING: SHUT OFF ENGINE AND REMOVE KEY!

Steps:

1. Take out the existing bearing by removing the two 1/8" cotter pins, two 5/8" nuts, and two 5/8" bolts. (See Figure 1.)

2. Insert the new bearing (item #1) into the 4 3/8" hole on the post (item #2).

3. Fasten the bearing to the post with two 5/8" bolts (item #3), two 5/8" nuts (item #4), and two 1/8" cotter pins (item #5).

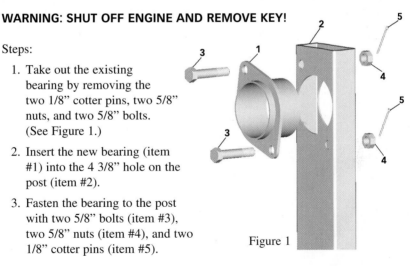

Figure 1

Note: For ease of installation, insert both of the bolts before tightening the nuts.

Caution: For safe installation, fasten the replacement bearing with the new bolts, nuts, and cotter pins included in the replacement kit.

"Experience is the worst teacher. It always gives the test first and the instruction afterward."

—Vernon Law

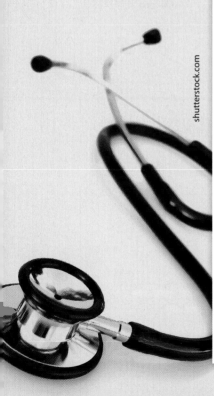

Checklist Instructions

Your goal is to break down a task into logical steps and describe those steps so clearly that a reader can do the task.

Ideas 9-16

____ identifies the task and lists all the parts, materials, and tools needed.
____ explains step-by-step what to do and how to do it.
____ uses accurate measurements of time, distance, length, height, and so on.
____ includes clear and appropriate *warnings, cautions,* and *notes.*

Organization 17-24

____ opens with a clear title and introduction that identify the procedure.
____ has a middle with numbered steps: each step has a single, clear action.
____ includes a conclusion that summarizes or clarifies the process.

Voice 25-32

____ writes clearly and confidently about the subject.
____ addresses sensitive issues directly, but tactfully.

Words 33-40

____ uses words appropriate for the situation and reader.
____ identifies parts using the same terms in lists, steps, and illustrations.
____ states *notes, cautions,* and *warnings* clearly, without alarm.

Sentences 41-50

____ states steps in crisp phrases or sentences using command verbs.
____ includes clear transitions where needed.

Correctness 51-58

____ cites accurate specifications, names, titles, quotations, and figures.
____ includes error-free grammar, punctuation, capitalization, and spelling.

Design 59-70

____ uses headings, numbers, and graphics to organize information.
____ includes illustrations that are labeled, readable, and set off with white space.
____ uses correct format for signal words such as *notes* (regular type), **cautions** (boldface), and **WARNINGS** (boldface and caps).

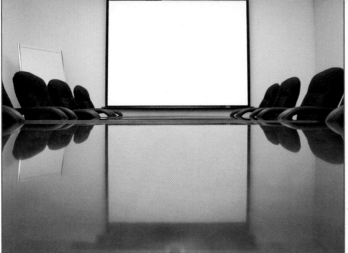

shutterstock.com

20
Presentations

In the course of doing business, people get together regularly to give presentations, offer proposals, debate topics, and make decisions. The challenge is being able to share ideas in a clear, concise, effective manner.

This chapter includes information that will help you plan, write, and deliver a presentation, whether it's a one-minute impromptu talk, or an hour-long report with presentation software. The chapter includes practical strategies for drafting an attention-grabbing introduction, organizing the body, and developing a focused conclusion. It also includes tips on how to use visual support and rehearse the delivery.

Giving Presentations

Regardless of the topic, form, or length of your presentation, you can follow the same basic steps to develop and present it.

Getting Started

The first step in preparing an oral presentation is getting an overview of the task. Begin by asking yourself *What is my subject? What is my purpose?* and *Who is my audience?* Answering these questions will help you write the presentation and shape its delivery.

1 **What is my subject?**
- What do I already know about the subject?
- What do I need to learn, and where can I find the information?
- What support materials (displays, computer projections, handouts) would help me present my message?

2 **What is my purpose?**
- Am I going to explain something
- Am I trying to persuade or inspire my audience to do something?
- Am I hoping to teach my audience about something?

3 **Who is my audience?**
- Is it an in-house group or an outside group?
- How many people are in the group, and what are their ages, backgrounds, and interests?
- What will people already know about the subject, and what will they want or need to know?
- What will their attitude be toward the subject and toward me?

Stating Your Main Point

Once you have defined your subject, purpose, and audience, you should write out your main point as a single sentence. Use this formula:

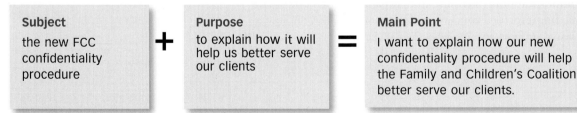

Subject
the new FCC confidentiality procedure

+

Purpose
to explain how it will help us better serve our clients

=

Main Point
I want to explain how our new confidentiality procedure will help the Family and Children's Coalition better serve our clients.

Note: The outline that develops this idea is on pages 222-223.

Planning Your Presentation

Drafting an Outline

After you've clarified your subject, purpose, and audience—and you've written out your main point—think about how to present your message. Begin by brainstorming points that you want to communicate, and then organize the points into a list or working outline. For a brief, informal presentation, this list or outline may be the only script you need.

On the other hand, for a longer, more challenging presentation, you may need to significantly revise and develop the outline as you research and write the script. This outline is your tool for gathering and organizing your thoughts. (See page 221.)

Gathering Information

Using your outline as a guide, gather the information you need. Begin by reviewing key documents, manuals, and company material related to the topic. If necessary, read current articles, review videos, explore the Internet, and talk with other people. What you gather will depend on your purpose, topic, resources, and available time.

For help in finding and organizing information, see pages 74-77.

Thinking About Support Materials

As you gather information, keep a list of graphics, displays, and handouts that could make your presentation clearer and more interesting. For example, charts, tables, and graphs can help an audience grasp the meaning of complex data. Technical drawings or sketches can help listeners visualize a product or site. Demonstrations or video clips can help listeners better understand a process or connect with the people involved.

Review the list below for items appropriate to your topic, audience, and setting (including available equipment). Then, as you do your research, make a note about an item that you could use and how you could use it (as a display, projection, handout, and so forth).

audio clip (music)	key quotation
bibliography	list of authorities
brochure	overhead
cartoon	photograph
chart	sample product
company document	sketch
demonstration	table
graph	technical drawing
handheld prop	video clip

Organizing Your Presentation

After you've gathered your information, you must organize and develop the message. How? Start by thinking about your presentation as having three distinct parts: (1) introduction, (2) body, and (3) conclusion. The guidelines on this page and the following two pages will help you integrate, organize, and refine all the parts so that they communicate the message and achieve your purpose.

> "What this country needs is more free speech worth listening to."
> —Hansell B. Duckett

Introduction ①

For any speaking situation, you should develop an introduction that does the following:

- greets the audience and grabs their attention.
- communicates your interest in them.
- introduces your topic and main idea.
- shows that you have something worthwhile to say.
- establishes an appropriate tone.

You may greet the audience in many ways, including the following: introducing yourself; thanking people for coming; or making appropriate comments about the occasion, the individuals present, or the setting. Following these comments, introduce your main point as quickly and as clearly as you can. For example, you could open with one of these attention-grabbing strategies:

- a little-known fact or statistic
- a series of questions
- a humorous story or anecdote
- an appropriate quotation
- a description of a serious problem
- a cartoon, picture, or drawing
- a short demonstration
- a statement about the topic's importance
- an eye-catching prop or display
- a video or an audio clip

"When high words confuse the talk,
low words will untangle it."
—Jobo proverb

2 Body

The body of your presentation should deliver the message—and supporting points—so clearly that the audience understands the presentation after hearing it only once. The key to developing such a clear message is choosing an organizational pattern that fits your purpose statement.

So before you outline the body, take a moment to review what you want your presentation to do: explain a problem? promote an idea? teach a process? Be sure the organizational pattern will help you do that. For example, if you want to teach a process, the outline should list the process steps in chronological order. If your outline is clear, you may begin to write. Organizational patterns for explaining a process and other purposes are listed below.

- **Chronological Order**: Arrange information according to the time order in which events (steps in a process) take place.

- **Order of Importance**: Arrange information according to its importance: greatest to least, or least to greatest.

- **Comparison/Contrast**: Give information about subjects by comparing and contrasting them.

- **Cause and Effect**: Give information about a situation or problem by showing (1) the causes and (2) the effects.

- **Order of Location**: Arrange information about subjects according to where things are located in relation to each other.

- **Problem/Solution**: Describe a problem and then present a solution for it.

After deciding how to organize your message, write it out in either outline or manuscript form. For help, see the tips at the right and the models on pages 222-225.

Body-Building Tips

1. Build your presentation around several key ideas. (Don't try to cover too much ground.)
2. Write with a personal, natural voice.
3. Support your main points with reliable facts and clear examples.
4. Present your information in short, easy-to-follow segments.
5. Use positive, respectful language. (Avoid jargon.)
6. Use graphic aids and handouts.

Conclusion (3)

A strong introduction and conclusion work like bookends supporting the body of the presentation. The introduction gets the audience's attention, sets the tone, states the main idea, and identifies the key points of the message. Almost in reverse, the conclusion reviews those points, restates the main idea, reinforces the tone, and refocuses the audience on what it should think about or do. Together, those bookends emphasize and clarify the message so that the audience understands and remembers it.

Here are some strategies—which you can use alone or in combination—for concluding a presentation:

- Review your main idea and key points.
- Issue a personal challenge.
- Come "full circle." (State those arguments or details that back up your original point.)
- Recommend a plan of action.
- Suggest additional sources of information.
- Thank the audience and ask for questions.

Q & A

Following your presentation, you may want to invite your audience to ask questions. Very often, a Q & A session is the real payoff for participants. They can ask for clarification of points or ask how your message applies to their personal situations. Audience members may even offer their own insights or solutions to problems mentioned in the presentation. The following suggestions will help you lead a good Q & A session:

- Listen carefully and think about each part of the question.
- Repeat or paraphrase questions for the benefit of the entire group.
- Answer the question concisely and clearly.
- Respond honestly when you don't know the answer, and offer to find an answer.
- Ask for a follow-up question if someone looks confused after your answer.
- Look directly at the group when you answer.
- Be prepared to pose an important question or two if no one asks a question.
- Conclude by thanking the audience for their participation.

"We cannot ignore tone of voice or attitude. These may be just as important as the words used."

—Maurice S. Trotter

Writing Your Presentation

How much of your presentation you actually write out depends on your subject, purpose, audience, and—of course—your personal style. The three most common forms to use to make a presentation are a list, an outline, and a manuscript.

List: Use a list for a short, informal speech such as an after-dinner introduction. Think about your purpose and then list the following:

- your opening sentence (or two)
- a summary phrase for each of your main points
- your closing sentence

1. Opening sentence or two
2. Phrase #1
    Phrase #2
    Phrase #3
3. Closing sentence

Outline: Use an outline for a more complex or formal topic. You can organize your material in greater detail without tying yourself to a word-for-word presentation. Here's one way you can do it:

- opening (complete sentences)
- all main points (sentences)
- supporting points (phrases)
- quotations (written out)
- all supporting technical details, statistics, and sources (listed)
- closing (complete sentences)
- notes on visual aids (in caps or boldface)

  I. Opening statement
     A. Point with support
     B. Point (purpose or goal)
        [VISUAL 1]
 II. Body (with 3-5 main points)
     A. Main point
        1. Supporting details
        2. Supporting details
     B. Main point
        1. Supporting details
        2. Supporting details
     C. Main point
        1. Supporting details
        2. Supporting details
III. Closing statement
     A. Point, including
        restatement of purpose
     B. Point, possibly a call to
        action [VISUAL 2]

Manuscript: Use the guidelines below if you plan to write out your presentation word for word as you plan to give it:

- double-space pages (or cards)
- number pages (or cards)
- use complete sentences on a page (do not run sentences from one page to another)
- mark difficult words for pronunciation
- mark script for interpretation (See symbols on page 227.)

Presentation in Outline Form

Opening

The opening is written out word for word and placed in boldface.

Italics and brackets signal a speaker's prompt.

Middle

Main points are stated as full sentences (word for word).

Supporting details are listed as phrases.

The speaker uses the phrases as cues and comments on each point.

Report on FACC's Confidentiality Procedure

I. Good afternoon, everyone. I appreciate this opportunity to report on our work here at the Family and Children's Coalition. Today I want to focus on one topic that impacts all of our work—the new Confidentiality Procedure that was adopted last week. We believe this procedure will help us serve our clients more effectively. We think it's an effective tool because . . .

- **it is based on sound policy,**
- **it will help the staff implement the policy in a uniform manner, and**
- **it will enable staff and clients to develop trusting relationships with each other.**

[*Identify the handout and read the policy.*]

II. First, let's examine four strengths of the policy on which the new procedure is based. Note how the policy . . .

- enables clients to control most personal information.
- calls for written records of who receives case-related information.
- satisfies legal requirements related to privacy issues.
- helps staff and clients develop trust.

[*Identify the handout and read the procedure.*]

III. Second, the Confidentiality Procedure will help staff members deal with confidentiality issues in a consistent, uniform manner. Note how the procedure . . .

- lists issues that counselors must explain to clients at intake.
- sets guidelines for releasing information to outside parties.
- explains a client's recourse to a staff member's breach of confidentiality.
- promotes the uniform application of the Confidentiality Policy— particularly by new staff and student interns.

2

Middle

Entire text is double-spaced for easy reading.

Quotations are written out word for word in boldface.

IV. **Third, the Confidentiality Procedure will help staff and clients establish the trusting relationships FACC needs in order to provide its services.**

- Clients needing a confidential advocate often come to intake sessions fearful and suspicious.
  - abused wife with child: *"How do I know he won't find out that we are here? He said if I say anything, . . . he'll kill me."*
  - pregnant teenager: *"Thanks for listening . . . I just had to tell somebody."*
- Clients become less fearful because they view the policy and procedure as contracts—that the information collected will be kept in confidence.
- Clients become less fearful because they feel information will be kept private from outsiders—staff can say that the Confidentiality Procedure does not allow them to release information.

Closing

The closing is written out and placed in boldface.

The speaker recaps main points and asks for questions.

V. **As you know, the work that we do at the Family and Children's Coalition requires that our staff and clients have trusting, confidential relationships with each other. To build such relationships, and to satisfy legal requirements related to privacy issues, FACC has long had a Confidentiality Policy. However, the staff believes that the new Confidentiality Procedure will help them provide better service to clients because the procedure (1) is based on sound policy, (2) improves uniform application of that policy, and (3) helps staff members and clients develop trusting relationships.**

Are there any questions?

Presentation in Manuscript Form

Opening

[SLIDE 1] The title is projected.

The speaker delivers the speech as it appears on the page.

Middle

[SLIDE 2] monument

[SLIDE 3] inscription

[SLIDES 4-8] people mentioned

[SLIDE 9] company headquarters

All points and supporting details are stated.

[SLIDE 1] **Abix Technologies: Finding the Right Solutions**

Good afternoon, everyone, and welcome to Abix Technologies! This is Lynn, your tour guide, and I'm Zachary Clark, Director of Public Relations at Abix. Lynn will soon be taking you on a walk through our Reception Center, a research lab, and a manufacturing facility. During that tour, she will give you a lot of information and answer all of your questions. However, before Lynn takes over, I want to personally welcome each of you to Abix. In addition, I'd like to introduce you to our company by saying a few things about who we are, what we produce, and the people we serve.

First, who are we? [SLIDE 2] The inscription on the monument that you passed when entering the building answers the question with these words: [SLIDE 3] "Abix Technologies is an international corporation that provides technological solutions to environmental wastewater problems." What does that mean? It means that at Abix Technologies, [SLIDE 4] we have scientists who research wastewater problems and propose solutions. [SLIDE 5] We have engineers who develop products to implement those solutions. [SLIDE 6] We have people who produce the products. [SLIDE 7] We have sales personnel who market our products around the world. [SLIDE 8] And finally, we have technicians who service what we sell, wherever we sell it.

[SLIDE 9] **Second, what do we produce?** While Abix Technologies makes a wide variety of products for many different applications, it specializes in technology that disinfects wastewater. These products are
- well researched,
- environmentally safe, and
- cost effective.

2

Middle

[SLIDE 10]
researchers

[SLIDE 11]
products

[SLIDES 12-19]
markets
mentioned

[SLIDE 20]
statement 1

[SLIDE 21]
statement 2

[SLIDE 22]
monument

[SLIDE 10] For example, as you tour the laboratory today, you'll meet researchers who have been working on a particularly challenging problem for more than 3 years. Though they needed only 10 months to find a solution, more than 2 years later, they're still refining it. Why? Because at Abix, products must not only solve problems—they must do so in ways that are environmentally safe and cost effective. [SLIDE 11]

Third, who uses our products? The short answer to this question is "Smart people around the world!" In fact, as you visit the Shipping Department today, you'll see crews packaging products that will be sent to sites on three continents.

However, the longer answer to the question about our customer base is that our markets include [SLIDE 12] the United States, [SLIDE 13] Canada, [SLIDE 14] South America, [SLIDE 15] Europe, [SLIDE 16] Australia, [SLIDE 17] New Zealand, [SLIDE 18] the Middle East, [SLIDE 19] and the Far East. While serving such a broad clientele is not easy, we do it well for two reasons: [SLIDE 20]

1. We carefully assess each customer's needs to make sure that the products we sell meet those needs. [SLIDE 21]
2. We have offices in Sydney, Australia; London, England; Flint, Michigan; and Toronto, Ontario. Each office has highly trained technicians who respond to our customers quickly and effectively. [SLIDE 22]

Closing

The main point
is restated and
polite close
is added.

While I'd like to tell you more, Lynn will show you these things for yourselves. So once again, welcome to Abix Technologies! I'm glad that you're here, and I hope that you enjoy the tour!

Developing Computer Presentations

Business people commonly use computers to make presentations because this multimedia approach can powerfully reinforce and clarify a message. To use presentation software effectively, follow the guidelines below.

1 Develop a design. Be sure your graphic design fits your topic and your audience—businesslike for a serious topic, casual for a team meeting, and so on.

2 Create pages. If a main idea has several parts, present each one on its own page. Each click of the mouse button (or computer key) should reveal a new detail.

3 Use transitions. Dissolves, fades, wipes, and other transitional effects refine a computer presentation and keep the audience's attention (as long as the devices don't detract from the message).

4 Try animation. Text can be animated to appear from off screen at just the right moment. Graphics can be made to appear one element at a time, and illustrations can change before the viewer's eyes. Remember to use special effects, especially animation, wisely.

5 Add sound. Just as graphics and animation can enhance a presentation, so, too, can sound. Music can serve as an intro or backdrop, and sound effects can add emphasis. Voice recordings can add authority and help drive home key points.

6 Fine-tune your presentation. Practice delivering your presentation while clicking through your pages. Try it with an audience of coworkers, if possible, and ask for their input.

7 Check for word choice and style. Make sure that the words on the screen are keywords. Use these words as talking points—don't try to cover any point word for word. Also, check that transitions, animations, and sounds are smooth and not disruptive.

8 Edit the final version. Check spelling, punctuation, usage, and other mechanics. Remember: On-screen errors are glaringly obvious to many people.

9 Rehearse. Practice running the equipment until you can use it with confidence.

10 Make a backup copy. Protect all the effort you invested in your presentation.

> "When you say something, make sure you have said it. The chances of having said it are only fair."
>
> —E. B. White

shutterstock.com

Practicing Your Delivery

Research shows that less than 40 percent of your message is communicated by your words. More than 60 percent is communicated by your delivery—your voice, body language, and attitude. In other words, rehearsing the delivery of a presentation is at least as important as revising the script.

Rehearsing Your Presentation

Keep going over your presentation until you're comfortable with it. Ask a family member or coworker to listen to you and offer feedback, or use a video recorder so that you can see and hear yourself. Practice these things:

1 **Maintain eye contact with your audience.**
It helps people feel that you care about them. It also helps you notice how people are responding to your message.

2 **Speak loudly and clearly.**
Also speak at an appropriate speed.

3 **Take your time.**
Glance at your notes when necessary.

4 **Use your hands to communicate.**
Practice using natural, unforced gestures.

5 **Maintain a comfortable, erect posture.**
Avoid the following:
- folding your arms across your chest.
- clasping your hands behind you.
- keeping your hands on your hips.
- rocking back and forth.
- fidgeting with objects.
- chewing gum.

6 **Use your voice effectively.**
You can mark your copy for vocal variety by using the techniques on the right.

Marking Your Script

Inflection
(arrows) . . . . for a rise in pitch,
for a drop in pitch

Emphasis
(underline or boldface) . . . . for additional
<u>drive</u> or **force**

Color
(curved line or italic) . . . . for additional
feeling or *emotion*

Pause
(diagonal) . . . . for a pause/or
break in the flow

Directions
(brackets) . . . . for movement
[walk to chart]
or use of visual aids
[hold up chart]

Pronunciation
(parentheses) . . . . for phonetic *(fō NE tic)*
spelling of words that are
difficult to pronounce

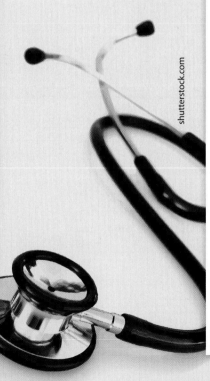

shutterstock.com

Checklist Overcoming Stage Fright

Your goal is to deliver your presentation with confidence, ease, and comfort.

While it's okay to feel a little nervous before a presentation (the emotion keeps you alert), stage fright can limit your ability to communicate. The remedy for stage fright follows:

Personal Presentation
____ Know your subject well.
____ Rehearse the presentation thoroughly, including the use of visuals.
____ Schedule your time carefully, making sure to arrive early.
____ Relax by stretching or doing a deep-breathing exercise.

The Room and Equipment
____ See that the room is clean, comfortable, and well lit.
____ Make sure tables and chairs are set up and arranged correctly.
____ Check that equipment is in place and working.
____ Test microphone volume.
____ Position the screen and displays for good visibility.

Personal Details
____ Check clothing and hair.
____ Arrange for drinking water to be available.
____ Put your script and handouts in place.

Speaking Strategies
____ Greet individuals as they arrive for the presentation.
____ Learn some people's names.
____ Be confident, positive, and energetic.
____ Provide for audience participation; survey the audience.
____ Speak up and speak clearly—don't rush.
____ Reword and clarify when necessary.
____ After the presentation, ask for questions and answer them clearly.
____ Thank the audience.

Senator Mark Warner from Flickr

21
Job-Search Documents

If the thought of creating a résumé gets your heart pounding, you aren't alone. Résumés make people nervous because so much is riding on them: A well-written résumé can mean a job, and a poorly written one can mean a missed opportunity. And where there's a résumé, there's a cover letter. It, too, can be daunting in its own way.

This chapter takes the guesswork out of writing résumés, cover letters, and other documents that will help you with your job search. Follow the guidelines for each form to create documents that make you stand out from the crowd.

Guidelines Application Letters

Your Goal ▶ Your goal is to convince the reader to study your résumé and invite you for an interview.

> "Choose a job you love, and you will never have to work a day in your life."
> —Confucius

1. Prewrite: (Ideas and Organization)
- What does the employer or company do?
- Which of your skills, academic degrees, or work experiences match the job requirements?

Think about your reader.
- Find the name, title, and address of the person you are writing to.
- Review the job description and your résumé.

2. Draft: (Ideas, Organization, and Voice)
Opening Use a courteous but confident voice.
- Refer to the job and tell how you learned about it.
- State your main qualification.

Middle Show that you're qualified.
- Tell how your education, experience, and skills fit the job. (Refer to your résumé.)
- Communicate your interest in and knowledge of the job and the company.

Closing Close by encouraging contact.
- Explain when and where you may be reached.
- Request an interview.

3. Revise: (Ideas, Organization, Voice, Words, and Sentences)
- ☐ Have you explained why you can do the job well?
- ☐ Have you delivered your message in clear, well-organized paragraphs?
- ☐ Have you used a courteous, confident, businesslike tone?

4. Refine: (Conventions and Design)
- ☐ Did you double-check names, titles, and addresses?
- ☐ Did you run a spell check, and then read carefully for additional spelling and usage errors?
- ☐ Did you print your letter on quality paper that matches the résumé?

shutterstock.com

Application Letter

3041 45th Avenue
Lake City, WA 98125-3722
November 17, 2010

Ms. Marla Tamor
Human Resources Director
Evergreen Medical Center
812 University Street
Seattle, WA 98105-6152

Dear Ms. Tamor:

Opening

Name the job
and the source
of the ad. Introduce
your qualifications.

In response to your advertisement in the *Seattle Times* on November 12, I am writing to apply for the position of Software-Training Specialist. For the past seven years, I have worked as a trainer in the health-care system at Pacific Way Hospital.

Middle

List specific
training,
experience,
and skills.

I have instructed individuals and groups on how to use the following systems/software: Microsoft Office, WordPerfect Office, Lotus Millennium, as well as mainframe/business-specific programs. I am also trained to instruct clients in CorelDRAW and Pagemaker products.

In addition to my work with software systems, I have developed job descriptions, recruited technical employees, and trained human-resources personnel. I believe this experience would help me address the needs of a growing health-care facility such as Evergreen Medical Center.

Closing

Invite follow-up,
provide contact
information, and
close politely.

Enclosed is my résumé, which further details my qualifications. I look forward to hearing from you and can be reached at (206) 555-0242 or at<jmvrtz@aol.com>.Thank you for your consideration.

Sincerely,

Jamie Vertz

Jamie Vertz

Enc.:Résumé

Post-Interview Thank-You Letter

Jack Delaney
442 Mesquite Drive
El Paso, TX 79903
August 20, 2010

Julia Villanueva
Human Resources Manager
Del Rio Hospital
4305 Westlake Avenue
El Paso, TX 79902

Dear Ms. Villanueva:

Opening

Thank the reader for the opportunity to interview.

Thank you for the interview yesterday. I enjoyed meeting you and the obstetric nurses at Del Rio Hospital.

Middle

Confirm interest in the position and show you would be a good fit.

I would enjoy contributing to the important work that you and other staff members do in this community. After touring your impressive obstetrics unit, I'm convinced that my recently completed internship at the neonatal unit of El Paso General would make me an asset to your team.

Closing

Restate thanks and provide an opportunity for follow-up.

I appreciate being considered for the position of registered nurse. If you have further questions, I am available at 823-9667 from 8:00 to 10:00 weekday mornings, or you may leave a message any time after that.

Yours sincerely,

Jack Delaney

Jack Delaney

Job-Acceptance Letter

Opening

Graciously accept the job that has been offered.

Middle

Clarify any remaining details.

Closing

Look to a bright future of work.

Dear Ms. Villanueva:

I am pleased to accept the position of registered nurse in the obstetrics unit of Del Rio Hospital, at the salary of $40,250.

As we discussed on the phone, a starting date of March 17 works well for me. Before then, I will complete the forms you sent and return them. I will also forward my Associate Degree in Nursing certification next week after Lone Star Technical College processes it.

I'm looking forward to caring for the patients of Del Rio.

Yours sincerely,

Jack Delaney

Job-Declining Letter

Opening

Politely decline the job that has been offered.

Middle

Provide a general reason for declining the job.

Closing

Thank the reader and end politely.

Dear Ms. Villanueva:

Thank you for offering me the registered nurse position at Del Rio Hospital. After carefully considering my options, however, I regret that I must decline the offer.

While Del Rio's obstetrics unit presents a challenging and exciting work opportunity, I have decided to accept a position that better suits my particular career goals.

I was honored by this job offer and greatly appreciate your kind attention throughout the interview process. I know that through people like you, Del Rio will continue to make a valuable contribution to the community it serves.

Best regards,

Jack Delaney

Jack Delaney

Guidelines Résumés

Your Goal ▶ Your goal is to show that your skills, knowledge, and experience match the requirements for a specific job.

"A résumé is a balance sheet with no liabilities."
—Robert Half

1. **Prewrite:** (Ideas and Organization)
   - Show that your skills and experience match the job requirements.
   - Choose the style of résumé that best highlights your qualifications (chronological features experience; functional features skills).
   - Choose the format (paper or electronic) that the employer prefers.

   Gather details about the following:
   - your career objective, worded to match the job description.
   - your educational experiences (schools, degrees, certification).
   - your work experiences (employers and dates; responsibilities, skills, and titles; special projects, leadership roles, and awards).
   - activities and interests directly or indirectly related to the job.
   - responsible people who are willing to recommend you.

2. **Draft:** (Ideas, Organization, and Voice)
   Opening List your contact information and job objective.
   Middle Write appropriate headings, and list educational and work experiences in parallel phrases or clauses. Refer to your training and skills with key words that match the job description (terms that could be identified by an employer's search).
   Closing List names, job titles, and contact information for your references; or state that references are available upon request.

3. **Revise:** (Ideas, Organization, Voice, Words, and Sentences)
   - ☐ Are skills, training, and key words listed in the job description?
   - ☐ Do you have clear organization, correct details, and a professional tone?
   - ☐ Do you use strong verbs, precise nouns, and parallel phrases?

4. **Refine:** (Conventions and Design)
   - ☐ Have you checked names, dates, grammar, and punctuation?
   - ☐ Have you checked format (divisions, headings, lists, spacing)?

shutterstock.com

Chronological Résumé

Opening

Present contact information.

State your employment objective.

Middle

List experiences, skills, and training (most recent first).

Use periods after clauses— including those with understood subjects.

Do not use periods after headings or phrases.

Keep all phrases and clauses parallel.

List awards and honors in order of importance.

Closing

Offer references.

LLOYD A. CLARK
1913 Linden Street
Charlotte, NC 28205-5611
(704) 555-2422
lloydac@erthlk.net

EMPLOYMENT OBJECTIVE
Law enforcement position that calls for technical skills, military experience, self-discipline, reliability, and people skills.

WORK EXPERIENCE
Positions held in the United States Marine Corps:
- Guard Supervisor—Sasebo Naval Base, Japan, 2005-2009
  Scheduled and supervised 24 guards.
- Marksmanship Instructor—Sasebo Naval Base, Japan, 2004-2005
  Trained personnel in small-arms marksmanship techniques.
- Company Clerk—Okinawa, Japan, 2002-2004
  Handled correspondence; prepared training schedules and assignments.

SKILLS AND QUALIFICATIONS
- In-depth knowledge of laws and regulations concerning apprehension, search and seizure, rules of evidence, and use of deadly force
- Knowledge of security-management principles, training methods, and countermeasures
- Experience in physical-training management, marksmanship, and weaponry
- Computer word-processing and database skills on an IBM-compatible system
- Excellent one-on-one skills and communication abilities

EDUCATION
- Arrest, Apprehension, and Riot Control Course, Sasebo, Japan, 2004
- Marksmanship Instructor Course, Okinawa, Japan, 2003
- Sexual-Harassment Sensitivity Training, Camp Lejeune, NC, 2002
- School of Infantry, Camp Pendleton, CA, 2002

AWARDS AND HONORS
- Promoted meritoriously from Private (E-1) to Lance Corporal (E-3); promoted meritoriously to final rank of Corporal (E-4) in less than 2 years.
- Achieved "Expert" rating for pistol at annual marksmanship qualifications (3 years).
- Represented Marine Barracks, Japan, in division shooting matches (placed in top half).

References available upon request

Opening

Present contact
information and
your employment
objective.

Middle

Feature skills
by referring to
educational
and work
experiences.

Put the most
important
skills first.

Use periods
after clauses—
including those
with understood
subjects—but not
after phrases.

Closing

Offer references.

MICHELLE MOORE
3448 Skyway Drive
Missoula, MT 59801-2883
(406) 555-2166
E-mail: mimoore@erthlk.net

EMPLOYMENT OBJECTIVE   Electrical Engineer—designing or developing digital
and/or microprocessor systems.

QUALIFICATIONS AND SKILLS

Design
- Wrote two "C" programs to increase production-lab efficiency.
- Built, tested, and modified prototypes in digital and analog circuit design.
- Designed and worked with CMOS components.
- Wrote code for specific set of requirements.
- Helped implement circuitry and hardware for a "bed-of-nails" test.

Troubleshooting and Repair
- Repaired circuit boards of peripheral computer products.
- Helped maintain equipment using circuit-board testing.
- Improved product quality by correcting recurring problems.
- Debugged IBM-XT/Fox Kit Microprocessor Trainer (Z80).

Management
- Trained and supervised production technicians.
- Facilitated smooth operation of production lab.
- Assisted in lab teaching for Microprocessors and Digital Circuits class.

EDUCATION
Montana State University, Bozeman, MT
- Bachelor of Science in Engineering, 2008
- Major: Electrical Engineering
- Independent Study: C programming, DOS and BIOS interrupts

EXPERIENCE

October 2008 to present	Production Engineer (full-time) Big Sky Computer Products, Inc., Missoula, MT
June 2008 to September 2008	Engineer (part-time) Western Labs, Missoula, MT
September 2007 to May 2008	Engineering Assistant Montana State University, Bozeman, MT
May 2006 to September 2007	Engineering Intern Montana State University, Bozeman, MT

References available upon request

Choosing a Résumé Format

As you consider which type of résumé to create, remember that . . .
- chronological résumés highlight work history.
- functional résumés emphasize job skills.

Follow your path through this flowchart to discover which type of résumé would work best for you.

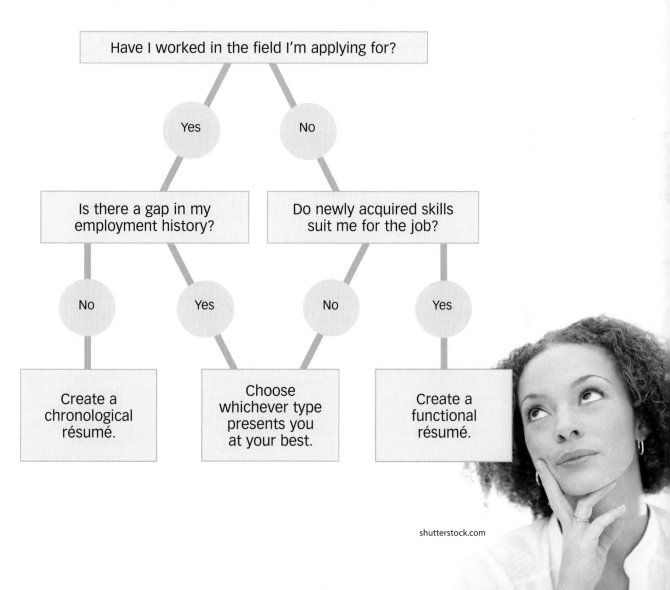

Have I worked in the field I'm applying for?

Yes   No

Is there a gap in my employment history?

Do newly acquired skills suit me for the job?

No   Yes   No   Yes

Create a chronological résumé.

Choose whichever type presents you at your best.

Create a functional résumé.

shutterstock.com

Preparing an E-Résumé

Whether you create a chronological or functional résumé, you should make it available in both paper and digital form. Large companies collect e-résumés into databases and use search engines to discover potential candidates. Smaller companies often search online résumé banks.

Keywords

Since e-résumés are selected by search engines, it's crucial that your résumé includes keywords that employers will look for—words related to degrees, job skills, experience, computer skills, and even your location. To gather keywords, first scan job listings and write down important nouns. Then brainstorm to expand your list of keywords.

shutterstock.com

Job Posting Keywords	Law Enforcement Keywords		
law enforcement	military	apprehension	evidence
police science	Marine	marksman	riot control
security management	instructor	marksmanship	database
self-discipline	supervisor	search	seizure

Submitting Electronically

Often, when you submit an electronic résumé, you'll need to copy and paste portions into an online form. If, however, you submit a complete document, save your résumé in a format that can be understood regardless of the reader's hardware or software:

- **PDF** (portable document format) allows your résumé to be viewed by anyone who has the free Adobe Reader. This format allows the best control over fonts, graphics, and page layout.
- **RTF** (rich text format) allows your résumé to include some basic formatting, such as bold and italic, and is readable by most word processors.
- **TXT** (text only) allows the document to be read by any computer, but it does not include bold, italics, or other special formatting.

Fyi Many employers request a specific type of file. Be sure to follow their directions.

It is a good idea to follow an e-résumé with a printed résumé, unless an employer specifically says otherwise.

Electronic Résumé

Opening

Present contact information and employment objectives.

Jonathan L. Greenlind
806 5th Avenue
Waterloo, IA 50701-9351
Phone: 319.555.6955
E-mail:grnlnd@aol.com

OBJECTIVE
Position as hydraulics supervisor that calls for hydraulics expertise, technical skills, mechanical knowledge, reliability, and enthusiasm.

Middle

List skills, experiences, and education using many key words.

SKILLS
Operation and repair specialist in main and auxiliary power systems, subsystems, landing gears, brakes and pneumatic systems, hydraulic motors, reservoirs, actuators, pumps, and cylinders from six types of hydraulic systems
Dependable, resourceful, strong leader, team worker

Format for e-mail, scanner, and Web site:

- one column
- asterisks as bullets
- simple sans-serif typeface
- flush left margin
- no italics, boldface, or underlining
- RTF text (readable by all computers)

EXPERIENCE
Aviation Hydraulics Technician
United States Navy (2006-present)
* Repair, test, and maintain basic hydraulics, distribution systems, and aircraft structural hydraulics systems.
* Manufacture low-, medium-, and high-pressure rubber and Teflon hydraulic hoses.
* Perform preflight, postflight, and other periodic aircraft inspections.
* Supervise personnel.
Aircraft Mechanic
Sioux Falls International Airport (2004-2006)
Sioux Falls, South Dakota
* Performed fueling, engine overhauls, minor repairs, and tire and oil changes of various aircraft.

EDUCATION
United States Navy (2006-2010)
Certificate in Hydraulic Technical School; GPA 3.8/4.0
Certificate in Hydraulic, Pneumatic Test Stand School; GPA 3.9/4.0
Courses in Corrosion Control, Hydraulic Tube Bender, Aviation Structural Mechanics
Equivalent of 10 semester hours in Hydraulic Systems Maintenance and Structural Repair

Closing

Offer references.

References available upon request

> "A chest full
> of medals is
> nothing more
> than a résumé
> in 3-D and
> Technicolor."
>
> —Owen
> Edwards

shutterstock.com

Checklist Résumés

Your goal is to show that your skills, knowledge, and experience match the requirements for a specific job.

Ideas 9-16
____ shows that you understand the prospective job and are qualified for it.
____ includes accurate and honest details about training, skills, awards, and experiences matched to the job requirements.

Organization 17-24
____ begins with your name, contact information, and objective.
____ follows with specific details starting with most recent (chronological) or most important (functional) and groups details under headings.
____ concludes with how the reader can access my references.

Voice 25-32
____ is confident and knowledgeable, but not arrogant.

Words 33-40
____ includes key words from the job description as well as related terms.
____ uses accurate terms for academic degrees, training programs, professional certifications, job titles, and tasks.
____ uses strong verbs, especially for a paper-only résumé.

Sentences 41-50
____ provides information in parallel lists, phrases, and clauses.
____ uses complete sentences only when needed to make a point.

Correctness 51-58
____ uses correct terms, names, dates, and titles.
____ includes no errors in grammar, punctuation, mechanics, or spelling.
____ uses periods after clauses (including those with understood subjects).

Design 59-70
____ *(paper)* uses bullets, boldface, underlining, and business typeface.
____ *(electronic)* uses RTF text, sans-serif typeface, single-column format—but no boldface or underlining.

The U.S. Army from Flickr

22
Management Writing

When employees write on the job, they often do so to communicate with individuals. When managers write on the job, they often do so to communicate with an entire department, division, or company. What they write has a direct and often profound effect on many people. That's why management writing should be well polished before it is presented.

This chapter can help. Whether you are setting policies and procedures, evaluating existing employees, or conducting a search for new employees, you'll find the management writing guidelines and models you need on the following pages.

Guidelines Policy Statements

Your Goal ▶ Your goal is to explain the organization's policy regarding a workplace issue.

shutterstock.com

"By definition, a government has no conscience. Sometimes it has a policy, but nothing more."

—Albert Camus

1. **Prewrite:** (Ideas and Organization)
   - What exactly is the issue (including its history), and how does the issue relate to your organization's mission, values, and priorities?
   - Who will read the policy statement now and in the future, and what will their concerns and attitudes be?

   Prepare to draft.
   - Review relevant company documents: mission statement, related policy statements, minutes, the employee handbook, and so forth.
   - Research the issue carefully: Interview people (other managers, legal council, and employees) knowledgeable about the topic; read reliable sources; and study other organizations' policies on this topic.

2. **Draft:** (Ideas, Organization, and Voice)
   Opening Introduce the policy and explain why it is adopted.
   Middle Explain the policy and its implementation.
   - Indicate what employees must do, when, where, and how.
   - Outline what the organization will do, when, where, and how.
   Closing List dates the policy is adopted and revised and any reference documents.

3. **Revise:** (Ideas, Organization, Voice, Words, and Sentences)
   - ☐ Is the policy correctly identified, clearly explained, and sufficiently supported?
   - ☐ Is the organization clear and logical?
   - ☐ Is the voice informed, reasoned, fair, and concerned?

4. **Refine:** (Conventions and Design)
   - ☐ Are names, titles, and dates correct?
   - ☐ Are spelling, punctuation, usage, and grammar correct?
   - ☐ Does the formatting provide easy access and use?

Policy
Statement
on Quality
Control

 UMI Manufacturing Inc.

5683 135th Avenue NE
Minneapolis, MN 55414-2899
(612) 555-1923
FAX: (612) 555-1924

Opening

State the policy's
name and subject.

Middle

Develop the policy
in greater detail.

Closing

List adoption and
revision dates.

Quality Policy

UMI Manufacturing Inc. aims to produce products that meet or exceed both industry standards and our customers' expectations for quality. Providing quality products and services is the heart of UMI's mission and success.

To that end, UMI Manufacturing, on an ongoing basis, commits to
- monitor and improve products based on customer needs.
- correct procedures that create problems for customers and document both the actions taken and the results.
- monitor and reduce process variation in order to decrease product costs.
- use environmentally sound practices.
- invest time and resources in employee training that supports product improvement and customer satisfaction.

Adopted: 3/21/08
Revised: 7/14/10

Guidelines Procedures

> "I had been told that the training procedure with cats was difficult. It's not. Mine had me trained in two days."
>
> —Bill Dana

Your Goal ▶ Your goal is to instruct readers about the procedure for carrying out a policy.

1. **Prewrite:** (Ideas and Organization)
   - What is the policy, and what must readers know in order to implement it?
   - What are the priorities and responsibilities of your readers? How will the procedure impact their work?
   - When, where, and how will the procedure be used?

   Prepare to draft.
   - Study relevant documents such as related policies and procedures as well as the minutes of the committee that adopted the policy that you're implementing.
   - Interview people familiar with the issues in the policies.
   - List necessary ingredients: people, tasks, tools, and materials. If possible, practice the procedure and take notes.
   - Consider timing: How long should the procedure take?

2. **Draft:** (Ideas, Organization, and Voice)
   Opening Identify and summarize the policy and procedure.
   Middle Give step-by-step instructions.
   - Spell out necessary actions.
   - Cite who must do each activity and by when.
   Closing State the outcome and any necessary follow-up.

3. **Revise:** (Ideas, Organization, Voice, Words, and Sentences)
   - ☐ Does the procedure accurately implement the policy?
   - ☐ Are safety, security, and legal issues correctly addressed?
   - ☐ Are steps, assignments, and due dates clear and correct?

4. **Refine:** (Conventions and Design)
   - ☐ Are names, titles, due dates, and procedural terms correct?
   - ☐ Does the procedure use action verbs, numbered steps, and an attractive format?
   - ☐ Are the spelling, punctuation, and grammar correct?

Procedure

Family and Children's Coalition Confidentiality Procedures

Opening

Identify the organization and topic; summarize the policy.

The Family and Children's Coalition Confidentiality Policy states that all clients have the right to confidentiality. Conduct your work in keeping with this policy by following the procedures below.

Middle

Use clear headings throughout.

List steps clearly, including which documents to complete and submit.

Client Intakes:
During the client intake, the Coalition counselor should discuss the conditions of confidentiality with the client. These conditions include the following:

1. Information will never be shared unless the client has given written permission using the Consent to Release Form.

2. Confidentiality may be limited or canceled if Coalition staff have serious concerns about child abuse or neglect, or if the client is a danger to herself or himself, or to others.

Outside Requests for Information:
Coalition counselors will handle outside requests for client information.

1. No client information will be shared without the client's written permission.

2. Clients will be notified of any outside requests for information. If the client gives permission, he or she must sign the Consent to Release Form and specifically indicate what information may be released and to whom. A Coalition counselor must also sign the release form.

Closing

Close with a fitting summary or restatement.

Breaches of Confidentiality:
If a client believes that Coalition staff have not observed the confidentiality policy and procedures, the client should be directed to follow the Client Grievance Process.

By carefully following the procedures above, Coalition staff can help clients while also respecting their rights to confidentiality.

Guidelines Employee Evaluations

Your Goal ▶ Your goal is to objectively evaluate a person's strengths and weaknesses.

> "There are four ways, and only four ways, in which we have contact with the world. We are evaluated and classified by these four contacts: what we do, how we look, what we say, and how we say it."
>
> —Dale Carnegie

shutterstock.com

1. Prewrite: (Ideas and Organization)
- Do you anticipate a positive, negative, or mixed review?
- Who will read the evaluation—the employee, HR staff, other managers? What will their concerns be?
- What is the employee's history with the company? What key forces and events have impacted this person's position during the review period?
- How must you present your evaluation—form, memo, e-mail, letter?

Gather details and prepare to write.
- Review key documents: job description, *Employee Handbook,* the employee's self-assessment, past evaluations, and work record.
- Measure recent performance (awards, productivity, projects completed, assessments by coworkers or clients); analyze reasons for success or difficulty; and brainstorm ways of building on strengths and resolving weaknesses.

2. Draft: (Ideas, Organization, and Voice)
Opening Provide important employee information.
Middle Present your evaluation.
- Use direct organization for a positive critique.
- Use indirect organization for a negative critique: (1) what led to the assessment, (2) the assessment, and (3) corrective steps.
Closing Sum up the assessment and anticipate future improvement.

3. Revise: (Ideas, Organization, Voice, Words, and Sentences)
- ☐ Are main points clear, correct, well organized, and supported?
- ☐ Is the tone objective, fair, genuine, and concerned?
- ☐ Is wording clear?

4. Refine: (Conventions and Design)
- ☐ Are grammar, spelling, punctuation, and usage correct?
- ☐ Does the evaluation follow the correct format?

Employee Evaluation (Short Form)

Opening

State the form's title and basic details describing the job and person.

Define the rating scale clearly.

Provide space for scores and comments.

When completing the form, include scores along with supporting details.

Empire Estates Employee Evaluation

Employee: <u>Larry Mott</u>   Supervisor: <u>Sarah Iverson</u>
Job Title: <u>Mortgage Specialist II</u>   Title: <u>Mortgage Specialist Supervisor</u>
Hire Date: <u>April 17, 2003</u>   Evaluation Date: <u>December 3, 2010</u>

Using the scale below, rate the employee's performance. (If an area does not apply to this position, write "NA.") Support your rating with details.

Rating Scale:

5 – EXCELLENT: Performance frequently exceeds requirements and expectations. Outstanding work.

4 – GOOD: Performance is above average. Employee is reliable and independent.

3 – ACCEPTABLE: Performance meets requirements and expectations. Goals met with normal supervision.

2 – MARGINAL: Performance needs improvement to meet job requirements and expectations.

1 – UNACCEPTABLE: Performance fails to meet job requirements and expectations. Not reliable, unable to work independently. Poor understanding of position.

<u>4</u> **Quality of Work**
Comments: <u>Larry is hardworking and regularly attends seminars to refine his skills.</u>

<u>3</u> **Analytical and Problem-Solving Skills**
Comments: <u>Larry has strong skills when handling standard mortgages but needs to learn greater flexibility with FHA or VA loans.</u>

<u>4</u> **Job Knowledge**
Comments: <u>Larry understands/applies information, instructions, and procedures. He has learned to do cash reservations, lockboxes, and CPI system balancing.</u>

<u>3</u> **Communication Skills**
Comments: <u>Larry sometimes finds it difficult to explain the technical aspects of mortgages to some clients.</u>

<u>3</u> **Interpersonal Skills**
Comments: <u>Larry is well liked by coworkers but needs to learn greater patience in dealing with clients.</u>

Employee Evaluation (Long Form)

Opening

State the organization, person, and key details about the job.

Middle

List the job's responsibilities in order of importance.

In the first column, succinctly respond to the topics listed.

In the second column, state additional details in a fair, objective voice.

Empire Estates Incorporated
Employee Evaluation

Employee: **Mary Lamont**   Supervisor: **Sam Everly**
Job Title: **Mortgage Specialist II**   Title: **Mortgage Specialist Supervisor**
Hire Date: **April 16, 2003**   Evaluation Date: **September 10, 2010**

Part A   **Job Responsibilities:** (List 3-5 key roles from job description.)
1. Reconciling A/A and S/S accounts
2. Reconciling FHLMC P & I accounts
3. CPI system balancing
4. Troubleshooting and technical advisor/supervisor

Part B   **Job Characteristics:** Rank the employee's performance (E for excellent, G for good, A for acceptable, M for marginal, U for unacceptable) and specify areas of strength and areas for improvement.

Job Characteristics

Evaluation/Comments:

1. Quality of work: **Produces consistent and correct work.**

   G Works steadily.

2. Productivity: **Produces an expected quantity of work on time.**

   G Production levels good; some delays due to troubleshooting.

3. Job Knowledge: **Understands, retains, and applies information, instructions, and procedures.**

   A Good analytical skills; needs training on Monarch and Access.

4. Communication Skills: **Communicates effectively. Writes clearly and concisely in language appropriate for the reader.**

   E Works well with customers; accommodating.

5. Decision-Making Skills: **Identifies problems and implements solutions.**

   A Solves problems well; needs to develop leadership skills.

6. Interpersonal Skills: **Works respectfully and cooperatively with coworkers and clients.**

   E Works well with both administrators and customers.

Part C   Performance Evaluation Summary: Review Parts A & B; then summarize the demonstrated strengths and areas for improvement.

Demonstrated Strengths

Mary's analytical skills help her serve as a department problem solver. She's a quick learner of new systems. In addition, Mary's excellent interpersonal and communication skills enable her to work well with colleagues and customers.

Areas for Improvement

Mary should receive further training to strengthen her knowledge of Monarch and Access. She also needs additional supervisory training to expand her skills in troubleshooting and problem solving.

Part D   Individual Development Plan: Establish an individual plan to further develop or improve skills. Plans may include additional training, seminars, on-the-job assignments, etc.

1. Fall 2010: Additional training in Monarch and Access
2. Spring 2011: Leadership seminars to strengthen supervisory skills

Part E   Employee Response:

I appreciate this fair evaluation and look forward to growing professionally through the suggested training and seminars.

Prepared by: Sam Everly, Mortgage Specialist Supervisor

Date: September 10, 2010

Reviewed by: Dan Levine, Mortgage Department Supervisor

Date: September 13, 2010

Employee Signature: Mary Lamont

Date: September 14, 2010

Note: The employee's signature above does not necessarily constitute agreement with this evaluation.

Margin notes:

Name the person's strengths and give details.

Cite weaknesses precisely and clearly.

List activities and dates.

Respond honestly but politely.

Closing

Sign and date as requested.

Guidelines Application Follow-Up Messages

Your Goal ▶ Your goal is to express appreciation for the application and to keep strong candidates interested.

> "Whenever you are asked if you can do a job, tell 'em, 'Certainly I can!' Then get busy and find out how to do it."
>
> —Theodore Roosevelt

shutterstock.com

1. **Prewrite:** (Ideas and Organization)
   - What are the applicant's strengths and weaknesses?
   - How does the applicant match the job requirements?
   - How does this applicant compare with others?

   Gather details and prepare to write.
   - Reread the job description and note details.
   - Review the application for key (or missing) information.
   - Note the person's current job situation, availability, and contact information.

2. **Draft:** (Ideas, Organization, and Voice)
   Opening Greet the reader, mention the application, and show appreciation.
   Middle Explain the selection process.
   - Encourage strong candidates.
   - For weak candidates, state objectively but courteously why they do not meet the job requirements.

   Closing State appreciation, and encourage strong candidates to complete the process.

3. **Revise:** (Ideas, Organization, Voice, Words, and Sentences)
   - ☐ Are details related to the applicant, job, and organization correct and complete?
   - ☐ Does the message have brief paragraphs and clear transitions?
   - ☐ Is the voice informed, confident, professional, and positive?
   - ☐ Is wording clear?

4. **Refine:** (Conventions and Design)
   - ☐ Are spelling, punctuation, and usage correct?
   - ☐ Is the format effective (parts, spacing, typography, and so forth)?

**Application
Follow-Up
(Strong
Candidate)**

TRIPLEX TECHNOLOGIES, INC.

3020 Gore Road • Imlay City, MI 48444-0981 • Phone: 616-555-8069

June 25, 2010

Mr. Marvin Greenfield
1554 Bastian Street
Lapeer, MI 48446-1601

Opening

Greet the reader
and acknowledge
the application.

Dear Mr. Greenfield:

Thank you for submitting your application and résumé for the position of
Chief Microbiologist at Triplex Technologies, Inc. Your academic research
on environmental hazards with the University of Michigan's Biology
Department and your subsequent work as a microbiologist for the EPA
indicate that you have much to offer our company.

Middle

Describe the status
of the process and
(if needed) request
information.

Evaluation of all applications is nearly complete, and we will begin
interviewing in two weeks. To help us gain a clearer view of your
qualifications, please send us a job description detailing your current work
responsibilities.

Closing

Express thanks and
encourage the
applicant.

Thank you again for your interest in Triplex Technologies. Your résumé and
credentials show you to be a deserving candidate for the position of Chief
Microbiologist. Please send the requested materials to our Human Resources
Department by Monday, July 9.

Sincerely,

Keith Ryster
Human Resources Manager

Levinsky and **Gring**   400 Talbot Avenue, NE, Oakland, CA 94623-1412

May 14, 2010

Mr. Frederick O'Brien
1525 Montgomery Street
Oakland, CA 94612-6315

Dear Mr. O'Brien:

Opening

Express
appreciation for
the application.

Thank you for submitting your application and résumé for the accounting position at Levinsky and Gring. We have reviewed your academic achievements and experience.

Middle

State your
disinterest in the
application
courteously.

You are probably aware that the competition is formidable for staff accounting positions in large firms. Although your background is commendable, it does not match our current needs. Experience working at a smaller firm could strengthen your résumé and increase your chances of employment in a large firm.

Closing

Reiterate your
appreciation and
wish success
elsewhere.

We do appreciate your interest and wish you success in securing a position.

Sincerely,

Ruby Unger
Director of Recruiting

Employer's Job-Offer Letter

TRIPLEX TECHNOLOGIES, INC.
3020 Gore Road • Imlay City, MI 48444-0981 • Phone: 616-555-8069

July 24, 2010

Mr. Marvin Greenfield
1554 Bastian Street
Lapeer, MI 48446-1601

Dear Mr. Greenfield:

Opening

Offer congratulations.

I am pleased to offer to you the position of Chief Microbiologist at Triplex Technologies. Our selection committee noted that your enthusiasm and range of experience set you apart from the other applicants whom we considered.

Middle

Affirm the person's strengths and state contract details.

Following are further details regarding this position:
1. Your salary will be $100,000, with a review based on your yearly performance appraisal.
2. The starting date is Monday, August 16, 2010,with a three-month probationary period.
3. An overview of employee benefits is enclosed. If you have questions, please call Judy Owen, Human Resources Assistant (616-555-8911).

Mr. Greenfield, we sincerely hope that you will accept our offer. We are eager to work with you and believe that our relationship will be mutually beneficial.

Closing

Encourage acceptance and note the date for the reader's decision.

Please inform me of your decision by August 2, 2010.You may call my office at 616-555-8948. Thank you again for your interest in Triplex Technologies, and I look forward to your reply.

Sincerely,

Keith Ryster

Keith Ryster
Human Resources Manager

Enc.: Employee Benefits

"Management
is nothing
more than
motivating
other people."

—Lee Iacocca

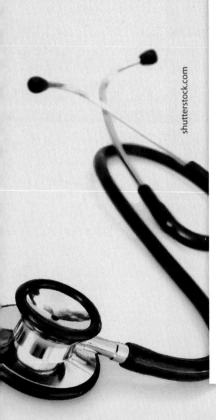

shutterstock.com

Checklist Management Forms

Your goal is to produce management writing that is clear, complete, correct, and professional.

Ideas 9-16
____ The main point is clearly stated.
____ Supporting details are complete and compelling.

Organization 17-24
____ The writing follows the appropriate form.
____ The beginning provides a strong introduction.
____ The middle includes details following an appropriate organizational pattern.
____ The ending sums up the form well.

Voice 25-32
____ The voice is positive, confident, and objective.
____ The voice connects to the intended audience.
____ The language is formal.

Words 33-40
____ Active verbs are used to be direct and passive verbs to be indirect.
____ Nouns are specific, and technical terms are defined.

Sentences 41-50
____ The sentences read smoothly and include logical transitions.

Correctness 51-58
____ The writing contains no errors in grammar, punctuation, usage, or spelling.

Design 59-70
____ The writing follows the expected format.
____ White space, typography, and other design features are used well.

Section 4:
Proofreader's Guide

In this section

23
Punctuation

Period

To End a Sentence

- Use a **period** to end a sentence that makes a statement, requests something, or gives a mild command.

    (Statement) **"A gold mine is a hole in the ground with a liar at the top."**
    —Mark Twain

    (Request) **Please arrange an on-site meeting.**

    (Mild Command) **"Concentrate on finding your goal; then concentrate on reaching it."**
    —Michael Friedsam

Note: Omit a period after a statement that has parentheses around it if it is part of another sentence.

    These early entrepreneurs (some of them were true visionaries) often met skepticism.

After an Initial or an Abbreviation

- A period should be placed after an initial and after most abbreviations.

    Ms.   Inc.   O.D.   M.A.
    C.E.   a.m.   U.S.A.   Joan Q.

Note: When an abbreviation is the last word in a sentence, do not add a second period.

    Tom recently received his M.B.A.

After an Indirect Question

- Use a period, not a question mark, after an indirect question.

    I wonder how much that will cost us.

Ellipsis

To Show Omitted Words

- Use an **ellipsis** (three spaced periods) to indicate that words have been omitted in a quoted passage. Leave one space before and after each period.

    (Original) **All new employees must fill out the standard work forms—Social Security, insurance, and payroll. The forms, which maybe obtained from your immediate supervisor, should be completed before beginning work. If you have any questions, please contact Rosa for assistance.**

    (Quotation) **"All new employees must fill out the standard work forms . . . which may be obtained from your immediate supervisor . . . before beginning work."**

At the End of a Sentence

- If words from a quoted passage are omitted at the end of a sentence, the ellipsis follows the period.

    "All new employees must fill out the standard work forms—Social Security, insurance, and payroll. . . . If you have any questions, please contact Rosa for assistance."

If the quoted material is a complete sentence (even if it was not in the original), use a period and then an ellipsis.

    "All new employees must fill out the standard work forms. . . . Please contact Rosa for assistance."

Note: The first word of a sentence following a period and an ellipsis may be capitalized, even though it was not capitalized in the original.

* * Success occurs when opportunity meets preparation. —Zig Ziglar * * *

Comma

To Separate Independent Clauses

- Use a **comma** before a coordinating conjunction (*and, but, or, nor, for, so, yet*) when it is used to link two independent clauses.

  Ability may get you to the top, but only character will keep you there.

  "A doctor can bury his mistakes, but an architect can only advise his client to plant vines."

  —Frank Lloyd Wright

Note: Do not mistake a sentence containing a compound verb for a compound sentence. (No comma is needed with a compound verb.)

  Marva quickly checked the document and corrected a few minor errors.

To Separate Phrases and Clauses

- A comma should follow an introductory adverb clause or a long introductory phrase.

  "If you don't learn from your mistakes, there's no sense making them."

  —Laurence J. Peter

Note: The comma is usually omitted if the phrase or adverb clause follows the independent clause.

  There's no sense making mistakes if you don't learn from them.

To Set Off Extra Information

- Commas are used to set off explanatory phrases.

  Drive-in banks, according to E. Joseph Cossman, were established so most of the cars could see their real owners.

To Set Off Contrasted Elements

- Commas are used to set off contrasted elements in a sentence.

  This is real life, not fantasy.

To Separate Adjectives

- Commas are used between two or more adjectives that modify the same noun *equally*.

  Using a database software package can be a reliable, efficient solution to many small-business problems.

A Closer Look

Use the tests below for help in deciding whether adjectives modify *equally*.

1. **Switch the order of the adjectives.**
   If the sentence is still clear, the adjectives modify equally. (If *reliable* and *efficient* were shifted in the example above, the sentence would still be clear; therefore, use a comma.)

2. **Place *and* between the adjectives.**
   Does the sentence still sound all right? If so, insert a comma (without *and*). (If *and* were inserted in the sentence above, it would still read well.)

For Items in a Series

- Commas are used to separate three or more items (words, phrases, or clauses) in a series.

  The best workplace chair is one with a padded seat, an adjustable backrest, and a lumbar support system.

Note: Do not use commas when all the items in a series are connected with *or, nor,* or *and.*

  Vision problems can be caused by improper lighting or by computer glare or even by letters that are difficult to read.

  The best workplace chair is one with a padded seat and an adjustable backrest and a lumbar support system.

In Addresses and Dates

- Commas are used to set off items in an address and in a date.

  Send for your personal copy of *Write for Business* before December 31, 2011, from UpWrite Press, 35115 West State Street, Burlington, Wisconsin 53105.

Note: No comma is placed between the state and ZIP code. Also, no comma is needed if only the month and year are given: *December 2011.*

To Separate a Vocative

- A comma is used to separate a **vocative** (noun of address) from the rest of the sentence. (A vocative is the noun that names the person or persons spoken to.)

  Jamie, would you like to join me for lunch today?

To Set Off Interruptions

- Commas are used to set off a word, a phrase, or a clause that interrupts the flow of a sentence. The following tests can help identify such expressions. The meaning of the sentence does not change if the expression is (1) omitted or (2) placed nearly anywhere in the sentence.

  The problems, in the final analysis, were due largely to a lack of planning.

  In the final analysis, the problems were due largely to a lack of planning.

For Clarity or Emphasis

- A comma may be used to clarify or to emphasize. Sometimes no specific rule calls for a comma, but one is needed to avoid confusion or to emphasize an important idea.

  What he says, says volumes.

To Set Off Exact Words

- Commas are used to set off the exact words of the speaker from the rest of the sentence.

  "Nothing in fine print is ever good news," quipped Andy Rooney.

Do not use a comma before an indirect quotation. (The comma circled below should not be used.)

  The computer technician said, that he would be here shortly. (misuse of a comma before an indirect quotation)

Comma (continued)

To Set Off Nonrestrictive Modifiers

- Commas are used to set off nonrestrictive phrases and clauses used as modifiers. Nonrestrictive phrases or clauses are those that are not essential to the basic meaning of the sentence.

  Roy, who is training to be a supervisor, is an asset to our service department. (nonrestrictive)

  Good service at a reasonable rate, which sums up the department's philosophy, is the reason for the dealership's success. (nonrestrictive)

Note: The two clauses shown above in red are merely additional information; they are *nonrestrictive* (not required). If the clauses were left out of the sentences, the meaning of the sentences would remain clear.

- Restrictive phrases or clauses—phrases or clauses that are needed in the sentence because they restrict or limit the meaning of the sentence—are not set off with commas.

  Employees who are praised for new ideas are apt to be creative. (restrictive)

  Companies that offer flexible hours usually have happier, more efficient workers. (restrictive)

Remember: Restrictive phrases are required in a sentence; *nonrestrictive* phrases are not required. Compare the following phrases:

  The humorist Will Rogers was born in Oklahoma. (*Will Rogers* is required; do *not* use commas.)

  Will Rogers, the humorist, was born in Oklahoma. (*The humorist* is not required; use commas.)

A Closer Look

  Which and That: Use *which* to introduce nonrestrictive (unnecessary) clauses; use *that* to introduce restrictive (necessary) clauses. Doing so will help the reader quickly distinguish essential information from nonessential information.

  The system that we implemented in March 2010 was selected after a year-long study.

Note: The clause beginning with *that* is necessary to identify which system.

  The new system, which was implemented in March, has already improved productivity 40 percent.

Note: The main clause tells the reader important information about the new system; the clause beginning with *which* gives additional or nonessential information.

To Set Off Appositives

- Commas are used to set off an **appositive**, a noun or phrase that identifies the noun or pronoun it follows. (A *restrictive appositive* is essential to the basic meaning of the sentence; do not set it off with commas. See the second example below.)

  Scott Erickson, a landscape designer, uses his laptop computer in the office and in the field. (nonrestrictive appositive)

  Landscape designer Scott Erickson uses his laptop computer in the office and in the field. (restrictive appositive)

* * * * * * * * * * * * * * * * Of all the things you wear,

In Large Numbers

- Commas are used to separate numerals, or digits, in large numbers. For numbers of four digits or more, place a comma before every third digit, counting from the right.

  This printer costs $3,045.

Note: In scientific writing, it is acceptable to omit the comma in numbers with only four digits.

Exceptions: Commas are not used in address numbers or in identification numbers.

  12345 Karry Place   room 5496

  invoice 17823

Note: Spaces, not commas, are used in metric measurements. (This avoids confusion in those countries where commas are used as decimal points.)

  14 267.9 hectares (U.S.A.) or
  14 267,9 hectares (European)

To Enclose a Title

- Commas are used to enclose initials, a title, or names that follow a surname.

  Mr. Anton Sellek, Sr., and James Matthews, Esq., will arrive at noon.

  Daly, C. U., and Herr, I. M., are not alphabetized correctly on this list.

Note: It is also acceptable to use *Jr.* and *Sr.* without commas.

  John Kennedy Jr. had a variety of careers.

Roman numeral suffixes are never set off by commas.

  John Williams III is the CEO.

Before Tag Sentences

- A comma is used before a tag sentence, which is a short statement or question at the end of a sentence.

  You took the job, didn't you?

To Separate Interjections

- A comma is used to separate an interjection or a weak exclamation from the rest of the sentence.

  OK, I'll pass the latest sales figures on to the Accounting Department.

A Closer Look

In addition to understanding when and where to use commas correctly, you should also know when *not* to use commas.

Do **not** use a comma between compound predicates.

  We started the van and discovered a problem.

Do **not** use a comma between a subject and a verb.

  Recent articles on Internet marketing are available online.

Do **not** use a comma between a verb and its object or complement.

  My supervisor said I should read *The Business Journal*.

Semicolon

To Join Two Independent Clauses

- A **semicolon** is used to join two related independent clauses. (*Remember:* Independent clauses can stand alone as separate sentences.)

  Business has been good; it really does pay to advertise.

Note: A comma may be used if the two clauses are short or express a contrast in ideas.

  Acquiring new technology is one thing, using it efficiently is another.

With a Conjunctive Adverb

- A semicolon is used before a conjunctive adverb (*also, besides, however, instead, then, therefore*) that connects two independent clauses; a comma is often used after the adverb.

  Too many overtime hours can lead to insanity; however, you'll probably be too busy to notice.

To Separate Items in a Series

- A semicolon is used between items in a series if any of those items already have commas.

  When renting a car, consider your budget restrictions; the model, type, and size of the car required; and any mileage, insurance, or additional charges that may apply.

To Separate Independent Clauses

- A semicolon is used to separate independent clauses joined by a coordinating conjunction if one or both of the clauses are long or contain commas.

  Tomorrow afternoon, please use the Main Street entrance; but after 5:00 p.m., use the First Street entrance.

Colon

After a Salutation

- A **colon** should be used in business communications after salutations and memo headings.

  Dear Mr. Buffet: **To: Jeani Schultz**

To Indicate Time and Ratios

- A colon is used between the parts of a number indicating time and between numbers in a ratio.

  1:00 p.m.   6:30 p.m.   7:50 p.m.

  The ratio of managers to workers is 1:15.

To Introduce Explanatory Material

- A colon may be used to introduce a word or words that explain or summarize the main clause.

  There is no future in any job: The future lies in the person who holds the job.

As a Formal Introduction

- A colon may be used following an independent clause that introduces a formal statement, a question, or a quotation.

  Malcolm Forbes once offered this thought: "Failure is success if we learn from it."

To Introduce a List

- A colon is used to introduce a list.

  A good employee needs two things: a positive attitude and a willingness to learn.

Note: Don't use a colon to introduce a list if no summary words are used. (In the sentence below, the summary words *two things* have been deleted; no colon is needed.)

  A good employee needs a positive attitude and a willingness to learn.

* * * * * * * * * * * * If it ain't broke, don't fix it—

Hyphen

To Join Words in Compound Numbers

- A **hyphen** is used to join compound numbers from twenty-one to ninety-nine when they must be written out. A hyphen is also used when the numbers in a ratio are spelled out.

  twenty-one   **sixty-six**

  "There are some people who, in a fifty-fifty proposition, insist on getting the hyphen, too."

  —Laurence J. Peter

To Make a Compound Noun

- A hyphen can be used to create a compound noun.

  secretary-treasurer   **city-state**

To Join Letters and Words

- A hyphen is used to join a capital or lowercase letter to a noun or a participle.

  O-ring   **G-rated**   **x-axis**

  x-rayed   **L-shaped**   **A-frame**

Between Numbers in a Fraction

- A hyphen is used between the numerator and denominator of a fraction but not when one or both of those elements are already hyphenated.

  one-third   **seven-eighths**

  twenty-one thirty-seconds

When Words Have Common Elements

- A hyphen is used when two or more words have one or more common elements that are omitted in all but the last term.

  The new travel policy applies to lower-, mid-, and upper-level management.

To Make a Compound Adjective

- A hyphen can be used to join two or more words that form a single adjective (a single grammatical unit) before a noun. Do not hyphenate the words forming the adjective when they follow the noun.

  Only double-insulated wire should be used in this situation.

  Only wire that is double insulated should be used in this situation.

Note: Do not use a hyphen when the first of these words is an adverb ending in *ly* or when a letter or number ends the grammatical unit.

  freshly painted conference room
  (adverb ending in *ly*)

  grade A milk
  (the letter *A* is the final element)

Also Note: When such a group of words is used as a noun, it is usually not hyphenated.

  She usually takes a middle-of-the-road position. (adjective)

  He usually takes the middle of the road. (noun)

To Create New Words

- A hyphen is usually used to form new words after the prefixes *self, ex, all,* and *half.* Also, a hyphen is used to connect any prefix to a proper noun, a proper adjective, or the official name of an office. A hyphen is also used with the suffix *elect.*

  self-portrait   **all-inclusive**

  half-finished   **ex-employee**

  mid-August   **post-Vietnam**

  governor-elect

**unless you are a consultant. —William Rossiter * * * * * * * *

Hyphen (continued)

To Divide a Word at the End of a Line

- The hyphen is used to divide a word at the end of a line of print. A word may be divided only between syllables.

A Closer Look

DIVIDE:

1. Always divide a compound word between its basic units: *attorney-at-law,* not *at-tor-ney-at-law.*

2. When a vowel is a syllable by itself, divide the word after the vowel: *ori-gin,* not *or-igin.*

3. Divide at the prefix or suffix whenever possible: *bi-lateral,* not *bilat-eral.*

DO NOT DIVIDE:

1. Never divide a word so that it is difficult to recognize.

2. Never divide a one-syllable word: *filed, trains, rough.*

3. Avoid dividing a word of five letters or fewer: *final, today, radar.*

4. Never leave a single letter at the end of a line: *omit-ted,* not *o-mitted.*

5. Never divide contractions or abbreviations: *couldn't,* not *could-n't.*

6. Avoid dividing a number written as a figure: *42,300,000,* not *42,300-000.*

7. Avoid dividing the last word in a paragraph.

8. Avoid ending two consecutive lines with a hyphen.

Dash

For Emphasis

- Dashes are used to set off material (a word, phrase, or clause) for emphasis.

> **Before you have an argument with your boss, take a good look at both sides—her side and the outside.**

> **If they try to rush me, I always say, "I've only got one other speed—and it's slower."**
> —Glenn Ford

To Set Off an Introductory Series

- A dash is used to introduce a statement that explains or summarizes a series or list before it.

> **Widgets, carburetors, or bologna sandwiches—she could successfully market anything.**

To Set Off Explanations and Examples

- A dash may be used to set off examples, explanations, and definitions.

> **Three of the applicants—James Johnson, Shiere Melin, and Santana Garcia—have been called back for second interviews.**

> **The new network—which will be installed tomorrow—will allow us to link directly to our Chicago office.**

To Indicate Interrupted Speech

- A dash is used to show interrupted or faltering dialogue in reports of speeches or conversations.

> **"The—ah—fourth item on the agenda is not really—is actually no longer a concern."**

* * * * * Success seems to be largely a matter of hanging

Question Mark

In a Direct Question

- A **question mark** is used after a direct question.

    Have you had any experience with *Expedite*?

Note: A question mark is *not* used after an indirect question.

    I asked him if he had any experience with *Expedite*.

When Two Clauses Ask Questions

- When a question ends with a quotation that is also a question, only one question mark is used; it is placed inside the quotation marks.

    On a day off, do you ever wake up in a panic, asking, "Am I late for work?"

To Show Uncertainty

- A question mark is placed within parentheses to show that an item (e.g., a date or number) is uncertain.

    This August will be the 25th (?) anniversary of the fax machine.

In a Series of Questions

- A question mark is used after each question in a series of questions.

    When can we expect the order? Monday? Tuesday? Next week?

For a Parenthetical Question

- A question mark is used for a short question within parentheses or a question set off by dashes.

    You must check your company handbook (do you have one?) for the dress code and sick-leave policy.

Exclamation Point

To Express Strong Feeling

- An **exclamation point** is used to convey strong feeling and should be used sparingly.

    Service! Service! Service! These are the three laws of business.

Note: When an interjection is mild, a comma or period may be used.

    Yes, we just found out that we got the account with no strings attached.

With Quotation Marks

- When used with quotation marks, the exclamation mark goes outside, unless the quotation itself is an exclamation.

    Remember what she said: "Service!" You absolutely must read her latest article, "We Are Here to Serve"!

A Closer Look

Exclamation points show special emphasis. If you overuse them, they lose their effect. Also, avoid combining exclamation points and question marks.

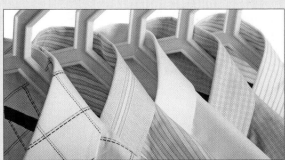

shutterstock.com

Quotation Marks

To Punctuate Titles

- **Quotation marks** are used to enclose titles of speeches, short stories, songs, poems, episodes of radio or television programs, chapters or sections of books, unpublished works, and articles found in magazines, journals, newspapers, or encyclopedias. (Also see page 268.)

  "Walk This Way" (song)

  "Over the Top" (short story)

  "Tricks of Trade" (magazine article)

  "Managing in the Dark" (chapter in a book)

  "Costo" (television episode)

  "Oh, My Aching Back" (encyclopedia article)

  "Ansett Blues" (poem)

  "Natural Gas Prices March Higher" (journal article)

Placement of Periods and Commas

- Periods and commas at the end of quoted material are always placed inside the quotation marks.

  "Double-check the hotel reservations, Dave," remarked Mr. Schmidt. "Our flight is going to be late."

Placement of Semicolons and Colons

- Semicolons and colons at the end of quoted material are always placed outside the quotation marks.

  I just read "Computers and Creativity"; the chapter talks about the role of computers in the arts.

Placement of Other Punctuation

- An exclamation point or a question mark is placed inside quotation marks when it is part of the quotation; it is placed outside when it is not part of the quotation.

  I almost laughed when he asked, "That won't be a problem, will it?"

  Did you hear Molly say, "Oh, no, sir"?

For Special Words

- Quotation marks also may be used (1) to show that a word is being referred to as the word itself; (2) to indicate that a word is jargon, slang, or a coined word; or (3) to indicate that a word is being used in a special sense.

  (1) What does the term "integrity" mean to you?

  (2) Oh man, that group is so "DOA"!

  (3) One person showed up for the "team" meeting.

Note: Italics may be used in place of quotation marks for special words. (See page 268.)

A Closer Look

  Do **not** use quotation marks as a way to emphasize key words.

  We offer "fast" and "friendly" service.

The quotation marks actually call into question whether the service is either fast or friendly.

---

* * * * * * * * * * * * * The difference between ordinary

Marking Quoted Material

1. Quotation marks are placed before and after the words in a direct quotation—a person's exact words—but are not used with indirect quotations.

   > **You may have heard Ms. Clark say that all supervisors should** *adopt* **the new report form. Actually, she said, "All supervisors should** *adapt* **the new report form for use in their departments."**

2. Quotation marks are placed before and after a quoted passage. Any word or punctuation mark that is not part of the original quotation must be placed inside brackets.

   > **(Original) All supervisors should adapt the new report form for use in their departments.**

   > **(Quotation) "All supervisors should adapt [not adopt] the new report form for use in their departments."**

Note: If only part of the original passage is quoted, make sure that the sentence is accurate and grammatically correct.

   > **Ms. Clark has directed all supervisors to "adapt the new report form for use in their departments."**

3. If more than one paragraph is quoted, quotation marks are placed before each paragraph and at the end of the last paragraph (Example A).

   Quotations that are more than four lines on a page are usually set off from the text by indenting 10 spaces from the left margin. Quotation marks are not used before or after the quoted material, unless they appear in the original passage (Example B).

   Example A   **Example B**

4. Single quotation marks are used to show a quotation within a quotation.

   > **Her exact words were "Bring your copy of the article 'Right for Business' to the afternoon work-shop."**

Italics

To Punctuate Titles

- **Italics** are used to indicate the titles of newspapers, magazines, journals, pamphlets, books, plays, films, radio and television programs, ballets, operas, lengthy musical compositions, cassettes, CD's, software programs, and legal cases, as well as the names of ships, trains, aircraft, and spacecraft. (Also see page 266.)

  Forbes (magazine)

  Our Town (play)

  It's a Wonderful Life (film)

  The First 20 Million Is Always the Hardest (book)

  Nova (television program)

  Washington Post (newspaper)

  Boston Business Journal (journal)

  Small Business Resource Guide (CD)

  Office Array (software program)

For Foreign Words and Phrases

- Italics are used for foreign words and phrases that have not been fully assimilated into the English language.

  All U.S. coins contain the phrase *e pluribus unum*. It means "out of many, one."

For a Word as a Word

- Italics (or quotation marks) are used to indicate that a word is being referred to as a word. (If the word is defined, the definition is placed in quotation marks.)

  In computer language, the term *cookie* means "a unique identifier used to track visitors on a Web site."

For Technical Words

- Italics (or quotation marks) are used to denote technical, scientific, or other specialized terms that may be unclear to most readers.

  Mail sent via the postal service is often referred to as *snail mail*.

Note: A technical term is italicized or set off by quotation marks only once; thereafter, it is set in regular type. For in-house reports or memos, technical terms that are commonly used within your company are not italicized.

Slash

To Form a Fraction

- A **slash** is used to separate the numerator from the denominator in a fraction.

  Lamar has been in this department only 2 1/2 months.

With Abbreviations

- The slash is sometimes used in abbreviations.

  c/o (in care of)   w/o (without)

To Express Alternatives and Two Functions

- The slash can be used in place of "or" to show alternatives; it can also be used to show two functions.

  his/her   either/or   and/or

  secretary/treasurer

  coach/general manager

* * * * * * * * * * * * * * * * * * * Where all think alike,

Parentheses

To Enclose References

- **Parentheses** are often used to enclose references to authors, titles, or pages.

  The latest numbers support our plan (see page 12) and show a need for expansion.

To Enclose Dates and Explanatory Material

- Parentheses are used to enclose dates or explanatory material that interrupts the normal sentence structure.

  The average worker works 128 days each year (from January 1 to May 7) to pay all federal, state, and local taxes.

  The Walk for Life event is set for early spring (Tuesday, March 12) and will be held at the Performing Arts Center.

Placement of Punctuation

- When a parenthetical sentence comes *after* the main sentence, capitalize and punctuate the parenthetical sentence the same way you would any other complete sentence.

  Depending on the meeting's purpose, you may want to use small groups. (Small groups promote discussion.)

  When adding a parenthetical sentence within another sentence, do not capitalize it or use a period inside the parentheses.

  The T-shaped setup (this can also accommodate small groups) is good for panel discussions.

Around Numerals in a Numbered List

- Parentheses are used to set off numerals or letters that introduce items in a list within a sentence.

  A good used car will have (1) low mileage, (2) new tires, and (3) a clean interior.

For Parentheses Within Parentheses

- For unavoidable parentheses within parentheses, use brackets.

  (. . . [. . .] . . .)

Brackets

Around Comments Added for Clarity

- **Brackets** are used before and after comments added to explain, clarify, or correct what another person has said or written.

  "They [20th Century Fox] said they had no interest in seeing a picture with the word 'star' in it."
  —Sidney Gains, on *Star Wars*

  "The funny thing is better [TV] shows don't cost that much more than lousy shows."
  —Warren Buffet

Note: The brackets point out that the words *20th Century Fox* and *TV* are not in the original quotations but were added for clarification.

Around the Word *sic*

- Brackets should be placed around the word *sic* (Latin for "thus" or "so") when it appears within a quoted passage. *Sic* indicates that an error was made by the original speaker or writer.

  "With this sales staff, your *[sic]* bound to succeed."

Apostrophe

In Place of Numbers or Letters

- An **apostrophe** is used to show that one or more numerals or letters have been left out of numbers or words that are spelled as they are actually spoken.

    class of '09 (*20* is left out)

    good mornin' (*g* is left out)

    they'll (*wi* is left out)

    I'm (*a* is left out)

To Form Plurals

- An apostrophe and *s* are used to form the plural of a letter, an abbreviation, a number, a sign, or a word referred to as a word.

    M's   8's   #'s   MD's   p's and q's

    This letter contains five *actually***'s and seven** *really***'s.**

Note: It is now acceptable to omit the apostrophe when forming the plurals of letters, numbers, and the like—as long as no confusion results (*CDs, Bs,* and *7s;* but *M's, i's,* and *U's*). Choose the best way to handle these plurals, following any preferences your company may have established—and be consistent.

Also Note: If the same word calls for two apostrophes, omit the second one.

    Please change the *can'ts* **[not** *can't's***] to** *can's.*

To Form Singular Possessives

- An apostrophe is used with a noun to show ownership. The possessive form of a singular noun is usually made by adding an apostrophe and *s.*

    Brent's résumé

    the office's main entrance

Note: When a singular noun of more than one syllable ends with an *s* or a *z* sound, the possessive may be formed by adding just an apostrophe. (If, however, the possessive form is pronounced with an extra syllable, it is acceptable to use an apostrophe and *s.* Choose the best way to form these possessives and be consistent.)

    Kansas' (or Kansas's) cornfields

    Dallas' (or Dallas's) skyline

    a waitress' (or waitress's) tips

Also Note: One-syllable nouns ending in an *s* or a *z* sound usually form the possessive by adding an apostrophe and *s.*

    Jones's work on Banks's portfolio

    the dress's length

To Show Joint Possession

- To indicate ownership shared by more than one noun, use the possessive form for only the last noun in the series.

    Yolanda, Sara, and Elana's project
    (All work together on one project.)

    Yolanda's, Sara's, and Elana's projects
    (Each works on her own project.)

* * * * * * * * * * * When you come to the end of your rope,

To Form Plural Possessives

- The possessive form of a plural noun ending in *s* or *es* is usually made by simply adding an apostrophe.

  the Smiths' family business

  bosses' assistants

Note: To punctuate correctly, keep in mind that the word immediately preceding the apostrophe is the "owner."

  coordinator's summary
  (*coordinator* is the owner)

  coordinators' summary
  (*coordinators* are the owners)

  class's instructor (*class* is the owner)

  classes' instructor (*classes* are the owners)

To Express Time or Amount

- An apostrophe and *s* are used with a singular noun that is part of an expression indicating time or amount. Use the apostrophe alone with a plural noun of this type.

  today's stock quotes   **two cents' worth**

  a year's experience

With Indefinite Pronouns

- The possessive form of an indefinite pronoun is made by adding an apostrophe and *s* to the pronoun. (See pages 305 and 306.)

  everyone's input   **anyone's guess**

  no one's fault

Note: In expressions using *else*, add the apostrophe and *s* after *else*.

  somebody else's turn

In Compound Nouns

- The possessive of a compound noun is made by placing the possessive ending after the last word.

  attorney-at-law's (singular) **advertisement**

  the attorneys-at-law's (plural) **advertisements**

  manager in training's (singular) **enthusiasm**

  the managers in training's (plural) **enthusiasm**

Note: It is usually a good idea to rephrase an awkward-sounding possessive.

  the advertisements of the attorneys-at-law

  the enthusiasm of the managers in training

With Descriptive Words

- Check a dictionary or your company's style book for descriptive words ending in *s*.

  traveler's check   **user's manual**

  writers club

With Names of Companies or Organizations

- The possessive of a company or organization name is formed by adding an apostrophe and *s*. If the name ends in an *s* or a *z* sound, it is acceptable to add only an apostrophe.

  The Bank of Madison's new building

  Siemens' (or Siemens's) employee benefit package

Note: If the last word in a company name is plural, simply add an apostrophe.

  Nolan Ventures' quarterly report

Apostrophe (continued)

With Stand-Alone Possessives

- Use an apostrophe with a possessive noun that appears without the word it modifies.

  The meeting will be at the Campbells'.

  This quarter's sales are running behind last quarter's.

In Holidays

- Most of the possessive holiday names are formed as if the names were singular nouns.

  Mother's Day   **New Year's Day**
  Valentine's Day

Note: There are a couple of exceptions to the rule.

  Presidents' Day   **April Fools' Day**

shutterstock.com

Punctuation Marks

´ (é)	Accent, acute	.....	Leaders
` (è)	Accent, grave	( )	Parentheses
'	Apostrophe	.	Period
*	Asterisk	?	Question mark
{ }	Braces	" "	Quotation marks (double)
[ ]	Brackets	' '	Quotation marks (single)
¸ (ç)	Cedilla	§	Section
^ (â)	Circumflex	;	Semicolon
:	Colon	/	Slash/Diagonal
,	Comma	~ (ñ)	Tilde
—	Dash	__	Underscore
¨ (ü)	Dieresis		
. . .	Ellipsis		
-	Hyphen		

* * * * * * * * * * * * * Nothing in life is to be feared;

24
Mechanics

The following information and examples will help you edit your writing with confidence. Use them to check capitalization, form plurals, use abbreviations, and improve your spelling. The chart on page 276 provides an overview of capitalization rules.

Capitalization

Proper Nouns and Proper Adjectives

- Capitalize all proper nouns and proper adjectives (adjectives formed from proper nouns).

> The owner, Lynn Taylor, would like to thank Rankin Technologies.

> I have a Cartesian philosophy: "I think, therefore I am . . . promoted."

First Words

- Capitalize the first word in a sentence and in a direct quotation.

> Advertising staffers gathered for the usual Monday meeting.

> Ms. Beggs began, "A lie may take care of the present, but it has no future."

Note: Also capitalize the first word of a saying, a slogan, a motto, or dialogue when it appears within a sentence. A question within another sentence may or may not be capitalized.

> Marsha believes the saying All's well that ends well.

> The first rule is, When in doubt, leave it out.

> My question is, How (or how) are we going to pay for this?

First Words in Lists

- Capitalize the first word in each item in a list typed in an outline style.

> Come to the meeting prepared to do the following:
> 1. Share your thoughts on the latest building plan.
> 2. Explain the changes to the original blueprint.
> 3. Provide an updated cost analysis and environmental impact statement.

Note: Do not capitalize the first words in such a list if all together the items compose a complete sentence.

> Come to the meeting prepared with the following:
> 1. a presentation of the latest building plan,
> 2. an explanation of the changes to the original blueprint, and
> 3. an updated cost analysis and environmental impact statement.

Salutation and Complimentary Closing

- Capitalize the first and all major words in the salutation of a letter, but only the first word in the complimentary closing.

> Dear Sherry,

> Dear Production Manager:

> Dear Sir or Madam:

> Best wishes,

> Sincerely yours,

it is only to be understood. —Marie Curie * * * * * * * * * *

First Words Enclosed in Parentheses

- Capitalize the first word in a sentence that is enclosed in parentheses, and does not appear within another sentence.

  Some writers were unsure of the product's worthiness. (Exaggerating seemed necessary.)

Note: *Do not* capitalize a sentence that is enclosed in parentheses and is located in the middle of another sentence.

  Pat and Meg both volunteered to do the copywriting (we were relieved), and they immediately began tossing ideas back and forth.

After a Colon

- Capitalize the first word in a complete sentence that follows a colon when that sentence is (1) a formal statement, (2) a quotation, or (3) a sentence you want to emphasize.

  It was Sydney Harris who said this about computers: "The real danger is not that computers will begin to think like people, but that people will begin to think like computers."

Organizations

- Capitalize the name of an organization or a team and its members.

  Toledo Mud Hens

  American Indian Movement

  Republican Party

  Business Products Association

Particular Sections of the Country

- Words that indicate sections of the country are proper nouns and should be capitalized; words that simply indicate direction are common nouns and should be lowercased.

  Many businesses are moving to the sunny South. (section of the country)

  Businesses move south to cut fuel costs and other expenses. (direction)

Abbreviations

- Capitalize abbreviations of titles and organizations. (A number of other abbreviations are also capitalized. See pages 281–283.)

FTC	BBB	P.A.	YWCA
SSA	OSHA	CEO	Dr.

Numerical Designations

- Nouns used with reference numbers or letters are often capitalized in business writing.

Flight 709	Model 312	Form 411
Appendix B	Chapter 6	Table A3

Letters Used to Indicate Form or Shape

- Capitalize the letters used to indicate form or shape.

B-pillar	A-frame	O-ring
T-bar	L-bracket	T-shirt

Note: Lowercase lesser divisions within such units.

page 3	paragraph 5	line 2

* * * * * * * * * * * * * * * You will do foolish things,

Words Used as Names

- Capitalize words like *dad, mother, aunt,* and *judge* when they are part of a title that includes a personal name, or when they are substituted for a proper noun (especially in direct address).

  Hi, Aunt Mae! (*Aunt* is part of the name.)

  My aunt is a doctor.

  The senator said his favorite legislator was Senator Hubert Humphrey.

  Please, Mom, stay for dinner.

A Closer Look

Here is a way to tell if a word is being substituted for a proper noun: read the sentence with a proper noun in place of the word. If the proper noun fits in the sentence, the word being tested should be capitalized. (*Note:* Generally the word is not capitalized if it follows a possessive noun or pronoun, such as *Tonya's, her, my.*)

  Did Dad (Alex) get the promotion? (*Alex* works in this sentence.)

  Did your dad (Alex) get the promotion? (*Alex* does not work here; also, the word *dad* follows the possessive *your.*)

Names for the Supreme Being

- Nouns that refer to the Supreme Being or the title of any holy book are capitalized.

God	**Jehovah**	**the Savior**
Allah	**Genesis**	**the Koran**

Titles

- Capitalize the first and last word of a title and every word in between with the following exceptions: articles (*a, an, the*), short prepositions, and coordinating conjunctions. This applies to titles of books, newspapers, periodicals, poems, plays, films, works of art, articles, and photographs.

  Write for Business

  Journal of Office Professionals

Formal Titles

- Capitalize the first letter of each major word of an employee's title when it precedes that person's name.

  Marketing Manager Diane Barnhart will give her report at today's meeting.

  The marketing manager will give her report at today's meeting.

Note: Also capitalize the formal names of entities within a company.

  Research and Development

  Human Resources

Titles of Specific Courses

- Words such as *history, business, science,* and *technology* are proper nouns when they are used in the titles of specific courses, but they are common nouns when they name a field of study.

  Professor Sajev teaches Global Business Ethics. (title of a specific course)

  Which professor teaches the biology course? (a field of study)

Note: Language classes and school subjects that are followed by a number should be capitalized.

  Ms. Ott teaches Spanish and Geography 101.

---

but do them with enthusiasm. —Sidonie Gabrielle Collete * * * *

Proper Nouns and Proper Adjectives

- Capitalize all proper nouns and all proper adjectives (adjectives formed from proper nouns). The chart below provides an overview of capitalization rules.

Capitalization at a Glance

Periods, events in history	Dark Ages, Great Depression
Special events	Vietnam War
Months	February, September, December
Days of the week	Wednesday, Thursday, Saturday
Holidays, holy days	Labor Day, Ash Wednesday, Kwanzaa
Political parties	Libertarian Party, Democratic Party
Government bodies	Congress, the House, the Senate
Official documents	Bill of Rights
Awards, honors	Academy Award, Nobel Prize
Corporations	Microsoft; Jackson Farms, Inc.
Trade names	Honda Civic, Krispy Kreme doughnut
Formal nicknames	Ivan the Terrible, the Big Three
Official titles	Senator Russ Feingold, Training Director John Thatch
Official state nicknames	the Keystone State, the Wolverine State

Geographical Names

Planets and other heavenly bodies	Mars, Earth, Big Dipper
Continents	Africa, North America
Sections of a country or the world	the Northwest, the Mideast
Countries	Peru, Congo, Malaysia
States, provinces	Idaho, Iowa, Manitoba
Cities, towns, villages	San Diego, Lyons, East Troy
Localities	the Loop, the Twin Cities
Streets, roads, highways	Sunset Boulevard, Highway 18, Pennsylvania Turnpike
Landforms	the Mojave Desert, the Alps
Bodies of water	the Chang and Huang rivers, Lake Superior, Hudson Bay
Public areas	Empire State Building, Denali National Park

* * * * * * * * * * To be a success in business, be daring,

Forming Plurals

Formed by Adding *s*

- The plurals of most nouns are formed by adding *s* to the singular.

  book—books

  pen—pens

Compound Nouns

- The plurals of compound nouns are usually formed by adding *s* or *es* to the important word in the compound.

  sisters-in-law   **attorneys-at-law**

  secretaries of state

Nouns Ending in *ch*, *s*, *sh*, *x*, and *z*

- The plurals of nouns ending in *ch*, *s*, *sh*, *x*, and *z* are made by adding *es* to the singular.

  business—businesses   **wish—wishes**

  fax—faxes

Nouns Ending in *y* Preceded by Consonants

- The plurals of common nouns ending in a *y* that's preceded by a consonant are formed by changing the *y* to *i* and adding *es*.

  phony—phonies

  balcony—balconies

Note: The plurals of proper nouns ending in *y* are formed by adding *s*

  the department has three Marys, two Randys, and four Bobbys

Nouns Ending in *y* Preceded by Vowels

- The plurals of nouns ending in a *y* that's preceded by a vowel are formed by adding only an *s*.

  key—keys   **bay—bays**

Nouns Ending in *o* Preceded by Vowels

- The plurals of nouns ending in an *o* that's preceded by a vowel are formed by adding only an *s*.

  cameo—cameos

  zoo—zoos

Nouns Ending in *o* Preceded by Consonants

- The plurals of most nouns ending in an *o* that's preceded by a consonant are formed by adding *es*.

  potato—potatoes

  embargo—embargoes

Exception: All musical terms ending in an *o* form plurals by adding only an *s*.

  soprano—sopranos   **duo—duos**

  piano—pianos

Other exceptions include *memos* and nouns ending in *o* that can form plurals by adding either *s* or *es*, such as *mementos/mementoes* and *cargos/cargoes*.

A Closer Look

A plural generic is capitalized when used before two or more names; it is usually lower-cased when used after two or more names.

  Lakes Michigan, Erie, and Huron

  Mounts Everest and McKinley

  the Nile and Euphrates rivers

be different, be first. —Henry Marchant * * * * * * * * * * * *

Symbols, Letters, Numbers, and Words Discussed as Words

- The plurals of symbols, letters, numbers, and words discussed as words are formed by adding an apostrophe and an *s*.

  Using &'s, @'s, and %'s in place of the words *and, at,* and *percent* will save room in this report. Don't forget to cross your *t*'s. And, avoid using too many *and*'s in your writing.

Note: It is permissible to omit the apostrophe when the omission does not cause confusion, but be consistent. Also, spelled-out numbers do not require an apostrophe.

  DVD's or DVDs   fives and sixes

Nouns Ending in *f* or *fe*

- The plurals of nouns ending in *f* or *fe* are formed in one of two ways: If the final *f* sound is still heard in the plural form of the word, add only an *s*; if the final *f* sound becomes a *v* sound, change the *f* to *ve* and add *s*.

  Plural ends with *f* sound:
  proof—proofs; safe—safes

  Plural ends with *v* sound:
  shelf—shelves; life—lives

  Plural ends with either sound:
  scarf—scarfs, scarves

Nouns Ending in *ful*

- The plurals of nouns ending with *ful* are formed by adding an *s*.

  four cupfuls   six pailfuls

Note: When referring to separate cups or pails full of something, use *four cups* full or *six pails full*.

Irregular Spelling

- Some English words, including many borrowed from Latin or Greek, form a plural by taking on an irregular spelling; others are now acceptable with the commonly used *s* or *es* ending.

  Foreign Words
  alumnus—alumni
  criterion—criteria (criterions)
  datum—data
  index—indexes
  phenomenon—phenomena (phenomenons)
  radius—radii (radiuses)

  English Words
  child—children
  mouse—mice
  foot—feet
  louse—lice
  tooth—teeth
  ox—oxen

shutterstock.com

* * * * * * * * * * * * * * * * * * Whoever cares to learn

Numbers

Writing Numbers

- Normally use words for numbers from one to nine and use numerals for numbers 10 and over.

  one   four   eight   12   530   2,113

Note: When several numbers appear in the same sentence, keep them in the same style.

> **Four vice presidents and twelve managers will conduct the sixteen meetings.**

> **The three tool attachments cost $1.85, $1.42, and $.59.** (For the sake of consistent style, use $.59, not 59¢.)

Addresses and Time

- Spell out the number *one* in addresses (One Elmbrook Blvd.). You may spell out even, half, and quarter hours in text, but do not use *a.m.* or *p.m.* in this case.

  quarter to four   nine o'clock tonight

  half past two   eleven thirty

Abbreviations and Symbols

- Use numerals with abbreviations and symbols.

  7° C   4 lbs.   3 oz.   2 tsp.

  12′6″   5 ft.   9%

Numbers in Different Forms

- Use numerals to express numbers in the following forms: money used with symbols ($ or ¢), decimals, percentages, chapters, pages, addresses, exact times, identification numbers, statistics, measurements used with abbreviations, and dates.

  Money . . . .$20.00 (but **twenty dollars**)

  Decimals 26.25

  Percentages . . . . .8 percent

  Chapters . . . . Chapter 7

  Pages . . . . pages 287–289

  Addresses . . . . .7100 Second Avenue

  Times . . . . 4:30 p.m., 8:00 this morning (but **eight o'clock**)

  Identification numbers . . . . .Serial No. 3126598

  Statistics . . . . .a vote of 23-4

  Measurements . . . . 24 mph, 2 tsp.

  Dates . . . . .44 B.C.E.; 79 C.E.; July 10, 1997 (domestic), 10 July 1997 (international)

will always find a teacher. —German Proverb * * * * * * * * * *

To Begin a Sentence

- Use words to express numbers when they begin a sentence.

  Twelve customers have complained so far.

Note: If this rule creates an awkward sentence, reword the sentence.

> *Clumsy:* **Seven hundred forty-two employees signed up for dental care last year.**

> *Better:* **Last year, 742 employees signed up for dental care.**

Before a Compound Modifier

- Unless they cannot be expressed in one or two words, use words for numbers that precede a compound modifier that includes another number.

  She sold twenty 35-millimeter cameras in one day.

  The prescription called for 120 25-milligram doses.

Note: You may use a combination of words and numerals for very large numbers.

6–8 million	**2 billion to 2.9 billion**
7 trillion	**$6–$8 trillion**

Hyphenating Numbers

- Hyphens are used to form compound modifiers indicating measurement. They are also used for inclusive numbers and fractions when written out.

  a 500-mile flight

  the fiscal year 2001–2002

  a two-thirds majority

  a three-hour drive

Dates

- In letters and most other business writing, dates are indicated by the month, day, and year with a comma separating the figures.

  June 15, 2002

  The military and most European companies use the day-month-year system with no commas.

  5 June 2002

Note: Using slashes between numbers in a date may cause confusion

  6/8/10 (This means August 6, 2010, in Europe; but June 8, 2010, in the U.S.)

Abbreviations

Acceptable Forms

- An abbreviation is the shortened form of a word or a phrase. In general, use abbreviations only in tables, graphs, charts—places where space must be conserved. The following abbreviations, however, are acceptable in any form of writing:

  Mr.   Ms.   Mrs.   Dr.   Jr.   a.m. (A.M.)

Note: In the body of a letter or a report, spell out the names of states, countries, months, days, or units of measure. Also spell out the words *Avenue, Street, Road, Company,* and similar words when they are part of a proper name. Use words rather than signs or symbols (&,%,#,@).

> **A Closer Look**
>
> If terms such as *Company* or *Corporation* are abbreviated in an official company name, use the abbreviated forms (*Co.* or *Corp.*) in your writing.

* * * * * As I grow older, I pay less attention to what people

Common Abbreviations

a.a.c. average annual cost
a.a.e. average annual earnings
abr. abridged; abridgment
acct. account; accountant
ACV actual cash value
addn. addition
addnl. additional
adm. administration; administrative
advt. advertisement
aff. affirmative
afft. affidavit
agcy. agency
agt. agent
a.k.a. also known as
A.M., a.m. before noon
amt. amount
ann. annual; annually
AP accounts payable
APR annual percentage rate
AR accounts receivable
ASAP as soon as possible
ASCII American Standard Code for Information Interchange
assn. association
asst. 1. assistant 2. assorted
attn. attention
atty. attorney
aux. auxiliary
avg., av. average
BBB Better Business Bureau
B.C.E. before the Common Era
biog. biographer; biographical; biography
BO back order

c. 1. circa (about) 2. cup(s)
CAD computer-aided design
cc carbon copies; copies
CDT, C.D.T. central daylight time
C.E. Common Era
CEO chief executive officer
CFO chief financial officer
chap. chapter
c.i.f. cost, insurance, and freight
ck. check
cm centimeter(s)
c/o care of
COD, c.o.d. collect on delivery
C of C Chamber of Commerce
COLA cost of living allowance
contd. continued
COO chief operating officer
co-op cooperative
Corp. Corporation
CPA certified public accountant
CPM cost per thousand
CST, C.S.T. central standard time
cu 1. cubic 2. cumulative
d/b/a, d.b.a. doing business as
dept. department
dev. development
disc. discount
doc. document
DST, D.S.T. daylight saving time
dup. duplicate
ea. each
ed. edition; editor
EDT, E.D.T. eastern daylight time
e.g. for example
EIN employer identification number

e.o.m. end of month
encl. enclosure
EST, E.S.T. eastern standard time
et al. and others
etc. and so forth
ex. example
exec. executive
FAQ frequently asked question
fin. finance; financial
F.O.B., f.o.b. free on board
FMV fair market value
ft. foot; feet
fwd. forward
FY fiscal year
FYI for your information
g gram(s)
gal. gallon(s)
gds. goods
GM general manager
GNP gross national product
govt. government
hdqrs. headquarters
hp horsepower
i.e. that is
illus. illustration
Inc. Incorporated
inst. institute
invt. inventory
IRA individual retirement account
IRS Internal Revenue Service
kc kilocycle(s)
kg kilogram(s)
km kilometer(s)
kw kilowatt(s)

say. I just watch what they do. —Dale Carnegie * * * * * * * *

Common Abbreviations

l liter(s)
lat. latitude
lb. pound(s)
l.c. lowercase
lg. large
L.L.C. limited liability company
long. longitude
Ltd., ltd. limited
m meter(s)
man. manual
Mc, mc megacycle(s)
mdse. merchandise
MDT, M.D.T. mountain daylight time
mfg. manufacturing
mgr. manager
mgt., mgmt. management
mi. 1.mile(s) 2.mill(s) (monetary unit)
misc. miscellaneous
mkt. market
mktg. marketing
ml milliliter(s)
mm millimeter(s)
mo. month(s)
mpg, m.p.g. miles per gallon
mph, m.p.h. miles per hour
MST, M.S.T. mountain standard time
mtg. meeting
N/A not available; not applicable
natl. national
neg. negative
N.S.F., n.s.f. not sufficient funds
num. number(s)

org. organization
orig. original
o.t., o/t overtime
oz, oz. ounce(s)
P & I principal and interest
P & L profit and loss
pat. patent
pct. percent
pd. paid
PDT, P.D.T. Pacific daylight time
P/E price or earnings
pg., p. page
pp. pages
PIN personal identification number
P.M., p.m. after noon
pmt. payment
PO purchase order
P.O. Post Office
POA power of attorney
POP point of purchase
ppd. 1. postpaid 2. prepaid
PR, P.R. public relations
p.s.i. pounds per square inch
PST, P.S.T. Pacific standard time
QA quality assurance
QTD quarter to date
qty. quantity
R&D research and development
recd. received
resp. respectively
retd. returned
ROI return on investment
r.p.m., rpm revolutions per minute
R.S.V.P., r.s.v.p. please reply

S&H shipping and handling
S&L savings and loan
sal. salary
SASE self-addressed stamped envelope
shpt. shipment
sm. small
SOP standard operating procedures
SRO, S.R.O. standing room only
SSN social security number
std. standard
syn. synonymous; synonym
tbs., tbsp. tablespoon(s)
TM trademark
tsp. teaspoon(s)
UHF, uhf ultra high frequency
v. 1. Physics: velocity
2. Electricity: voltage
3. volume
VA, V.A. Veterans Administration
VIP very important person
vol. 1. volume 2. volunteer
vp vice president
vs. versus
whse., whs. warehouse
whsle. wholesale
wkly. weekly
w/o without
wt. weight
yd. yard(s) (measurement)
yr. year(s)
YTD year to date

* * * * * * * * * * * * * * Not to know is bad; not to wish

Acronyms

- An acronym is a word formed from the first or first few letters of each word in a compound term. Periods are not used with acronyms.

  LAN—Local Area Network

  radar—radio detecting and ranging

  RICO—Racketeer Influenced and Corrupt Organizations (Act)

  scuba—self-contained underwater breathing apparatus

Initialisms

- An initialism is similar to an acronym except that the initials are pronounced as individual letters.

  FDA—Food and Drug Administration

  ICC—Interstate Commerce Commission

  SUV—Sport-Utility Vehicle

Note: Spell out the term the first time you use it, followed by its acronym or initialism in parentheses. Once the term has been identified in this way, you may use just the abbreviation.

Common Acronyms and Initialisms

AFL	American Federation of Labor	**MADD**	Mothers Against Drunk Driving
AIDS	acquired immunodeficiency syndrome	**NASA**	National Aeronautics and Space Administration
BBB	Better Business Bureau	**NATO**	North Atlantic Treaty Organization
CIA	Central Intelligence Agency	**NYSE**	New York Stock Exchange
CT	Computerized Tomography	**OEO**	Office of Economic Opportunity
CAT	Computerized Axial Tomography	**OEP**	Office of Emergency Preparedness
DOD	Department of Defense	**OPEC**	Organization of Petroleum Exporting Countries
EPA	Environmental Protection Agency		
FAA	Federal Aviation Administration	**OSHA**	Occupational Safety and Health Administration
FBI	Federal Bureau of Investigation		
FCC	Federal Communications Commission	**PAC**	political action committee
FDA	Food and Drug Administration	**PIN**	personal identification number
FDIC	Federal Deposit Insurance Corporation	**PSA**	public service announcement
FHA	Federal Housing Administration	**REA**	Rural Electrification Administration
FICA	Federal Insurance Contributions Act	**ROTC**	Reserve Officers' Training Corps
FmHA	Farmers Home Administration	**SEC**	Securities and Exchange Commission
FTC	Federal Trade Commission	**SSA**	Social Security Administration
GAO	General Accounting Office	**SWAT**	Special Weapons and Tactics
HUD	Housing and Urban Development	**VISTA**	Volunteers in Service to America
IRS	Internal Revenue Service		

to know is worse. —Nigerian Proverb * * * * * * * * * * * * *

Spelling Rules

i Before *e*

- Use *i* before *e* except after *c*, or when sounded like *a* as in *eighty* and *freight*.

  deceit   ceiling   belief   piece

Exceptions: This sentence can help you remember eight exceptions.

  Neither sheik dared leisurely seize either weird species of financiers.

Final Consonant

- If a single-syllable word (for example, *sad*) ends with a consonant *(d)* preceded by a single vowel *(a)*, double the final consonant before adding a suffix beginning with a vowel *(saddest)*.

  tap—tapping   plan—planner

  If a multisyllable word *(admit)* ends in a consonant *(t)* preceded by a single vowel *(i)*, the accent is on the last syllable *(ad-mit´)*, and the suffix begins with a vowel *(ed)*—the same rule holds true: double the final consonant *(admitted)*.

  occur—occurrence

  refer—referring

Silent *e*

- If a word ends with a silent *e*, keep the *e* when adding a suffix beginning with a consonant. Drop the *e* when adding a suffix beginning with a vowel.

  hope—hopeful—hoping

  care—careless—caring

  value—valueless—valuable

  love—lovelorn—lovable

Exceptions: courageous, noticeable, judgment

y as the Last Letter

- If a word ends in a *y* preceded by a consonant, change the *y* to *i* before adding any suffix, unless the suffix is *ing*.

  worry—worrisome—worrying

  study—studious—studying

  lazy—laziness

  try—tried—trying

- If a word ends in a *y* preceded by a vowel, form the plural by simply adding an *s*.

  key—keys   day—days

  play—plays

shutterstock.com

* * * * * * * * * A wise man will make more opportunity

25
Usage

This list contains words that are easily confused and thus misused. The definitions and examples will help clarify how these challenging words ought to be used in your writing.

a, an

- *A* is used before words beginning with a consonant sound; *an* is used before words beginning with a vowel sound.

  a hotel   an understanding
  a unified team   an honest mistake

accept, except

- The verb *accept* means "to receive" or "to believe." The preposition *except* means "other than"; the conjunction means "unless"; and the verb means "leave out."

  The supervisor accepted Lu's reason for being late for work.

  Everyone—except Lu and the supervisor—had remembered to switch to daylight savings time.

  Only in rare cases are employees excepted from the policy on punctuality.

adapt, adept, adopt

- *Adapt* means "to modify to make suitable"; *adopt* means "to take and treat as one's own" (as with a concept or a child). *Adept* is an adjective meaning "proficient or well trained."

  We adopted Business Plus accounting software. Now we need an adept accountant to adapt our bookkeeping system to the new software.

adverse, averse

- *Adverse* means "hostile, unfavorable, or harmful." *Averse* means "to have a definite feeling of distaste; disinclined."

  Adverse weather conditions grounded all airplanes.

  The tired staff was averse to the idea of working till midnight.

advice, advise

- *Advice* is a noun that means "recommendation or information"; *advise* is a verb meaning "to counsel or recommend."

  He advised me to value good advice.

affect, effect

- *Affect* is a verb that means "to influence." As a noun, *effect* means "the result"; as a verb, it means "to bring about."

  Your performance in the coming year will directly affect the amount of your bonus.

  The effect of the economy is hard to predict.

  The new procedure will effect significant savings in time and cost.

aid, aide

- As a verb, *aid* means "to help"; as a noun, *aid* means "the help given." *Aide* is a person who acts as an assistant.

  This book will aid anyone who wants to improve his or her writing.

  Mr. Young is an aide to the vice president.

than he finds. —Francis Bacon * * * * * * * * * * * * * * *

allot, alot, a lot

- *Allot* means "to assign a portion or piece." *Alot* is not a word; *a lot* (two words) is correct, but should be used sparingly—especially in formal writing.

allude, elude, refer

- *Allude* means "to indirectly refer to something," *elude* "to escape attention or understanding altogether," and *refer* "to directly call attention to something."

   Don't just allude to proper conduct; instead, refer specifically to required behavior. That way your expectations will not elude your staff.

allusion, illusion

- *Allusion* is an indirect reference; *illusion* is a false impression or image.

   Are you under the illusion that most people understand your allusions to the works of Aristotle?

already, all ready

- *Already* is an adverb meaning "before or by the specified time." *All ready* is an adjective form meaning "completely prepared." (Use *all ready* if you can substitute *ready* alone in the sentence.)

   The shipment already arrived this morning.

   The sales staff is all ready to take orders.

alright, all right

- *Alright* is an incorrect form of *all right*. (Please note that the following words are spelled correctly: *always, altogether, already, almost.*)

alter, altar

- *Alter* means "to change something"; *altar* is a table or raised area used in worship.

   The secretary altered the form of the company letterhead.

   The couple stood in front of the altar.

alternate, alternative

- *Alternate* is a noun meaning "something or someone that can be used or put in place of another"; it is also a verb meaning "to change back and forth between two things." An *alternative* is a choice derived from two or more possibilities.

   If I'm still sick, Mary can go to the meeting as my alternate.

   Earl and I alternate shifts.

   One alternative to a meeting is a conference call.

altogether, all together

- *Altogether* means "wholly, completely." *All together* means "in a group" or "all at once." (Use *all together* if you can substitute *together* alone in a sentence.)

   All together there are 5,000 jobs listed.

   That's altogether too many to consider.

among, between

- *Among* refers to groups of more than two persons or things; *between* refers to only two.

   Personal-leave days are listed among the benefits offered by this company.

   Communication between workers and management is candid.

* * * * * * * * * * Don't be irreplaceable. If you can't be

amount, number

- *Amount* refers to things in bulk or mass. *Number* refers to separate units that can be counted. (See also *fewer, less.*)

  The number of new workers hired next year will depend upon the amount of revenue raised by sales.

and, etc.

- Don't use *and* before *etc.* (See also *etc.*)

  Did you confirm prices, costs, profits, etc.?

annual, biannual, semiannual, biennial, perennial

- *Annual* means "occurring once every year." *Biannual* and *semiannual* mean "twice a year." *Biennial* means "every two years." *Perennial* means "throughout the year, every year."

anxious (about), eager (to)

- *Anxious* indicates that one is worrying; *eager,* that one is gladly anticipating something.

  Margarete is anxious about speaking in public, but she is eager to share her new findings with the research department.

any one (of), anyone

- *Any one* means "a singular thing or person from a group"; *anyone* is a pronoun meaning "any person."

  Choose any one of the proposed weekend schedules. Anyone wishing to work on Saturday instead of Sunday may do so.

any way, anyway, anyways

- *Any way* means "any route, method, or course of action"; *anyway* is an adverb meaning "in any case." (*Anyways* is an incorrect form of *anyway.*)

  Matt couldn't think of any way to change his schedule. I didn't really need a ride from him anyway.

appraise, apprise

- *Appraise* means "to estimate the worth of something." *Apprise* means "to inform."

  The man appraised the house at $150,000 and apprised the owners of its worth.

as, as if, like (See *like*.)

ascent, assent (to)

- *Ascent* refers to rising or advancement; *assent* refers to agreement.

  The ascent of Mt. Everest is treacherous.

  Because of your inexperience, I cannot assent to your going on the expedition.

assure, ensure, insure (See *insure*.)

augment, supplement

- Although both words mean "to add something," *augment* indicates a simple increase in size or degree, and *supplement* indicates making something that was deficient, complete.

  Flood warnings augmented the importance of the levee reports.

  This manual supplements the program we purchased last month.

replaced, you can't be promoted. —Anonymous * * * * * * * * * *

average, median

- The *average* and *median* of a series of numbers can be explained by this example: Seven workers used 0, 2, 3, 3, 5, 7, and 8 sick days respectively. The *average* number of sick days used is the total (28) divided by the number of workers (7): **4**. The *median*, or middle number in the series, is 3: 0, 2, 3, **3**, 5, 7, 8.

bad, badly

- *Bad* is an adjective and can be used after linking verbs.

  The **bad** day would not end.

  I feel **bad**, look **bad**, and smell **bad**.

  Badly is an adverb.

  He was driving **badly**, so I called the 800 number on the truck's bumper sticker.

base, bass

- *Base* is the lowest part or the foundation. *Bass* (when pronounced like *case*) is a low-pitched sound. *Bass* (when pronounced like *pass*) is a fish.

beside, besides

- *Beside* is a preposition that means "next to." *Besides* is an adverb that means "in addition to."

  Put the file cabinet **beside** the desk.

  Besides the new cabinet, we need better lighting.

between, among (See *among*.)

biannual, biennial (See *annual*.)

bring, take

- *Bring* refers to movement toward the writer or speaker; *take* refers to movement away from the writer or speaker.

  Please **bring** the new product data to the meeting, and remember to **take** the disks to Personnel beforehand.

by, bye, buy

- *By* is a preposition or an adverb. *Bye*, an interjection, is short for "good-bye." *Buy* is a verb meaning "to purchase."

  I cannot walk **by** a candy store without having an urge to **buy** some chocolate.

can, may

- *Can* implies ability; *may* indicates permission.

  "I **can** take your order" literally means "I am physically or mentally able to take the order."

  "**May** I take your order?" asks permission to take the order.

capital, capitol

- As a noun, *capital* refers to wealth (money or goods) or to a chief city. The adjective *capital* means "important, excellent, or serious." *Capitol* refers to a government building.

  Capitol buildings are generally in the center of **capital** cities.

  She grew used to making decisions of **capital** importance.

  Thought, not money, is the real business **capital**.

  —Harvey Firestone

  New investments contributed **capital** for the building fund.

* * * * * * * * * * The by-product is sometimes more valuable

censor, censure

- *Censor* means "to examine in order to delete anything objectionable." *Censure* means "to condemn or criticize."

   After the letter was censored, there was little left to read.

   The problematic open-campus policy was censured by the school board.

cent, sent, scent

- *Cent* is the value of a penny; *sent* is the past tense of the verb *send*; *scent* is a fragrance or a smell.

   The perfume company sent out 75-cent postcards to announce their new scent.

chair, chairperson

- The terms *chair* and *chairperson* refer to the presiding officer of a meeting or board. Use either term, but do not use *chairman* or *chairwoman;* the latter terms are sexually biased.

choose, chose

- *Choose* (chüz) means "to select"; *chose* (chōz) is the past tense of *choose.*

   After being warned to choose her words carefully, Fiona chose to remain silent.

chord, cord

- *Chord* means "the combination of three or more tones sounded at the same time," as with a guitar *chord*. It can also mean "an emotion or a feeling." A *cord* is a string, a rope, or a small electrical cable.

   The guitar player strummed the opening chord to the group's hit song, which struck a responsive chord with the audience.

   The worn electrical cord for my space heater should be replaced.

cite, sight, site (See *sight.*)

climactic, climatic

- *Climactic* refers to the climax, or high point, of an event; *climatic* refers to the climate or weather conditions.

   Because we are using the open-air amphitheater, climatic conditions in these foothills will just about guarantee the wind gusts we need for the climactic third act.

clothes, cloths, close

- The word *clothes* means "a covering or garments meant to be worn." *Cloths* are fabrics. As an adjective, *close* means "very near." As a verb, it means "to shut" or "bring to an end."

coarse, course

- *Coarse* is an adjective meaning "common, rough, or crude." The noun *course* can mean "a direction or route taken" or "a class on a certain subject." The verb *course* means "to move swiftly."

   Burlap is a very coarse fabric.

   The ship's captain mapped out a new course to avoid the hurricane.

   I'm taking an Internet course.

compare with, compare to

- Things of the same class are *compared with* each other; things of different classes are *compared to* each other.

   Compare your responses with mine.

   Ben compared his computer to a sloth.

Note: Compared to can also mean "in relation to."

   Roberta is Internet savvy compared to me.

than the product. —Havelock Ellis * * * * * * * * * * * * *

complement, compliment

- *Complement* means "to complete or go well with." *Compliment* means "to give praise." Both words can also be used as nouns. The adjective *complementary* means "serving to fill out or complete." *Complimentary* means "given free as a favor."

  "Some folks pay a compliment like they expect a receipt."
  —Frank McKinney Hubbard

  A fine grape jelly is a complement to any peanut butter.

comprehensible, comprehensive

- *Comprehensible* means "capable of being understood"; *comprehensive* means "covering a broad range, or inclusive."

  If the report is comprehensible to the laypeople, it's a great report.

  Comprehensive training sessions ensured the program's success.

comprise, compose

- *Comprise* means "to contain or consist of"; *compose* means "to create or form by bringing parts together."

  The research team comprises three Ph.D.'s and one high school student.

  The research team is composed of [not comprised of] three Ph.D.'s and one high school student.

concave, convex

- *Concave* refers to an object curved inward like the inner surface of a ball; *convex* refers to an object curved outward like the outer surface of a ball.

confidant, confident

- A *confidant* is someone you trust. *Confident* means "self-assured."

  Mr. Barker had no confidant with whom he could share his ideas.

  Confident of her talent, Sharon leapt at any chance to speak.

conscience, conscious

- A *conscience* gives one the capacity to know right from wrong. *Conscious* means "awake or alert, not sleeping or comatose."

  Your conscience will guide you.

  Mr. Kreutz needs two cups of coffee to be fully conscious at this hour.

consequently, subsequently

- *Consequently* means "as a result of"; *subsequently* means "following closely in time or order."

  We were late for the meeting; consequently, we missed the reading of the minutes.

  The general had retired to his study but was subsequently interrupted by a knock at the door.

consul (See *counsel*.)

continual, continuous

- *Continual* refers to something that happens at intervals over a long period; *continuous* refers to something that happens without stopping.

  The continual interruptions impaired her concentration.

  The company suffered a continuous slump that lasted for five months.

* * * * * * * * It is true, all of us are standing in the mud,

controller, comptroller

- *Controller* refers to someone who either controls air traffic or is the chief accountant in a business or an institution. *Comptroller* refers only to the latter position.

counsel, council, consul

- As a noun, *counsel* means "advice" or "a legal or professional adviser"; as a verb, *counsel* means "to advise." *Council* refers to a group that governs, administers, or advises. A *consul* is a government official appointed to a position in a foreign country.

  The consul appointed to Brazil counseled the trade minister there about our new tariff laws.

  The corporate counsel knew the pollution laws by heart.

  The building council offers counsel to dissatisfied tenants.

credible, creditable

- *Credible* refers to someone or something you can believe. *Creditable* means "deserving of commercial credit or limited praise."

  The auditor examined two credible reports.

  The bank believes Joy's Shoe Mart is a creditable business.

criteria, criterion

- *Criteria* is the plural form of *criterion*, a standard on which a judgment is made.

  The most important criterion in the pie judge's mind was taste.

  The exclusive club has a long list of membership criteria.

data, datum

- Informally, the term *data* often defines a single collection of facts.

  The data given in this report *is* interesting and very convincing. (Informal)

  In formal writing, if your emphasis is on the individual facts, *data* is used as the plural form of the singular *datum*.

  These data were collected during months of research. (Formal, scientific)

decent, descent, dissent

- *Decent* means "good." *Descent* is the process of going or stepping downward. *Dissent* means "disagreement."

  The plane's descent into the airport was quick and smooth.

  There is clear-cut dissent over which airline offers decent business service.

defective, deficient

- *Defective* means "faulty or imperfect"; *deficient* means "lacking something necessary" and indicates a shortage.

  The defective part caused the sudden engine failure.

  Our winter food stores were deficient.

device, devise

- *Device* is an invention for a particular purpose or a means to do something. *Devise* means "to form, plan, or arrange."

  That paint-mixing device no longer works.

  He was asked to devise a sales plan for the fourth quarter.

but some of us are looking at the stars. —Oscar Wilde * * * *

different from, different than

- Use *different from* in most cases; use *different than* when it is followed by a clause.

  His car is different from mine.

  The elevator smells different than it smelled yesterday.

disburse, disperse

- *Disburse* means "to pay out funds"; *disperse* means "to spread out or break up."

  The trustee is the only person who can disburse the inheritance.

  The riot police dispersed the crowd.

discreet, discrete

- *Discreet* means "showing good judgment, modest, unobtrusive"; *discrete* means "distinct, separate."

  The new office dress code mandated businesslike, discreet attire.

  Her advice to me was to keep my home life discrete from my career.

disinterested (See *uninterested*.)

- Both words mean "not interested." However, *disinterested* is also used to mean "unbiased."

effect, affect (See *affect*.)

elicit, illicit

- *Elicit* is a verb meaning "to bring out"; *illicit* is an adjective meaning "unlawful."

  The manager's confidence in the team seems to elicit strong morale.

  Illicit home use of shop equipment has been uncovered.

eminent, imminent, emanate

- *Eminent* means "prominent, conspicuous, or famous"; *imminent* means "ready or threatening to happen"; *emanate* is a verb that means "coming from a particular source."

  Several eminent CEO's will be flying in for the meeting. A merger of the companies is imminent.

envelop, envelope

- *Envelop* means "to cover or surround"; an *envelope* is a flat paper folder or case (usually for a letter).

  Fog envelops our seaside cottage each morning in summer.

  The letter arrived in a hot-pink envelope.

etc.

- *Etc.* is an abbreviation for *et cetera*, which means "and others" or "and so forth." Never use *and* before *etc.* (See also **and, etc.**)

example, sample

- The noun *example* means "prototype, or something that serves as a pattern"; the noun *sample* means a "representative item from a larger whole." As a verb, *sample* means "to take a sample of or from."

  Mr. Dorrit will compose a collection letter to be used as an example for the rest of the clerks.

  Before you purchase the pepper sausage, taste a sample.

except, accept (See *accept*.)

* * When ideas fail, words come in handy. —Johann von Goethe *

explicit, implicit

- *Explicit* means "expressed directly, or clearly defined"; *implicit* means "implied, or unstated."

  The directions were explicit and easy for us to follow.

  The implicit message in the boss's glance was understood by all.

fair, fare

- *Fair*, as an adjective, refers to a pleasing appearance; as a noun, it refers to a gathering for buying and selling goods. *Fare* is the charge levied for transportation.

farther, further

- *Farther* refers to physical distance; *further* means "to a greater degree or extent."

  When we investigated further, we discovered that they had traveled farther than initially thought.

female, woman

- Use *female* in scientific or legal materials; in most other contexts, *woman* is the more personal, acceptable term.

  The female subject received the placebo.

  Women of varying economic backgrounds have been polled.

fewer, less

- *Fewer* refers to a number of countable units; *less* refers to value, degree, or bulk quantity. (See also *amount, number*.)

  Despite fewer benefits and less pay, department morale rose.

first, firstly

- Both words are adverbs meaning "before another in time" or "in the first place." However, do not use *firstly*, which is stiff and unnatural sounding.

  Incorrect: **Firstly, I want to see the manager.**

  Correct: **First, I want to see the manager.**

  When enumerating, use the forms *first, second, third, next, last*—without the "ly."

fiscal, physical

- *Fiscal* means "related to financial matters"; *physical* means "related to material things."

  Physical health requires regular exercise; fiscal health requires careful budgeting.

for, fore, four

- *For* is a preposition meaning "because of," "directed to," or "in favor of." As an adjective, *fore* means "earlier" or "forward"; as a noun, it means "the front." *Four* is the number 4.

  For pity's sake, move to the fore of the boat before this thing capsizes and the four of us take a cold dip!

former, latter

- When speaking of two things, *former* refers to the first thing and *latter* to the second. (See also *later*.)

  Of the two speeches, the former was more polished, but the latter was more entertaining.

  Former means "from an earlier time"; *latter* means "closer to the end" or "recent."

  This latter decision was never even hinted at in their former correspondence.

* * Words are what hold society together. —Stuart Chase* * * *

good, well

- *Good* is an adjective, never an adverb. *Well* is nearly always an adverb; however, when used to indicate state of health, *well* is an adjective.

  Good work should be well rewarded.

  Please go home if you're not feeling well.

guarantee, guaranty

- A *guarantee* is an agreement or assurance that a product or a service will maintain a certain standard. A *guaranty* is an agreement that one will pay another's debt if that person fails to pay.

  The guarantee says I must be completely satisfied with this stove or I'll get my money back.

  My parents signed a guaranty when I got my first car loan.

healthful, healthy

- *Healthful* means "promoting good health"; *healthy* means "possessing good health."

  She has a healthy heart because of her healthful diet.

hear, here

- *Hear* is a verb meaning "to perceive by the ear." *Here* is an adverb meaning "of or in this place."

heard, herd

- *Heard* is the past tense of the verb "hear." As a noun, *herd* means a "group of animals"; as a verb, it means "to keep or move a group of animals."

  When we heard the thundering herd of cattle, we knew it was time to get out of the way.

hole, whole

- *Hole* is a noun meaning "an opening or a gap." As an adjective, *whole* means "complete or entire"; as a noun, it means "an entire or complete entity."

illicit, elicit (See *elicit*.)

illusion, allusion (See *allusion*.)

immigrate (to), emigrate (from)

- *Immigrate* means "to come into a new country to reside here." *Emigrate* means "to leave one country to live in another."

  Her family emigrated from Nigeria in 1987.

  Knowing English made it easy for her to immigrate to the United States.

imminent, eminent (See *eminent*.)

imply, infer

- *Imply* means "to suggest, hint, or communicate indirectly"; *infer* means "to deduce or conclude from." (Writers and speakers *imply*; readers and listeners *infer*.)

  I thought she was implying that I would receive a raise; apparently I inferred incorrectly.

insight, incite

- *Insight* is the ability to see the truth in a situation. *Incite* means "to provoke or encourage."

  The new employee's insight proved extremely helpful.

  Poor communication can incite distrust in a company.

* * * * * * * * * * A pessimist is a person who looks both ways

insure, ensure, assure

- *Insure* means "to secure from harm or loss"; *ensure* means "to make certain of something"; and *assure* means "to put someone's mind at rest."

  We assured Mr. Finn that the drilling would be painless; and to ensure that promise, the dentist used her strongest anesthetic.

  One more gold crown, and I'm going to insure this mouth.

interstate, intrastate

- *Interstate* means "connecting or existing between two or more states"; *intrastate* means "occurring or existing within a state."

irregardless, regardless

- *Irregardless* is the substandard form of *regardless*.

  Incorrect: **Irregardless of the weather, we will go.**

  Correct: **Regardless of the weather, we will go.**

it's, its

- *It's* is the contraction of "it is" or "it has." *Its* is the possessive form of "it."

  It's about time for another staff meeting.

  The medical clinic finally remodeled its outdated waiting room.

kind of, sort of

- These phrases are used informally to mean "somewhat" or "rather"; avoid using them in formal business communications.

  Unacceptable: **Sales have been kind of slow this quarter.**

  Acceptable: **Sales have been somewhat slow this quarter.**

knew, new

- *Knew* is the past tense of the verb "know." *New* means "recent, original, or fresh."

  We are wondering if he knew about the new logo before we did.

later, latter

- As an adverb, *later* means "after a period of time"; as an adjective, it is the comparative form of "late." *Latter* is a noun referring to the second of two things mentioned. (See also *former, latter*.)

  We can write the agenda later.

  This report was submitted later than that one.

  Of the two proposals just presented, the latter offers a more workable solution.

lay, lie

- *Lay* means "to put or place something." It is a transitive verb, which means it must be followed by a direct object. (See page 311.) Its principal parts are *lay, laid, laid.*

  Please do not lay that report there.

  Harley's assistant laid down the new carpeting yesterday.

  She had laid down the law about photocopies.

  Lie means "to rest or recline." It is an intransitive verb, which means it does not take a direct object. (See page 311.) Its principal parts are *lie, lay, lain.*

  George likes to lie down for a nap after lunch. He lay down Monday at 12:30, but often he has lain down by 12:15.

before crossing a one-way street. —Laurence J. Peter * * * * *

lead, led

- *Lead* (lēd) is the present tense of the verb meaning "to guide or direct." The past tense of the verb is *led* (lĕd). The adjective *lead* (lēd) means "first." The noun *lead* (lĕd) refers to a heavy metal or graphite.

lean, lien

- As a verb, *lean* means "to incline or bend." As an adjective, *lean* means "having little or no fat." A *lien* is a legal charge or hold on property.

learn, teach

- *Learn* means "to acquire knowledge"; *teach* means "to impart knowledge."

    Someone who learns easily may not possess the patience to teach others.

leave, let

- *Leave* means "to depart from" or "to let something remain behind." *Let* means "to permit or allow."

    Leave your work at the office. Don't let it ruin your weekend.

lend, borrow

- *Lend* means "to give or allow the use of temporarily"; *borrow* means "to obtain or receive for temporary use."

    At Thursday's meeting, Rob asked to borrow a copy of the new manual. Laura was happy to lend it.

less, fewer (See *fewer*.)

liable, libel, likely

- *Liable* means "responsible according to the law" or "exposed to an adverse action"; *libel* is a false or unfavorable written statement about someone; *likely* means "very probable" or "reliable."

    If you take the expressway, you will likely be late.

    Being entirely at fault, Graham was liable for the damages.

    Claiming the charges were untrue, Maria sued for libel.

like, as, as if

- In formal writing, use *as* or *as if* (conjunctions) to introduce clauses.

    Prepare the report as [not like] you were instructed.

    It looks as if [not like] we will need two more tickets.

    Use *like* (a preposition) to introduce a phrase.

    Your office looks like an oversized closet!

loose, loosen, lose, loss

- The adjective *loose* (lüs) means "unfastened or free." The verbs *loosen* and *loose* mean "to release." *Lose* (lüz) is a verb meaning "to misplace" or "to fail to keep control of." *Loss* (lôs) means "deprivation" or "the act of losing possession."

man, mankind

- Do not use the words *man* or *mankind* to mean "the human race" because the terms exclude women. Instead, use *humankind*, *humans*, or *humanity*. (Also see page 38.)

* * * * * * * * * * * * * * * * * * It's what you learn after

medal, metal

- *Medal* is a small metal award. *Metal* is a hard substance like silver or aluminum.

media, medium

- *Media* is the plural form of *medium*.

    The **media** are relentlessly exposing fraud.

    Radio has been an important news **medium** throughout the world.

miner, minor

- A *miner* is a person who digs for ore. As a noun, *minor* means "someone who is not yet legally an adult." As an adjective, *minor* means "of lesser importance or size."

    The **miners** were rescued from a shaft 300 feet underground.

    Try to solve **minor** problems before they become serious.

    A responsible **minor** has an excellent chance of becoming a responsible adult.

moral, morale

- *Moral* refers to what is right or wrong, or to the lesson a story or situation teaches. *Morale* is a person's attitude or mental condition.

    Human cloning raises a **moral** question.

    Office **morale** seems to peak on payday.

number, amount (See *amount*.)

OK, okay

- This expression (*OK* or *okay*) is used informally; however, avoid using it in formal correspondence of any kind.

oral, verbal

- *Oral* means "uttered with the mouth"; *verbal* means "relating to or consisting of words and the comprehension of words" and can refer to something oral or written.

    Writing a clear, interesting report requires strong **verbal** skills.

    Delivering the report from the podium takes **oral** skill.

partly, partially

- *Partially* is an adverb meaning "to some extent but not totally"; *partly* is an adverb meaning "in some but not all parts."

passed, past

- *Passed* (the past tense of the verb "to pass") means "went by" or "gone by." *Past* can be used as a noun ("time gone by"), an adjective ("preceding"), or a preposition ("after" or "beyond").

    The company **passed** last year's sales in early December. (verb)

    Clinging to policies of the **past** can be a detriment to the future. (noun)

    For the **past** two weeks I've entered data into our new computer system. (adjective)

    It takes steel determination to walk **past** that pastry cart. (preposition)

percent, percentage

- *Percent* means a "part of a hundred" and is used with a specific number. *Percentage* refers to a portion of the whole and is not used with a specific number.

    Maria saves 20 **percent** of her paycheck each week. That **percentage** was recommended by her accountant.

you know it all that counts. —John Wooden * * * * * * * * * *

personal, personnel

- *Personal* means "private" or "individual." *Personnel* are workers in a particular business or other organization.

  The Human Relations Department keeps a list of all the company's personnel. Some personal information, such as address, phone number, and social security number, is included in the list.

perspective, prospective

- *Perspective* is a person's mental vision or outlook on things; *prospective* is an adjective meaning "expected in or related to the future."

  From my perspective as a recent dorm dweller, your apartment is pure luxury.

  We interviewed five prospective copywriters today.

plain, plane

- As a noun, *plain* means "a large area of level land." As an adjective, it means "easily understood or seen" or "ordinary."

  "The rain in Spain stays mainly on the plain."
  —Alan Jay Lerner

  "There are no plain women on television."
  —Anna Ford

  As an adjective, *plane* means "flat, level, and even." As a noun, it means a "flat surface" or "a tool used to smooth the surface of wood"; it also can mean "airplane."

  The surface of the new desk was a plane; not even a marble would roll off.

  A plane must be sharpened frequently when used on hardwood.

pore, pour, poor

- As a noun, *pore* means "a minute opening"; as a verb, it means "to read intently." *Pour* is a verb meaning "to cause to flow in a stream." *Poor* means "lacking wealth" or "inferior."

  This new fabric is full of pores that let moisture escape.

  Pour yourself some more coffee.

  The poor morale was causing problems.

precede, proceed

- To *precede* means "to go or come before," while *proceed* means "to move on or go ahead."

  A memo that preceded today's meeting told us to proceed with stage two.

preventive, preventative

- These words are synonyms, but *preventive* is the preferred form, meaning "something that prevents or hinders a certain action or disease."

  Preventive measures were taken to avoid the takeover.

principal, principle

- As an adjective, *principal* means "primary or main." As a noun, it can mean "highest-ranking person" or "a sum of invested money." *Principle* is a noun meaning "a guiding doctrine" or "a scientific law."

  His principal gripe is boredom. (adjective)

  Most high school principals are concerned about much more than academics. (noun)

  The buyers made extra payments to more quickly lower the principal. (noun)

  The principle of *caveat emptor* is "let the buyer beware."

* * * * * * * * * * * * * * * * * Rudeness is the weak man's

quiet, quit, quite

- As an adjective, *quiet* means "free from noise"; it can also be a noun or a verb. *Quit* is a verb meaning "to stop" or "to leave." *Quite* is an adjective meaning "completely" or "to a considerable extent; rather."

    My office is quiet and quite comfortable.

    I'll miss it when I quit.

quote, quotation

- In formal writing, *quote* should be used as a verb; *quotation* is always a noun.

    The quotation used in your report was very effective, but in your next report, you should also quote what your foreman said to you.

real, very, really

- *Real* is usually used as an adjective meaning "authentic." Do not use it in place of the adverbs *very* or *really*.

    "Real life seems to have no plot."
    —Dame Ivy Compton-Burnett

    Raul's forecasts turned out to be very [not real] accurate.

    The controller was not really in control of that situation.

reason . . . is because, reason why

- Don't use either of these phrases, because they are redundant. The words *because* and *why* both repeat the idea of cause unnecessarily. Instead, use *reason . . . that* or simply *because*.

    The reason I'm late is that I missed the train.

    I'm late because I missed the train.

respectfully, respectively

- *Respectfully* means "showing a high regard for"; *respectively* means "each in the order mentioned."

    The young man respectfully shared his views with his father.

    Awards were given to Mira, John, and Roland respectively.

right, write, wright, rite

- As an adjective, *right* means "righteous, correct, or appropriate"; as a noun, it means "that which is just or legal." *Write* means "to inscribe or compose." A *wright* is someone who builds or repairs something. *Rite* is a ceremonial act.

    Write the memo again, but this time use the right form.

    Get the wheelwright to repair the spokes.

    The initiation rites need to be reviewed.

scene, seen

- *Scene* is a noun that means "a view," "a place where something happens," or "a spectacle." *Seen* is a form of the verb "see."

    Have you seen Hannah's office? It looks like the scene of a disaster.

seam, seem

- *Seam* (noun) is a line formed by joining two pieces. *Seem* (verb) means "to give the impression of being."

    The stuffing was coming out of the seams on her chair.

    You seem to be capable of handling this yourself.

imitation of strength. —Eric Hofer * * * * * * * * * * * * *

set, sit

- The verb *sit* means "to assume a seated position." The verb *set* means "to place or put down." *Set* is transitive (it must take a direct object); *sit* is intransitive (it does not take a direct object).

  Jay set the package on the scale.

  Please sit over there while I do this.

sight, cite, site

- As a noun, *sight* means "the ability to see" or "something seen"; as a verb, it means "to see something." *Cite* means "to quote," "to officially commend," or "to summon before a court." *Site* means "a place."

  Before they reached the construction site, they were cited for speeding.

  Carolyn had a tendency to cite Dickens when observing the sights of London.

sole, soul

- As an adjective, *sole* means "single, one and only"; as a noun, *sole* refers to the bottom surface of the foot or a shoe. *Soul* refers to the spiritual part of a person.

  The sole reason for the success of this paper is that it prints the truth.

  Certain experiences nourish the soul.

some, sum

- *Some* (adjective) refers to unspecified things or numbers. *Sum* means "the whole amount, the total."

  Some reporters are at the door.

  The sum is too high for our budget.

stationary, stationery

- *Stationary* is an adjective meaning "immobile"; *stationery* is a noun referring to writing materials used in letters.

subsequently (See *consequently*.)

tenant, tenet

- A *tenant* is one who rents or leases property from a landlord; a *tenet* is a principle, belief, or doctrine.

than, then

- *Than* (conjunction) indicates a comparison; *then* (usually an adverb) refers to time.

  Michael did not know any more about this than I did.

  First write your résumé; then look for a job.

their, there, they're

- *Their* is a possessive pronoun. As a pronoun, *there* is used to introduce a clause; as an adverb, it is used to indicate place. *They're* is the contraction for "they are."

  They're planning to leave immediately after their presentation.

  "If there isn't a law, there will be."

  —Harold Farber

threw, through

- *Threw* (verb) is the past tense of "throw." *Through* (preposition) means "in one side and out the other"; *through* (adjective) means "extending from one place to another."

  After Marcus threw the ball, he heard it crash through a window.

* * * * * * * * * * * * * The surest way to be late is to have

to, too, two

- *To* (preposition) indicates direction; it is also used to form an infinitive. *Too* (adverb) means "also," "very," or "excessively." *Two* is the number 2.

  The **two** friends headed **to** the cafeteria **to** eat lunch, which smelled **too** good **to** pass up.

toward, towards

- These words are synonyms, but *toward* is the preferred form, meaning "in the direction of" or "in relation to."

  Please point me **toward** the fitness center.

uninterested, disinterested

- Both words mean "not interested"; *disinterested*, however, is also used to mean "unbiased or impartial."

  A judge is never **uninterested** in the facts of the case but must hand down a **disinterested** decision.

vain, vane, vein

- *Vain* (adjective) can mean "valueless" or "fruitless" or "conceited." *In vain* means "to no avail." *Vane* (noun) is an instrument that shows which way the wind blows. *Vein* (noun) refers to a blood vessel or an ore deposit.

  The weather **vane** twirled about during the spring storm.

  A rich silver **vein** was discovered beneath the town.

  We searched in **vain** for the disks.

vary, very

- *Vary* is a verb meaning "to change"; *very* is an adverb meaning "to a high degree."

  When you **vary** the speed like that, you take a **very** great risk.

waist, waste

- *Waist* is the part of the body between the rib cage and the hips. As a verb, *waste* means "to use carelessly" or "to cause to lose energy." As a noun, *waste* refers to either a worthless by-product or an act of wasting.

  "**Waste** neither time nor money, but make the best use of both."
  —Benjamin Franklin

  One's **waist** size is largely a function of diet and exercise.

wait, weight

- *Wait* (verb) means "to remain somewhere expecting something or someone." As a noun, *wait* refers to the act of waiting. *Weight* is a noun referring to a measure of heaviness.

ware, wear, where

- *Ware* is a noun that refers to manufactured goods. As a verb, *wear* means "to have on one's person"; as a noun, it means "clothing." *Where* refers to location; it can be an adverb, a conjunction, or a noun.

  Where do you plan to sell your **wares**?

  I never know what I should **wear** on casual Fridays.

plenty of time. —Leo Kenney * * * * * * * * * * * * * * * *

waver, waiver

- *Waver* refers to faltering due to a lack of decision making; *waiver* is a conscious surrender of rights or privileges.

    When Ms. Stewart was asked to make a final decision, she wavered.

    Many ski resorts require skiers to sign a liability waiver.

way, weigh

- *Way* is a noun meaning "path or route"; avoid using it as an adverb meaning "to a great degree." *Weigh* means "to measure weight" or "to evaluate."

    After weighing the possibilities, Kenton decided to take the easy way out.

weather, whether

- *Weather* refers to the condition of the atmosphere. *Whether* refers to a possibility.

    "Everybody talks about the weather, but nobody does anything about it."
    —Mark Twain

    Tell me whether you agree or not.

who, which, that

- *Who* always refers to people. *Which* refers to nonliving objects or animals, never to people. *That* may refer to people, animals, or nonliving objects. In formal writing, use *that* to introduce restrictive (necessary) clauses and *which* to introduce nonrestrictive (unnecessary) clauses. (See page 260.)

    The Altina Fitness Center, which was built last year, is filled to capacity after work.

    The exercise and yoga classes that are offered there are especially popular.

who, whom

- *Who* is used as the subject of a clause; *whom* is used as the object of a verb (direct object) or of a preposition.

    To whom should I give this Internet proposal? Give it to Ms. Brown, who is in charge of information technology services.

who's, whose

- *Who's* is the contraction of "who is" or "who has." *Whose* is a possessive pronoun.

    Who's in charge of cleanup?

    "Whose life is it anyway?"
    —Brian Clark

wood, would

- *Wood* is a noun or an adjective referring to the material trees are made of; *would* is a form of the verb "will."

    I would not buy that wood to make the filing cabinets.

your, you're

- *Your* is a possessive pronoun showing ownership. *You're* is the contraction of "you are."

    "Your job is only as big as you are."
    —George C. Hubbs

    "You're never wrong to do the right thing."
    —Malcolm Forbes

* * * * * * * * * * * * * Sometimes you have to be silent

26
Grammar

To understand and use grammar correctly, you need to understand the eight parts of speech and the role each plays in a sentence. Knowing this can help you boost your writing skills.

Noun

A **noun** is a word that names something.

People: David Cameron, politician
Places: South Africa, nation
Things: *Working Woman,* magazine
Ideas: business ethics, value system

Classes of Nouns

Nouns are divided into five classes: *proper, common, concrete, abstract,* and *collective.*

Proper Noun

- A **proper noun** names a specific person, place, thing, or idea and is always capitalized.

Bill Gates	Ivory Coast
Willis Tower	World Federalism

Common Noun

- A **common noun** is a general name for a person, a place, a thing, or an idea and is lowercased.

entrepreneur	stock exchange
skyscraper	ideology

Concrete Noun

- A **concrete noun** names something tangible. It can be seen, touched, heard, smelled or tasted.

odor	desk	piano
Yosemite	Lake Erie	Alabama

Abstract Noun

- An **abstract noun** names something that cannot be seen, touched, heard, smelled, or tasted. It is usually an idea, a condition, or a feeling.

War on Poverty	democracy	Buddhism
freedom	success	happiness

Collective Noun

- A **collective noun** names a group or a unit. Collective nouns can be used in either the singular or the plural form. (See page 304.)

herd	Green Bay Packers	committee
staff	Human Resources Department	

Forms of Nouns

Nouns are grouped according to their *gender, case,* and *number.*

Gender of a Noun

- **Gender** of a noun indicates whether a noun is masculine, feminine, neuter, or indefinite. (Also see page 38.)

Masculine: father, nephew, buck, drake

Feminine: sister, niece, doe, hen

Neuter (without sex): rock, keyboard, lake

Indefinite (masculine or feminine): mayor, firefighter, deer

A Closer Look

The eight parts of speech are *noun, pronoun, verb, adjective, adverb, preposition, conjunction,* and *interjection.* See page 316.

---

to be heard. —Stanislaw J. Lec * * * * * * * * * * * * * *

Case of a Noun

Case tells how a noun functions in a sentence. Three cases of nouns are nominative, possessive, and objective.

- **Nominative** case describes a noun used as the subject of a clause.

  Bill Gates heads a multibillion-dollar software company that he founded.

  Nominative case also describes a noun when it is used as a *predicate noun* (or predicate nominative). A predicate noun follows a form of the *be* verb (for example, *is, are, was, were, been*) and repeats or renames the subject.

  Business handbooks are useful tools for every office.

- **Possessive case** describes a noun that shows possession or ownership.

  An employee's desk is a construction site.

Note: Be sure to follow the rules of punctuation when it comes to possessives, especially the placement of apostrophes in plural words or words expressing joint ownership. (See pages 270–271.)

- **Objective case** describes a noun used as a direct object, an indirect object, or an object of a preposition.

  The delete key can give writers nightmares.
  (*Nightmares* is the direct object of *can give*; *writers* is the indirect object.)

  But writing without a delete key is also scary.
  (*Delete key* is the object of the preposition, *without*.)

Number of a Noun

Number indicates whether a noun is singular or plural. (See pages 323 and 325.)

- A **singular noun** refers to one person, place, thing, or idea.

  supervisor   warehouse   monitor

- A **plural noun** refers to more than one person, place, thing, or idea.

  secretaries   closets   calculators

A Closer Look

When it comes to their number, some nouns are not what they appear to be. For example, *earnings* refers to a single thing, but it is actually a plural noun.

Our third-quarter earnings were better than expected.

Singular nouns that appear to be plural:

economics, news, mathematics, mumps, measles, lens, summons

Plural nouns that refer to a single thing:

assets, earnings, media, premises, proceeds, quarters, scissors, trousers, goods, grounds, thanks, dues

Nouns that can be **singular or plural** (depending upon how they are used):

corps, headquarters, gross, means, ethics, data, species, series, class, group, staff, company, committee, board, public

* * * * * * * * * * * * * Opportunity lies in the person,

Pronoun

A **pronoun** is a word used to emphasize or replace a noun.

I	you	she	it
that	myself	someone	who

Almost all pronouns have **antecedents**. An antecedent is the noun that the pronoun refers to or replaces.

> The workers acted as though they had forgotten the proper procedure.
> (*Workers* is the antecedent of *they*.)

Note: Each pronoun must agree with its antecedent in number (singular or plural), in person (first, second, or third), and in gender (masculine, feminine, or neuter). (See page 307.)

Classes of Pronouns

All pronouns fall into one of seven classes: *personal, relative, interrogative, demonstrative, indefinite, reflexive,* or *intensive.*

Personal Pronoun

- A **personal pronoun** (*I, you, he, she, it*) takes the place of a noun.

  > Rita Worth is a CEO; she likes to go fishing on her days off.

Relative Pronoun

- A **relative pronoun** (*who, whose, whom, which, that*) introduces a clause related to another word in the sentence.

  > The person who leaves last should lock the office door. (The clause beginning with *who* describes *person*.)

Interrogative Pronoun

- An **interrogative pronoun** (*who, whose, whom, which, what*) introduces a question.

  > Who will write the report?

Demonstrative Pronoun

- A **demonstrative pronoun** (*this, that, these, those*) points out something.

  > This is great! These are our best year-end numbers ever.

Indefinite Pronoun

- An **indefinite pronoun** (*all, another, any, anyone, anything, both, each, either, everyone, few, many, most, neither, none, no one, one, several, some*) refers to an unspecified person, thing, or group.

  > All are invited to the seminar.

Reflexive Pronoun

- A **reflexive pronoun** (*myself, yourself, himself*) refers to the subject or the doer of the action.

  > Letta drives herself too hard.

Intensive Pronoun

- An **intensive pronoun** is a reflexive pronoun (*myself, yourself, himself*) that is used only to emphasize the noun or pronoun it refers to.

  > The club members themselves voted yes on this proposition.

A Closer Look

See the chart on page 306 for a list of pronouns categorized to help you make better use of them in your writing.

not in the job. —Anonymous * * * * * * * * * * * * *

Classes of Pronouns

Personal

I, me, my, mine, we, us, our, ours, you, your, yours, they, them, their, theirs
he, him, his, she, her, hers, it, its

Relative

who, whose, whom, which, what, that, whoever, whatever, whomever

Interrogative

who, whose, whom, which, what, whoever, whatever, whomever

Demonstrative

this, that, these, those

Indefinite

all	anyone	each one	everything	much	no one	several	something
another	anything	either	few	neither	nothing	some	such
any	both	everybody	many	nobody	one	somebody	
anybody	each	everyone	most	none	other	someone	

Reflexive and Intensive

myself, himself, herself, itself, yourself, themselves, ourselves, yourselves

Forms of Pronouns

	Forms of Singular Pronouns			Forms of Plural Pronouns		
	Subjective Pronouns	**Possessive Pronouns**	**Objective Pronouns**	**Subjective Pronouns**	**Possessive Pronouns**	**Objective Pronouns**
First Person	I	my, mine	me	we	our, ours	us
Second Person	you	your, yours	you	you	your, yours	you
Third Person	he she it	his her, hers its	him her it	they	their, theirs	them

* * * * * * * * * * * * * * * * * * Whether you think you can

Forms of Personal Pronouns

The form of a personal pronoun indicates its *number* (singular or plural), its *person* (first, second, or third), its *case* (nominative, possessive, or objective), and its *gender* (masculine, feminine, or neuter).

Number of a Pronoun

- The **number** of a pronoun can be either singular or plural. Singular personal pronouns include *I*, *you*, *he*, *she*, *it*. Plural personal pronouns include *we*, *you*, *they*. Notice that the pronoun *you* can be singular or plural.

    Have you (singular) **completed the tax forms?**

    Looking at the applicants, he said, "I will contact each of you (plural) **within a week."**

Person of a Pronoun

- The **person** of a pronoun indicates whether that pronoun is speaking, is spoken to, or is spoken about. (See page 306.)

	Singular	Plural
First Person	I (am)	we (are)
Second Person	you (are)	you (are)
Third Person	he / she / it (is)	they (are)

A Closer Look

A pronoun must agree with its antecedent in both *number* and *person*. (See page 325.)

Nicole greeted the committee with her distinctive smile. (Both the pronoun *her* and its antecedent *Nicole* are singular third person.)

Case of a Pronoun

The **case** of a pronoun indicates how it is used in a sentence. There are three cases of personal pronouns: *nominative* (or *subjective*), *objective*, and *possessive*.

- **Nominative case** pronouns are used in two ways—as subjects and as subject complements (following the linking verbs *am*, *is*, *are*, *was*, *were*, *be*, *being*, *been*).

    I appreciate a pat on the back when I deserve it. (subjects)

    It was Adam's idea, so the real hero is he. (subject complement)

- **Objective case** pronouns are used in three ways—as direct objects, indirect objects, and objects of prepositions.

    Alex saw it. (direct object)

    Max handed her two cups. (indirect object)

    The manager talked with him. (object of a preposition)

Note: Do not use objective pronouns as subjects.

> *Incorrect:* **Maria and me arrived early.**
>
> *Correct:* **Maria and I arrived early.**

- **Possessive case** pronouns are used in one way—to show possession or ownership.

    Their parents have been business partners for years.

Gender of a Pronoun

- The gender of a pronoun can be masculine, feminine, or neuter.

    He told her about it.

---

or think you can't, you are right. —Henry Ford * * * * * * * * *

Verb

A **verb** expresses either action (*run, flip, twist*) or state of being (*is, are, seem*).

The different forms of a verb indicate its *number* (singular or plural); *person* (first, second, or third); *voice* (active or passive); and *tense* (present, past, future, present perfect, past perfect, or future perfect).

Number and Person of a Verb

Number indicates whether a verb is singular or plural. **Person** indicates whether the verb is correctly used with a first-, second-, or third-person subject.

	Singular	Plural
First Person	(I) **am.**	(We) **are.**
Second Person	(You) **are.**	(You) **are.**
Third Person	(She) **is.**	(They) **are.**

Voice of a Verb

Voice of a verb indicates whether the subject acts or is acted upon.

Active Voice

- **Active voice** means that the subject acts or does something.

  The partners **talked** all afternoon.

Passive Voice

- **Passive voice** means that the subject is acted upon. (Passive verbs always begin with a form of "be"— *am, are, is, was, were, be, being, been,* and so on)

  Many topics **were discussed.**

Tense of a Verb

The **tense** of a verb indicates when the action is taking place or when the condition exists.

Present Tense

- **Present tense** indicates action that is happening at the present time or that happens continually.

  More people **work** in the service industry than in any other industry.

Past Tense

- **Past tense** indicates action that was completed in the past.

  In the early twentieth century, heavy industry **employed** most of the workforce.

Note: Usually the past tense of a verb is formed by adding *ed;* however, many irregular verbs do not follow this pattern. (See page 310.)

Future Tense

- **Future tense** indicates action that will take place in the future.

  Many workers wonder if Social Security **will survive** baby-boomer retirees.

Fyi In most cases, using active voice instead of passive voice will make your writing more direct, lively, and engaging. Reserve passive voice for special types of writing. (See pages 35 and 122.)

* * * * * * * * * * * * * * * * There is no job so simple

Present Perfect Tense

- **Present perfect tense** indicates action that began in the past but continues in the present or is completed in the present.

    Lately, airlines **have struggled** with rising costs and fewer customers.

Past Perfect Tense

- **Past perfect tense** indicates a past action that began and was completed in the past.

    The investors **had expected** to see returns.

Future Perfect Tense

- **Future perfect tense** indicates action that will begin in and be completed by a specific time in the future.

    By the end of December, the company **will have been sold.**

Classes of Verbs

Verbs can be divided into these classes: *auxiliary* (or helping), *linking*, *transitive*, and *intransitive*.

Auxiliary Verbs

- **Auxiliary verbs** (*am, is, are, was, were*) help to form some of the tenses and the voice of the main verb.

    Forming tense:

    I **enjoy** skiing. (present tense verb)

    I **will enjoy** skiing. (future tense verb formed by adding the auxiliary verb will)

    Forming voice:

    The kids **devoured** your lasagna! (active voice verb)

    Your lasagna **was devoured** in no time! (passive voice verb formed by adding the auxiliary verb *was*)

Tense	Active Voice Singular	Active Voice Plural	Passive Voice Singular	Passive Voice Plural
Present	I see you see he/she/it sees	we see you see they see	I am seen you are seen he/she/it is seen	we are seen you are seen they are seen
Past	I saw you saw he saw	we saw you saw they saw	I was seen you were seen It was seen	we were seen you were seen they were seen
Future	I will see you will see he will see	we will see you will see they will see	I will be seen you will be seen it will be seen	we will be seen you will be seen they will be seen
Present Perfect	I have seen you have seen he has seen	we have seen you have seen they have seen	I have been seen you have been seen it has been seen	we have been seen you have been seen they have been seen
Past Perfect	I had seen you had seen he had seen	we had seen you had seen they had seen	I had been seen you had been seen it had been seen	we had been seen you had been seen they had been seen
Future Perfect	I will have seen you will have seen he will have seen	we will have seen you will have seen they will have seen	I will have been seen you will have been seen it will have been seen	we will have been seen you will have been seen they will have been seen

that it cannot be done wrong. —Perrussel's Law * * * * * * * * *

Common Irregular Verbs

Present Tense	Past Tense	Past Participle	Present Tense	Past Tense	Past Participle
am, be	was, were	been	know	knew	known
arise	arose	arisen	lay (put)	laid	laid
bear	bore	borne	lead	led	led
begin	began	begun	lend	lent	lent
bind	bound	bound	lie (deceive)	lied	lied
bite	bit	bitten, bit	lie (recline)	lay	lain
blow	blew	blown	light	lit, lighted	lit, lighted
break	broke	broken	mistake	mistook	mistaken
bring	brought	brought	prove	proved	proved, proven
build	built	built	ride	rode	ridden
burst	burst	burst	ring	rang	rung
catch	caught	caught	rise (get up)	rose	risen
choose	chose	chosen	run	ran	run
cling	clung	clung	see	saw	seen
come	came	come	seek	sought	sought
deal	dealt	dealt	set (place)	set	set
dive	dived, dove	dived	shake	shook	shaken
do	did	done	shine (emit light)	shone	shone
draw	drew	drawn	show	showed	shown
dream	dreamed	dreamed	shrink	shrank	shrunk
dream	dreamt	dreamt	sing	sang	sung
drink	drank	drunk	sink	sank	sunk
drive	drove	driven	sit	sat	sat
eat	ate	eaten	slay	slew	slain
fall	fell	fallen	speak	spoke	spoken
feed	fed	fed	spring	sprang	sprung
fight	fought	fought	steal	stole	stolen
find	found	found	strike	struck	struck, stricken
flee	fled	fled	swear	swore	sworn
fly	flew	flown	swim	swam	swum
forbid	forbade	forbidden	swing	swung	swung
forgive	forgave	forgiven	take	took	taken
freeze	froze	frozen	tear	tore	torn
give	gave	given	throw	threw	thrown
go	went	gone	wake	woke, waked	woken, waked
grow	grew	grown	wear	wore	worn
hang (execute)	hanged	hanged	weave	wove	woven
hang (suspend)	hung	hung	wring	wrung	wrung
hide	hid	hidden	write	wrote	written

* * * * * * * * * * * * * * * * * * Forget the past; no one

Linking Verbs

- A **linking verb** is a special type of intransitive verb that links a subject to its complement—a noun, a pronoun, or an adjective in the predicate of a sentence.

  Poorly organized reports are not very helpful. (The subject *reports* is linked to the predicate adjective *helpful*.)

  Incorrect: **This is her.** (A linking verb cannot connect the objective pronoun *her* to the subjective pronoun *this*.)

  Correct: **This is she.** (A linking verb can connect the subjective pronoun *she* to the subjective pronoun *this*.)

  Common Linking Verbs: am, is, are, was, were, be, being, been, smell, look, seem, grow, become, appear, sound, taste, feel, remain

Transitive Verbs

- A **transitive verb** indicates action transferred to an object (or, in the passive voice, the subject). In the active voice, a transitive verb transfers its action to a direct object.

  Many people enjoy their jobs. (*Jobs* is the direct object of the verb *enjoy*.)

  A transitive verb may also have an indirect object, which receives the action indirectly.

  Samantha gave Matthew a reassuring glance. (*Glance* is the direct object of the verb *gave*, and *Matthew* is the indirect object.)

  In the passive voice, a transitive verb transfers the action to the subject of the sentence.

  An attempt to fix the copier was made by the receptionist. (The subject *attempt* receives the action of the verb *was made*.)

Intransitive Verbs

- An **intransitive verb** indicates action that is not transferred to anyone or anything. This verb does not need a direct object.

  The worst public speakers mumble and dawdle.

Special Verb Forms

A **verbal** is derived from a verb but functions as a noun, an adjective, or an adverb. There are three types of verbals: *gerunds, infinitives,* and *participles.* (See page 319 for information on verbal phrases.)

Gerunds

- A **gerund** ends in *ing* and is used as a noun.

  Arriving at work on time is important. (subject)

  Another key to success is accomplishing your tasks. (predicate noun)

Infinitives

- An **infinitive** is usually introduced by the word "to" and can be used as a noun, an adjective, or an adverb.

  To write well is not always easy. (noun)

  This is an important point to remember. (adjective)

  Writers are wise to practice their writing often. (adverb)

Participles

- A **participle** ends in *ing* or *ed* and is used as an adjective.

  That employee making clay models is very creative. The completed models will be on display in the coming weeks. (*Making* modifies *employee*; *completed* modifies *models*.)

becomes successful in the past. —Josh Billings * * * * * * * * *

Adjective

An **adjective** is a word that describes, limits, or in any other way modifies a noun or a pronoun. (The articles *a, an,* and *the* are adjectives.)

Adjectives can appear in different positions. They often come before the words they modify; but as predicate adjectives, they come after the words they modify.

> **The beautiful day ended with Marcia in tears. She was overjoyed.** (*The* and *beautiful* modify the noun *day; overjoyed* is a predicate adjective and modifies the pronoun *she.*)

Common and Proper Adjectives

- Like nouns, adjectives can be **common** (lower-cased) or **proper** (capitalized).

> **The professors at Oxford University agreed that Americanized English was unusual.**

Note: Since *Americanized* is derived from the proper noun *America,* it is considered a proper adjective and is always capitalized. *The* and *unusual* are common adjectives; *the* is capitalized only because it is the first word of the sentence.

A Closer Look

Don't add adjectives to nouns that don't need them. The adjectives listed below are unnecessary and only repeat what the noun already says.

> **basic necessities, end result, exact replica, final outcome, foreign imports, free gift, joint cooperation, mutual cooperation, past history, sum total**

Forms of Adjectives

Adjectives have three forms: *positive, comparative,* and *superlative.*

Positive

- The **positive form** describes without making any comparisons.

> **Good employees are important assets.**

Comparative

- The **comparative form** (*-er, more,* or *less*) compares two persons, places, things, or ideas.

> **Good employees are a more important asset than good buildings.**

Superlative

- The **superlative form** (*-est, most,* or *least*) compares three or more persons, places, things, or ideas.

> **Good employees are the most important asset a business can possess.**

Note: Most one-syllable and some two-syllable adjectives take the *er* and *est* endings. Most two-syllable and most three-syllable adjectives use *more* and *most* (and *less* and *least*).

Positive	Comparative	Superlative
good	better	best
bad	worse	worst
cold	colder	coldest
crabby	crabbier	crabbiest
impressive	more impressive	most impressive

* * * * * * * * * * * * * * * Many people quit looking for

Adverb

An **adverb** is a word that modifies a verb (or verbal), an adjective, or another adverb. Adverbs tell *how, when, where, why, how often,* or *how much.* (*Not* and *never* are adverbs.)

> **The business was sold quickly.** (*Quickly* modifies the verb *was sold.*)

> **The staff was extremely concerned.** (*Extremely* modifies the adjective *concerned.*)

> **Management moved very quickly to reassign employees.** (*Very* modifies the adverb *quickly,* which modifies the verb *moved.*)

Note: Most adverbs have an *ly* ending. Some adverbs can be written either with or without an *ly*; when in doubt, use the *ly* form.

> **deep, deeply; tight, tightly; loud, loudly**

A Closer Look

Adverbs can be placed in different positions in a sentence. Usually, they appear in front of the words they modify, but they can correctly follow the words as well. *Caution:* Adverbs should not be placed between a verb and its direct object.

> **The secretary carefully prepared the report.** (adverb before the verb)

> **The secretary prepared the report carefully.** (adverb after the verb and its direct object)

> **If the problem isn't addressed, these customers will definitely leave.** (adverb between verbs)

Forms of Adverbs

Adverbs have three forms: *positive, comparative,* and *superlative.*

Positive

- The **positive form** describes an action without making any comparisons.

  > **This copier operates efficiently.**

Comparative

- The **comparative form** (*-er, more,* or *less*) compares the actions of two persons, places, things, or ideas.

  > **This copier operates more efficiently than the one downstairs.**

Superlative

- The **superlative form** (*-est, most,* or *least*) compares the actions of three or more persons, places, things, or ideas.

  > **This copier operates most efficiently of all the copiers in the building.**

Special Adverb Form

Conjunctive Adverbs

- A **conjunctive adverb** can both modify and connect words, phrases, and clauses. It can be used at the beginning, in the middle, or at the end of a sentence.

  > **Consequently, we believe the profit/earnings ratio will not meet our expectations. We do wish, however, to evaluate your stock again in six months. We will buy another stock instead.**

work when they find a job. —Steven Wright * * * * * * * * * * *

Preposition

A **preposition** is a word (or word group) used in front of a noun or a pronoun to form a phrase that modifies some other word in the sentence.

The paperwork has been piled onto the file cabinet. (The preposition *onto* begins a phrase that acts as an adverb modifying the verb *has been piled*.)

Prepositional Phrase

- A **prepositional phrase** consists of a preposition, the object of that preposition, and the modifiers of the object.

  The flowers on the luncheon table are wilted. (preposition *on*, object *table*, and modifiers *the* and *luncheon*)

Common Prepositions

aboard	back of	excepting	notwithstanding	since
about	because of	for	of	subsequent to
above	before	from	off	together with
according to	behind	from among	on	through
across	below	from between	on account of	throughout
across from	beneath	from under	on behalf of	till
after	beside	in	onto	to
against	besides	in addition to	on top of	toward
ahead of	between	in back of	opposite	under
along	beyond	in behalf of	out	underneath
alongside	by	in case of	out of	unlike
alongside of	by means of	in front of	outside	until
along with	concerning	in place of	outside of	unto
amid	considering	in regard to	over	up
among	contrary to	inside	over to	upon
apart from	despite	inside of	owing to	up to
around	down	in spite of	past	via
as	down from	instead of	prior to	with
as for	due to	into	regarding	within
aside from	during	like	round	without
at	except	near	round about	
away from	except for	near to	save	

* * * * * * * * * * * * * * Everyone is ignorant, only on

Conjunction

A **conjunction** is the part of speech used to connect words, phrases, clauses, or sentences. Used properly, conjunctions can add continuity to your writing.

Kinds of Conjunctions

Subordinating Conjunctions

- **Subordinating conjunctions** connect a dependent clause to an independent clause, completing the meaning of the dependent clause.

   If the trailer is still here tomorrow, it will be impounded. (The dependent clause *if the trailer is still here tomorrow* depends on the rest of the sentence to complete its meaning.)

Correlative Conjunctions

- **Correlative conjunctions** are always used in pairs, linking items of equal weight.

   She decided to neither buy nor lease a new car.

Coordinating Conjunctions

- **Coordinating conjunctions** connect grammatically equivalent elements, that is, a word to a word, a phrase to a phrase, or a clause to a clause. The coordinating conjunctions are *and, but, or, nor, for, so,* and *yet.*

   "It's not the most intellectual job in the world, but I do have to know the letters."
   —Vanna White

Interjection

- An **interjection** is a word or phrase that expresses strong emotion or surprise. Punctuation (usually a comma or an exclamation point) sets off an interjection from the rest of the sentence.

   Help! The elevator is stuck!

   Oh my, that happens often.

Caution: Use strong interjections sparingly. Like shouting, they can distract from rather than enhance your message.

Kinds of Conjunctions

Coordinating

and, but, or, nor, for, so, yet

Correlative

either, or; neither, nor; not only, but also; both, and; whether, or; though, yet

Subordinating

after	as long as	before	provided that	that	unless	where
although	as though	if	since	though	until	whereas
as	because	in order that	so that	till	when	while

---

different subjects. —Will Rogers * * * * * * * * * * * * *

Parts of Speech

1. A **noun** is a word that names something: a person, a place, a thing, or an idea.

   David Cameron/prime minister   South Africa/country
   Working Woman/magazine   World Federalism/ideology

2. A **pronoun** is a word used in place of a noun.

I	you	she	it	which	themselves
me	that	he	they	whoever	whatever
my	mine	ours			

3. A **verb** is a word that expresses action or state of being.

fight	walk	drive	rip	dive	jump
play	write	lift	type	call	work
is	are	was	were		

4. An **adjective** describes or modifies a noun or pronoun. (The articles *a, an,* and *the* are adjectives.)

good	bad	tall	wide	clear	fast

5. An **adverb** modifies a verb, an adjective, or another adverb. An adverb tells *how, when, where, why, how often,* or *how much.* (*Not* and *never* are adverbs.)

tomorrow	near	far	perfectly	well	completely
surely	regularly	greatly	partly	slowly	quickly

6. A **preposition** is a word (or group of words) used in front of a noun or a pronoun to form a phrase that modifies some other word in the sentence.

above	across	after	with	by	for
from	in	of	off	on	out
over	through	to	until	up	away from

7. A **conjunction** connects individual words or groups of words.

and	but	or	nor	for	yet
so	because	when	though	whereas	while

8. An **interjection** expresses strong emotion or surprise.

Help!	Yikes!	Wow!

* * You can observe a lot just by watching. —Yogi Berra * * *

27
Sentences

The Sentence

A **sentence** is one or more words that express a complete thought.

> "Chop your wood, and it will warm you twice."
> —Henry Ford, Sr.

Subject and Predicate

- A sentence must have a subject and a predicate. The **subject** tells who or what the sentence is about. The **predicate**, which contains the verb, tells or asks something about the subject.

> "The Edsel is here to stay."
> —Henry Ford II

Note: In the sentence above, *Edsel* is the subject—the sentence talks about the Edsel. *Is here to stay* is the predicate—it says something about the subject.

Understood Subject and Predicate

- Either the subject or the predicate or both may be "absent" from a sentence in informal writing; however, both must be clearly understood.

> "What seems to be wrong?"
> (*What* is the subject; *seems to be wrong* is the predicate.)

> "Everything."
> (*Everything* is the subject; the predicate *is wrong* is understood.)

> "Be more specific."
> (The subject *you* is understood; *be more specific* is the predicate.)

The Subject

The **subject** is a word, phrase, or clause that tells *who* or *what* the sentence is about. It can be a noun, a pronoun, an infinitive, an infinitive phrase, a gerund, a gerund phrase, or a noun clause.

> **Technology has changed the way business is done.** (noun)

> **I can get that for you wholesale.** (pronoun)

> **To cut costs has been her primary goal.** (infinitive phrase)

> **Finding that document will be difficult.** (gerund phrase)

> **When your samples arrive is the time to begin calling.** (noun clause)

Simple Subject

- A **simple subject** is the subject without the words that modify it.

> "The greatest **test** of courage on earth is to bear defeat without losing courage."
> —Robert G. Intersoll

Complete Subject

- A **complete subject** is the simple subject and all the words that modify it.

> "**The greatest test of courage on earth** is to bear defeat without losing courage."
> —Robert G. Intersoll

Compound Subject

- A **compound subject** has two or more simple subjects.

> **Decisiveness and determination are key ingredients to any successful venture.**

* * * * * If there is no wind, row. —Latin proverb * * * * * *

The Predicate

A **predicate** is the sentence part that tells or asks something about the subject; it always contains a verb.

> **"Good management consists in showing average people how to do the work of superior people."**
> —John D. Rockefeller, Sr.

Simple Predicate

- A **simple predicate** is the verb without the words that modify it.

> **"Those who give too much attention to trifling things become generally incapable of great ones."**
> —Francois, Duke of Rochefoucauld

Complete Predicate

- A **complete predicate** is the simple predicate (the verb) and all the words that modify it.

> **"Those who give too much attention to trifling things become generally incapable of great ones."**
> —Francois, Duke of Rochefoucauld

Compound Predicate

- A **compound predicate** consists of two or more simple predicates.

> **Jackie added the figures in both columns and surprised us with the astonishing total.**

Direct Object

- A direct object receives the action of the verb. It's a noun or a noun substitute that answers *what* or *whom* after a verb. (See page 304.)

> **Please prepare the income statements.**

Using Phrases

A **phrase** is a group of related words that lacks a subject, a predicate, or both. It functions as a single part of speech but does not express a complete thought.

> **will be running** (verb phrase; no subject)
>
> **in the race** (prepositional phrase; no subject or predicate)
>
> **Marie will be running in the race.** (These two phrases plus a subject make a sentence.)

Types of Phrases

There are six types of phrases: *noun, appositive, verb, prepositional, absolute,* and *verbal.*

Noun Phrase

- A **noun phrase** includes a noun or pronoun plus all related modifiers. It can function as a subject, an object, a complement, or an appositive.

Appositive Phrase

- An **appositive phrase** follows a noun or a pronoun and identifies or explains it; it includes a noun and its modifiers.

> **Denzel, the director of our art department, has been with the company for ten years.**

Verb Phrase

- A **verb phrase** includes a main verb and the preceding helping verb or verbs.

> **Money orders are being issued at the bank and the post office.**

* * * * * * * * * If people listened to themselves more often,

Prepositional Phrase

- A **prepositional phrase** includes a preposition, its object, and any modifiers of the object. It functions as an adjective or an adverb.

  Worthwhile projects are only accomplished with hard work.
  (The prepositional phrase is used as an adverb modifying the verb *are accomplished*.)

  Luck is not a main ingredient in the recipe for success.
  (The prepositional phrase *in the recipe* is used as an adjective modifying the noun *ingredient*; the phrase *for success* is used as an adjective modifying the noun *recipe*.)

Absolute Phrase

- An **absolute phrase** includes a noun or a pronoun and a participle, as well as any modifiers (including any object of the participle).

  His voice rising above the noise, the manager encouraged his team.
  (The noun *voice* is modified by *rising*, a present participle. The entire absolute phrase modifies *manager*.)

Verbal Phrases:
Gerund, Infinitive, Participial

- A **gerund phrase** is a verbal phrase that includes a gerund and its modifiers. It functions as a noun.

  Making rubber tires was once a hot, exhausting job. (The gerund phrase acts as the subject.)

  Workers grew weary of sweating through their shifts. (The gerund phrase is the object of the preposition *of*.)

- An **infinitive phrase** includes an infinitive and its modifiers. It functions as a noun, an adjective, or an adverb.

  To walk outside was a welcomed break.
  (Acting as a noun, this infinitive phrase is the subject of the sentence.)

  After the holiday rush, we wanted some time to relax. (Acting as an adjective, this phrase modifies the noun *time*.)

  He rubbed a rough hand through his bristly white hair to jog his memory. (Acting as an adverb, this phrase modifies *rubbed*.)

- A **participial phrase** includes a past or a present participle and its modifiers. It functions as an adjective.

  Recalling the name of his favorite mystery writer, the man smiled. (The participial phrase modifies *man*.)

  This laborer, retired recently, takes refuge in books. (The phrase modifies *laborer*.)

A Closer Look

Be careful to place participial phrases next to the nouns or pronouns they modify so that you don't create a dangling or misplaced modifier. (See page 327.)

Panicked by the turbulence, I reminded my seatmate to breathe deeply. (This misplaced modifier is confusing: Is it *I* or *my seatmate* who is panicked?)

Panicked by the turbulence, my seatmate needed to be reminded to breathe deeply. (Clear)

---

they would talk less. —Courtois's Rule * * * * * * * * * * * * *

Using Clauses

Independent Clause

- An **independent clause** has both a subject and a predicate and expresses a complete thought; it can stand alone as a sentence.

  An answering machine can record messages, but voice mail can do so much more.

Note: The above sentence has two clauses; each independent clause can stand alone as a sentence.

Dependent Clause

- A **dependent clause** cannot stand alone. It can, however, add important detail to a sentence.

  When there's no one available to take calls, your voice-mail system can take a message.

Adverb Clause

- An **adverb clause** answers *how, where, when, why, how much,* or *under what condition.* Adverb clauses begin with a subordinating conjunction. (See 315.)

  When your sales staff is on the road, voice mail enables you to leave timely messages.

Adjective Clause

- An **adjective clause** is used to modify a noun or a pronoun by answering the questions *what kind* or *which one.*

  The person who invented the telephone would marvel at communications today.

Noun Clause

- A **noun clause** functions as a noun and can be used as a subject, an object, or a complement.

  What makes voice mail so efficient is the combination of the telephone and the computer.

Using Sentence Variety

Function of Sentences

As a writer, it makes sense to use sentences of varying function, including *declarative, interrogative, imperative, exclamatory,* and *conditional* sentences.

Declarative

- **Declarative sentences** simply state information about a person, a place, a thing, or an idea.

  "Consumers are the most merciless, meanest, toughest market disciplinarians I know."
  —Edwin S. Bingham

Interrogative

- **Interrogative sentences** ask questions.

  Why do some people flit from one job to another, while others stay for decades?

Imperative

- **Imperative sentences** give commands or make requests. Often the subject (you) is understood.

  Never rely on your memory—or a computer's.

Exclamatory

- **Exclamatory sentences** express strong emotion.

  Always have a backup plan! Always!

Conditional

- **Conditional sentences** state wishes ("if . . . then" statements) or conditions contrary to fact.

  "If Patrick Henry thought that taxation without representation was bad, he should see how bad it is with representation."
  —*Old Farmer's Almanac*

---

* * * * * * * * * * Don't talk about yourself; it will be done

Structure of Sentences

The structure of a sentence is *simple, compound, complex,* or *compound-complex.* This depends on the relationship between the independent and dependent clauses in it.

Simple

- A **simple sentence** has only one clause, which is independent; thus, it has only one subject and one predicate. The subject and/or predicate may be single or compound.

  My dogs bark.
  (single subject; single predicate)

  My dogs and my cat fraternize.
  (compound subject; single predicate)

  Their barking and yowling can startle and annoy.
  (compound subject; compound predicate)

Compound

- A **compound sentence** has two or more independent clauses without any dependent clauses. The clauses are most often joined by a coordinating conjunction (*and, or, so, but*), by punctuation, or by both.

  The dogs get weekly baths, so what is that smell?

  It can't be the cat; Missy is a fastidious self-groomer.

Note: Correlative conjunctions are also used to join the clauses in a compound sentence. (See page 315.)

  Either the dogs got into the garbage or Missy's been mouse hunting.

In addition, semicolons and conjunctive adverbs can be used in compound sentences.

  Cats and dogs can be "friends"; still, there are certain limitations.

Complex

- A **complex sentence** has only one independent clause (in red) and one or more dependent clauses (in italics). Dependent clauses usually begin with relative pronouns or subordinating conjunctions. (See pages 305 and 315.)

  ***When the weather is nice,* I walk the dogs for several miles.**
  (one dependent clause; one independent clause)

  ***When we get to the parkway, and if there are only a few people around,* Felix and Hairy can run free.**
  (two dependent clauses; one independent clause)

Compound-Complex

- A **compound-complex sentence** has two or more independent clauses (in red) and one or more dependent clauses (in italics).

  ***If I'm feeling spunky,* I run , too, but I can never keep up with the dogs.**
  (one dependent clause; two independent clauses)

A Closer Look

In general, varying sentence structure will enhance your writing style, making it more interesting and engaging. Remember, though, that clarity is still the single most important quality of good writing.

when you leave. —Wilson Mizner * * * * * * * * * * * * * *

Arrangement of Sentences

By arranging words in a particular way, the writer creates a point of emphasis. These arrangements may be classified as *loose, cumulative, periodic,* or *balanced.*

Loose

- In a **loose sentence**, the point of emphasis comes at the beginning. Explanatory material is added as needed.

  The press release is a vital tool often used to increase public visibility, to create a positive image, and to market services or products.

Cumulative

- A **cumulative sentence** places the point to be made in the main clause and gives it emphasis with modifying words, phrases, or clauses placed before it, after it, or in the middle of it.

  While double-checking the facts for accuracy, press-release writers look for the critical information, the newsworthy data, the new answers to old questions.

Periodic

- A **periodic sentence** begins with specific examples and ends with the main idea.

  With the editor lopping lines here and there and cutting off the end of the news release to make it fit the space, you will soon see the wisdom of putting critical information in the first paragraph.

Balanced

- A **balanced sentence** features a parallel structure that emphasizes a similarity or a contrast between two or more grammatically equal parts (words, phrases, or clauses).

  When writing a press release, start with the most important information and end with the least important data.

Note: Parallelism means "putting elements of equal value into similar constructions." Parallelism can make your sentences especially clear and add emphasis to your ideas.

  His first full-time job meant the end of impossible budgeting, with an easier life ahead. (Unparallel)

  His first full-time job meant the end of impossible budgeting and the beginning of an easier life. (Parallel)

Fyi Be careful when working with sentences. It's very easy to fall into the trap of writing run-on or rambling sentences. A short, clear sentence beats a long, wordy one every time. (See pages 30 and 36.)

* * * * * * * * * * * If there's a harder way to do something,

28
Sentence Errors

Agreement of Subject and Verb

The subject and verb of any clause must agree in both person and number. Checking sentences for agreement requires a close look at everything you write. The following guidelines should help.

- A verb must agree with its subject in number (singular or plural).

  The members were proud of their sales record. (Both the subject *members* and the verb *were* are plural; they agree in number.)

Note: Do not be confused by words that come between the subject and verb.

  Our director, along with most of the associate directors, finds the new procedure awkward at best. (*Director,* not *associate directors,* is the subject.)

Delayed Subjects

- **Delayed subjects** result when the verb precedes the subject (an inverted sentence). In such sentences, the true (delayed) subject must agree with the verb.

  There are many interesting stops along the way. There is no smoking on the bus. (*Stops* and *smoking* are the subjects of these sentences, not *there.*)

Compound Subjects

- Compound subjects connected with *and* almost always take a plural verb.

  Hard work and attention to detail are her greatest strengths.

Subjects with *or/nor*

- Singular subjects joined by *or* or *nor* require a singular verb.

  Either Spencer or Laura is expected to attend the meeting.

Note: Sometimes one of the subjects joined by *or* or *nor* is singular and one is plural; the verb should agree with the subject closer to the verb.

  Neither his complaints nor his attitude was the reason I changed my mind.
  (The singular subject *attitude* is closer to the verb; therefore, the singular verb *was* is used to agree with *attitude.*)

Indefinite Pronouns

- The indefinite pronouns *each, either, neither, one, everybody, another, anybody, anyone, anything, everyone, everything, nobody, somebody,* and *someone* are singular; they require a singular verb.

  Everybody is required to leave early today.

Note: Do not be confused by words or phrases that come between the indefinite pronoun and the verb.

  Each of the attendants is [not are] required to bring a notepad and pens to the briefing.

- The indefinite pronouns *both, few, several,* and *many* are plural; they require a plural verb.

  Many are calling in sick and several have been hospitalized.

someone will find it. —R. E. Roos * * * * * * * * * * * * * *

Indefinite Pronouns with Singular or Plural Verbs

- The indefinite pronouns *all, any, most, none,* and *some* may be either singular or plural. These pronouns are singular if the object of the preposition in the phrase that follows the pronoun is singular; they are plural if the object is plural.

    Most of the manuals were missing. (*Manuals,* the object of the preposition, is plural; therefore, the pronoun *most* is considered plural and takes a plural verb, *were.*

    Much of the meeting was over by the time we arrived. (Because *meeting* is singular, *much* is also singular and requires the singular verb *was.*)

    All of the members are expected to attend.

Collective Nouns

- Collective nouns (*class, faculty, family, committee, team, species, band, crowd, pair, squad*) can be singular or plural in meaning. They require a singular verb when they refer to a group as a unit; they require a plural verb when they refer to the group members as individuals.

    The team is [not are] required to submit an expense report for the road trip.
    (*Team* refers to a group as a unit; it requires the singular verb *is.*)

    The faculty are [not is] highly experienced.
    (In this example, *faculty* refers to the individuals within the group. If the word *individuals* were substituted for *faculty,* it would become clear that the plural verb *are* is needed.)

Nouns That Are Plural in Form

- Some nouns that are plural in form but singular in meaning require a singular verb: *economics, news, mathematics, summons, mumps,* and so on.

    Economics is a social science, not a pure science.

Exceptions: scissors, earnings, premises, proceeds (These plural-form nouns, though singular in meaning, use a plural verb.)

    Last year's earnings were up from 2001!

    The proceeds do not cover the cost of the banquet.

Relative Pronouns

- When a relative pronoun (*which, who, that*) is used to introduce a dependent clause, the number of the verb must agree with the pronoun's antecedent. (See pages 307 and 325.)

    This is one of the reports that are required for this project. (The relative pronoun *that* takes the plural verb *are* because the pronoun's antecedent, *reports,* is plural. To test this type of sentence, read the *of* phrase first: *Of the reports that are . . .)*

"Be" Verbs

- If a form of the *be* verb is used and a predicate noun follows it, the verb must agree with the subject, even if the predicate noun is different in number.

    The cause of his health problem was his bad eating habits.

    His bad eating habits were the cause of his health problem.

* * * * * It's not easy taking my problems one at a time when

Agreement of Pronoun and Antecedent

A pronoun must agree with its *antecedent* in number, person, and gender. (The antecedent is the word or words to which the pronoun refers.)

Susan paid cash for her lunch.

Note: The antecedent in this sentence is *Susan*; it is to *Susan* that the pronoun *her* refers. Both the pronoun and its antecedent are singular, third person, and feminine; therefore, the pronoun is said to agree with its antecedent.

Singular Pronouns

- Use a singular pronoun to refer to antecedents such as *either, neither, each, one, anyone, everyone, everybody, somebody, nobody, another, none,* and *a person.*

    One of the reports is missing its [not their] cover.

Note: When *a person* or *everyone* is used to refer to both sexes or either sex, you will have to choose whether to offer optional pronouns or to rewrite the sentence.

    Everyone will turn in her or his time card. (optional pronouns)

    All employees will turn in their time cards. (rewritten in plural form)

Plural Pronouns

- When a plural pronoun is mistakenly used with a singular indefinite antecedent, you need to change one or the other.

    Incorrect: **Everyone must turn in their reports.**

    Corrected: **Everyone must turn in his or her report.**

Singular and Plural Antecedents

- If one of the antecedents joined by *or* or *nor* is singular and one is plural, the pronoun is made to agree with the closer antecedent.

    Neither the employer nor his employees were ready for their [not his] trip.

Two or More Antecedents

- Two or more antecedents joined by *and* are considered plural; two or more singular antecedents joined by *or* or *nor* take a singular pronoun.

    Jane and Florence opened their briefcases.

    Either Fred or Stan forgot his laptop today.

Masculine and Feminine Antecedents

- If one of the antecedents is masculine and one is feminine, the pronouns should also be masculine and feminine.

    Ask either Sandra or Rob to return her or his extra laptop battery.

Collective Noun Antecedents

- Use a singular pronoun in place of a collective noun that refers to a group as a unit. Use a plural pronoun when the collective noun refers to the individuals in the group.

    The committee reported that it will present its agenda to the board of directors at noon. (group as a unit)

    The committee must sign their names to the document before they leave. (group as individuals)

they refuse to get in line. —Ashleigh Brilliant * * * * * * *

Shifts in Sentence Construction

A **shift** is an improper change in structure midway through a sentence. The following examples will help you identify and avoid several different kinds of shifts in your writing.

Shift in Number

- **Shift in number** is using both a singular and plural pronoun to refer to the same person or group.

> **When people get special training, he or she should share what they have learned with their coworkers.**
> (The sentence shifts from the single pronouns *he* or *she* to the plural pronoun *they*.)

> **When people get special training, they should share what they have learned with their coworkers.**
> (The sentence now contains the plural forms *people* and *they*.)

Shift in Person

- **Shift in person** is improperly mixing first, second, or third person within a sentence.

> **Customers can pay for the items when ordering or when you receive them.**
> (The sentence shifts from third person, *customers*, to second person, *you*.)

> **You can pay for the items when ordering or when you receive them.**
> (Both subjects remain in second person.)

> **Customers can pay when ordering or when they receive the items.** (*Customers*, a third person plural noun, requires a third person plural pronoun, *they*.)

Shift in Tense

- **Shift in tense** is using more than one tense in a sentence when only one tense is needed.

> **We are currently replacing the regulators in the serial link boxes, even though these units operated satisfactorily.** (*Are replacing* is present tense, but *operated* is past tense.)

> **We are currently replacing the regulators in the serial link boxes, even though these units are operating satisfactorily.** (*Are replacing* and *are operating* are both present tense.)

Shift in Voice

- **Shift in voice** is mixing active with passive voice.

> **As we searched the warehouse for damage, a broken window was discovered.** (*Searched* is in the active voice, while *was discovered* is in the passive voice.)

> **As we searched the warehouse for damage, we discovered a broken window.**
> (Both verbs are in the active voice.)

Unparallel Construction

- **Unparallel construction** occurs when the kind of words or phrases being used shifts or changes in the middle of a sentence.

> **All products must be tested, approval, and labeled before shipment.**
> (The sentence shifts from *tested* to *approval* to *labeled*.)

> **All products must be tested, approved, and labeled before shipment.**
> (All three verbs end with *ed*—they are consistent or parallel.)

* * * * * * An honest executive is one who shares the credit

Ambiguous Wording

Ambiguous wording occurs when the words used in a piece of writing are unclear to the reader because they can have two or more possible meanings. Learn to recognize and avoid ambiguous writing by studying the examples that follow.

Misplaced Modifiers

- **Misplaced modifiers** are words or phrases that are so separated from what they are describing that the reader may be confused.

   The copier has nearly been running three hours straight. (Does the sentence mean the copier has *nearly been running?*)

   The copier has been running nearly three hours straight. (This sentence says the copier has been running for *nearly* three hours.)

Dangling Modifiers

- **Dangling modifiers** are descriptive words or phrases that appear to modify the wrong noun. Dangling modifiers often occur as phrases or clauses containing *ing* words.

   After analyzing all the data, our supervisor asked us for our report.
   (It sounds as if the supervisor has been *analyzing all the data.*)

   After we analyzed all the data, our supervisor asked us for our report.
   (This sentence clarifies who *analyzed all the data.*)

Indefinite Pronoun Reference

- An **indefinite reference** is a problem caused by careless use of pronouns. There must always be a word or phrase nearby that a pronoun clearly replaces.

   When the forklift operator placed the pallet on the scale, it broke. (The pronoun *it* could refer to the *scale* or the *pallet.*)

   The pallet broke when the forklift operator placed it on the scale.
   (Now it is clear which item *broke.*)

Incomplete Comparisons

- **Incomplete comparisons**—leaving out words that show exactly what is being compared to what—can confuse readers.

   The office manager said the U150 is faster.
   (The *U150* is faster than what?)

   The office manager said the U150 is faster than the R33. (*Than the R33* completes the comparison.)

Unclear Wording

- One type of ambiguous writing is wording that has two or more possible meanings due to an unclear reference to something.

   Daniel wanted to complete his report after reading the latest research, but he didn't.
   (It is unclear what Daniel didn't do— *complete his report* or *read the latest research.*)

   Daniel wanted to read the latest research before completing his report, but he didn't have time to do the reading.
   (This sentence makes it clear that Daniel completed his *report* but not his *reading.*)

with the people who did the work. —Anonymous * * * * * * *

Nonstandard Language

Nonstandard language is language that does not conform to the standards set by schools, businesses, media, and public institutions. It is often acceptable in everyday conversation and in fictional writing, but seldom in formal speech or in formal writing.

Colloquial Language

- **Colloquial language** is wording used in informal conversation that is unacceptable in formal writing.

    How's it goin'? (Colloquial)

    How are you today? (Standard)

Slang

- Avoid the use of slang or any "in" words in formal writing.

    During the staff meeting, I really got ticked off. (Slang)

    During the staff meeting, I got very angry. (Standard)

Double Preposition

- The use of certain double prepositions—*off of, off to, from off*—is unacceptable.

    Place the file up on the shelf. (Double preposition)

    Place the file on the shelf. (Standard)

Substitution

- Avoid substituting *and* for *to*.

    Try and save all the data related to the Swanson project. (Substitution)

    Try to save all the data related to the Swanson project. (Standard)

Double Negative

- A **double negative** is an expression that contains two negative words used to convey a single negative idea. Double negatives are unacceptable in all writing.

    After examining the labels, I don't think none of them are good. (A double negative is created by using *don't* and *none* together.)

    After examining the labels, I don't think any of them are good. (Standard)

    She didn't barely have time to finish her presentation. (A double negative is created by using *didn't* and *barely* together.)

    She barely had time to finish her presentation. (Standard)

Sentence Fragment

- A **sentence fragment** is a group of words that lacks a subject, a predicate, or both.

    Raised the expectation of investors. (lacks a subject)

    All the reports since last year. (lacks a predicate)

    Quite an encouragement. (lacks a subject and predicate)

Note: Repair a sentence fragment by supplying what it lacks.

    The first-quarter earnings raised the expectations of investors.

    All the reports since last year indicate higher profits.

    The sales figures are quite an encouragement.

* No distance is greater

29
ELL Parts of Speech

This chapter provides English language learners with specific rules and examples that explain some of the oddities of English parts of speech.

Nouns

Count Nouns

- Some nouns name things that can be counted. Such count nouns can be preceded by numbers or articles (*a*, *an*, and *the*). Count nouns can be singular or plural.

  Singular: **cherry**   **bowl**

  Plural: **cherries** **bowls**

  I put 35 **cherries** in a bowl.

Noncount Nouns

- Other nouns name things that can't be counted. Such noncount nouns cannot be preceded by numbers or by *a* or *an* (but *the* is acceptable). Noncount nouns do not have a plural form.

  furniture   **equipment**   **luggage**

  We assembled the **furniture**, set up the **equipment**, and unpacked our **luggage**.

shutterstock.com

A Closer Look at Noncount Nouns

Materials

wood	wool	glass
cloth	steel	leather
ice	aluminum	porcelain
plastic	metal	

Foods

water	sugar	cheese
milk	rice	flour
wine	meat	

Activities

reading	swimming	poetry
boating	soccer	homework
smoking	hockey	
dancing	photography	

Science

oxygen	electricity	mathematics
weather	lightning	economics
heat	biology	air
sunshine	history	

Languages

Spanish	Mandarin
English	Farsi

Abstractions

happiness	publicity	health
harm	advice	

Two-Way Nouns

- Some nouns can be count or noncount, depending on how they are used. These are two-way nouns.

  I cut the **grass**, and then spread new seed with a mix of **grasses**.

than that between advice and help. —Anonymous * * * * * * *

Articles

English uses three types of articles—or short adjectives—before nouns to give more information about them.

Definite Article

- The definite article *the* comes before a noun, indicating that a specific noun is meant.

  Bring me the book.

  (I want a specific book.)

Note: The can be used with most nouns—count nouns and noncount nouns, alike—but avoid using it with most proper nouns.

   Incorrect: **The James Thurber wrote the *My Life and Hard Times.***

   Correct: **James Thurber wrote *My Life and Hard Times.***

Indefinite Articles

- The indefinite article *a* or *an* comes before a noun to indicate that the noun is not specific. Use *a* before nouns that begin with consonants and *an* before nouns that begin with vowels.

  Bring me a book.

  (I want any book.)

Note: A or *an* can be used with singular count nouns, but do not use them with plural count nouns or noncount nouns.

   Incorrect: **I have a health.**

   Correct: **I have my health.**

   Incorrect: **Hand me a flour.**

   Correct: **Hand me the flour.**

Using *A* or *An* with Different Starting Sounds

- If a word starts with a constant sound (such as the *h* sound) use *a*.

a home	**a hog**	**a history**
a handshake	**a helicopter**	

If a word starts with a vowel sound (such as *h* pronounced without the *h* sound) use *an*.

an herb	**an hour**	**an honor**
an hors d'oeuvre	**an honest person**	

Other Noun Markers

Other words can be used to give more information about nouns.

Possessive Adjectives

- Possessive adjectives show ownership of nouns. Possessive adjectives are formed from nouns by adding *'s*. If the noun is plural and ends in *s*, add just *'*.

  Carla's bag was full of books, but none of the books were Juan's.

Possessive Adjectives from Pronouns

	Singular		Plural	
	Before	After	Before	After
First Person	my	mine	our	ours
Second Person	your	yours	your	yours
Third Person	his	his	their	theirs
	her	hers	their	theirs
	its	its	their	theirs

Special forms of pronouns are also used as possessive adjectives. Note that one form is used if the adjective comes before the noun, and often a different form is used if the adjective follows the noun.

   my bike   **The bike is mine.**

   His plan is the same as hers.

* A leader is

Indefinite Adjectives

- Some adjectives show that the noun is not refer-ring to a specific person, place, or thing. These words are indefinite adjectives. Some indefinite adjectives mark count nouns and others mark noncount nouns.

    Many students take math.

    Much tutoring is needed.

With Count Nouns		
all	every	most
any	few	neither
each	many	several
either	more	some
With Noncount Nouns		
all	more	much
any	most	some

Quantifiers

- Quantifiers tell *how many* or *how much* there is of something. Some expressions work with count nouns and others with noncount nouns, and some can work with either.

With Count Nouns		
each	a couple of	several
every	a number of	many
both	a few	nine
With Noncount Nouns		
a bag of	a little	
a bowl of	much	
a piece of	a great deal of	
With Count or Noncount		
no	a lot of	most
not any	lots of	all
some	plenty of	

Demonstrative Adjectives

- Demonstrative adjectives (*this, that, these, those*) make a noun very specific: They *demonstrate* exactly which one is meant and so are stronger than the definite article *the*.

    This card came from that shop.

    These kids want those suckers.

Present-Tense Singular Verbs

The base form of most present-tense verbs is the plural form: *they sit, they see, they say.* To create the singular form, you add an *s* or *es* to the base form.

Add *es* when the verb . . .

- ends in *ch, sh, s, x,* or *z.*

latch—latches	**wash—washes**
harass—harasses	**fix—fixes**
buzz—buzzes	

    is *go* or *do.*

go—goes	**do—does**

Change *y* to *i* and add *es* when the verb . . .

- ends in a *y* after a consonant.

rely—relies	**fly—flies**
qualify—qualifies	**cry—cries**

Add *s* to most other verbs, including those that . . .

- end in *e* or in *y* after a vowel.

bite—bites	**tote—totes**
buy—buys	**say—says**

a dealer in hope. —Napoleon Bonaparte * * * * * * * * * *

Past-Tense Verbs

Most verbs form their past tense by adding *ed* or *d*. Follow these rules.

Add *ed* when the verb ends in . . .

- two consonants.

  latch—latched   thank—thanked

  start—started   learn—learned
- a consonant after two vowels.

  look—looked   reveal—revealed

  treat—treated   applaud—applauded
- a consonant after one vowel if the last syllable is not stressed.

  muster—mustered   budget—budgeted

  falter—faltered   fidget —fidgeted
- a *y* after a vowel.

  stay—stayed   fray—frayed

  destroy—destroyed   enjoy—enjoyed

Double the last consonant and add *ed* when the verb ends in . . .

- a consonant preceded by a vowel in a stressed syllable.

  stop—stopped   step—stepped

  admit—admitted   confer—conferred

Change *y* to *i* and add *ed* when the verb ends in . . .

- a *y* after a consonant.

  satisfy—satisfied   reply—replied

  try—tried   marry—married

Add *d* when the verb ends with . . .

- *e* or *ie*.

  tame—tamed   die—died

  love—loved   remove—removed

Note: Irregular verbs form their past tenses by changing the form of the verb: *has* becomes *had*, *swim* becomes *swam*, *eat* becomes *ate*. (See page 310.)

Progressive Verb Tenses

Progressive verbs express ongoing or continuous action in the past, present, or future. Progressive tenses are created by using helping verbs and the *ing* form of the verb.

Past Progressive Tense

- Form the past progressive tense by using the helping verb *was* or *were* before the *ing* form of the main verb.

  In 1913, workers were building the Smith Tower in downtown Seattle.

  The city was expanding up as well as out.

Present Progressive Tense

- Form the present progressive tense by using the helping verb *am, is,* or *are* before the *ing* form of the main verb.

  Many wheelchair athletes are competing in the Boston Marathon this year.

* * * * * * * * * * * * * Success is the sum of small efforts,

We are cheering them on excitedly.

Future Progressive Tense

- Form the future progressive tense by using the helping verbs *will be* before the *ing* form of the main verb.

    Someday, people will be living on a terraformed Mars.

> *Note:* The progressive tense is generally not used for the following verbs:
>
> | Thought | Appearance | Ownership | Inclusion |
> |---------|------------|-----------|-----------|
> | know | seem | possess | contain |
> | understand | resemble | own | hold |
> | want | look | have | comprise |
> | prefer | appear | belong | include |

They will be riding space elevators to orbiting stations.

Adding *ing* to Verbs

In English, ongoing action is shown by including a helping verb (*is, are, was, were, will be*) before the main verb and adding *ing* to the main verb.

shutterstock.com

Verbs in their *ing* form can also serve as participles or gerunds. Here are the rules for adding *ing*.

Add *ing* when the verb ends in . . .

- two consonants.

latch—latching	thank—thanking
start—starting	learn—learning

- a consonant after two vowels.

look—looking	reveal—revealing
treat—treating	applaud—applauding

- a consonant after one vowel if the last syllable is not stressed.

muster—mustering	budget—budgeting
falter—faltering	fidget—fidgeting

- a *y* after a vowel.

stay—staying	fray—fraying
destroy—destroying	enjoy—enjoying

Drop the *e* and add *ing* when the verb ends in *e*.

live—living	arrive—arriving
tape—taping	describe—describing

Double the final consonant and add *ing* when the verb ends in . . .

- a consonant preceded by a single vowel in a stressed syllable.

pat—patting	hop—hopping
permit—permitting	begin—beginning

Change *ie* to *y* and add *ing* when a verb ends with *ie*:

die—dying	lie—lying	tie—tying

repeated day in and day out. —Robert Collier * * * * * * * * * *

Modal Auxiliary Verbs

Modal auxiliary verbs work with the base form of a verb to express a special meaning. Here is a list of meanings expressed and the modals used to express them.

Meaning	Present-Tense Modal	Past-Tense Modal
possibility	*may, might, could*	*may have, might have, could have*
	You *may work* overtime.	You *may have worked* overtime.
	You *might work* overtime.	You *might have worked* overtime.
	You *could work* overtime.	You *could have worked* overtime.
advisability	*should*	*should have*
	You *should register.*	You *should have registered.*
necessity	*have to, must*	*had to*
	You *have to arrive* on time.	You *had to arrive* on time.
	You *must arrive* on time.	
request	*may, might, would, could, will, can*	
	May I *ask* a favor?	
	Might I *request* one change?	
	Would you *watch* my dog?	
	Could you *lend* a hand?	
	Can you *help* this week?	
ability	*can*	*could*
	I *can see* the Big Dipper.	I *could see* the Big Dipper.
intent	*shall, will*	*would have*
	We *shall see* who wins.	We *would have seen* who won.
	We *will see* who wins.	
expectation	*should*	*should have*
	I *should arrive* soon.	I *should have arrived* by now.
assumption	*must*	*must have*
	I *must be* lost.	I *must have been* lost.
repeated action		*would*
		I *would walk* by the lake.

* Take calculated risks.

Phrasal Verbs

A phrasal verb looks like a verb joined with a preposition (or an adverb), but it has a different meaning than the verb and preposition alone would have. Here is a list of phrasal verbs and their meanings, along with example sentences.

Phrasal Verb	Meaning	Example
break down	stop working, fall apart, examine	The car may **break down** in this heat. Let's **break down** the expenses.
call off	cancel	The police **called off** the manhunt.
call up	bring forward	**Call up** the main menu.
catch up with*	reach, pull alongside	We soon **caught up with** Charlie.
clear out	vacate, evacuate	**Clear out** your locker.
cross out	delete	**Cross out** the error and correct it.
figure out	decipher, solve	Can you **figure out** this remote?
fill in/out	complete	Please **fill out** the application.
find out*	discover	I will **find out** who called.
get over*	recover from	I can't wait to **get over** this cold.
give back	return, repay	I like to **give back** to my community.
give in/up	quit, surrender	We **gave up** the house hunt.
hang up	end a phone call	I **hung up** when the machine answered.
leave out	omit, exclude	The recipe **left out** the shortening.
look down on*	despise, disparage	The neighbors **look down on** us.
look forward to*	anticipate	I **look forward to** Thanksgiving.
look up	find information	Let's **look up** the street address.
look up to*	appreciate, admire	I **look up to** my father.
mix up	confuse, switch	You've **mixed up** the students.
pick out	select, choose	She **picked out** her favorite blouse.
point out	indicate, show	He **pointed out** his apartment building.
put off	delay, postpone	He **put off** filing his taxes.
put up with*	endure	We **put up with** the racket all day.
run out of	deplete, use up	The team **ran out of** pencils.
take after*	resemble	You **take after** your mother.
take part*	participate	Let's **take part** in the protest.
try on	put on to test-fit	**Try on** the pants before buying them.
turn down	refuse	I **turned down** his proposal.
turn up	appear, raise volume	The lost comb **turned up** yesterday.

* Do not split this phrasal verb with a direct object.

That is quite different from being rash. —George S. Patton * *

Objects—Infinitives and Gerunds

In English, some verbs take direct objects, which are nouns or noun forms. Some verbs are particular about what noun forms can follow them:

Verbs That Take Infinitives

- Most verbs take infinitives (*to* plus a verb) as objects.

  I appear to be next in line.
  [Not *appear being*]

  He decided to buy the torque wrench.
  [Not *decided buying*]

  The weld failed to hold the plates together
  [Not *failed holding*]

Note: Some verbs must include an indirect object.

  I authorize you to sign the check.
  [Not *authorize to sign*]

Use an Infinitive After . . .		
agree	deserve	pretend
appear	endeavor	promise
ask	expect	refuse
attempt	fail	seem
beg	hesitate	tend
bother	hope	venture
choose	intend	volunteer
claim	need	want
consent	offer	wish
decide	plan	
demand	prepare	

Verbs That Take Gerunds

- A few verbs take gerunds (*ing* form of verb) as objects.

  He imagines owning his own business.
  [Not *imagines to own.*]

  That idea would be worth writing down.
  [Not *would be worth to write*]

  I can't help thinking I am special.
  [Not *can't help to think*]

Use Gerunds After . . .		
admit	dislike	recall
appreciate	enjoy	recommend
avoid	finish	regret
be worth	imagine	resist
can't help	keep	risk
consider	miss	suggest
delay	postpone	tolerate
deny	practice	
discuss	quit	

Verbs That Take Infinitives or Gerunds

- A small group of verbs take gerunds or infinitives as objects.

  I love to walk in the rain.

  I love walking in the rain.

Sometimes a gerund creates a different meaning from the infinitive.

  I stopped eating.   **I stopped to eat.**

Use Infinitives or Gerunds After . . .		
begin	love	stop
continue	prefer	try
hate	remember	
like	start	

* * * * * * * * * * * * * Work spares us from three evils:

Adjective Placement

In English, adjectives often appear before the noun they modify. When more than one adjective is used, however, they need to appear in a specific order. Here is the accepted order of adjective placement:

First, start with . . .	
1. **articles**	a, an, the
demonstrative adjectives	that, this, these, those
possessives	my, our, her, their, Bill's
Next, place adjectives that tell . . .	
2. **time**	first, second, next, last
3. **how many**	some, few, many
4. **value**	lovely, fine, distinguished
5. **size**	huge, tiny, towering
6. **shape**	blocky, round, cubic
7. **condition**	ratty, tidy, bright
8. **age**	new, old, vintage, antique
9. **color**	brown, purple, green
10. **nationality**	Cuban, Kenyan, Japanese
11. **religion**	Jewish, Catholic, Islamic
12. **material**	steel, canvas, wooden
Finally, place . . .	
13. **nouns used as adjectives**	pencil [case], car [seat]

Example:
those multicolored plastic beach chairs
(1 + 9 + 12 + 13 + noun)

Note: It is best not to use too many adjectives before a noun. An article and one or two adjectives are usually plenty. More adjectives become difficult to keep track of, and difficult to include in the correct order:

Awkward: **My first few lovely small cubic bright new green Kenyan steel pencil cases arrived.**

Effective: **My lovely green pencil cases arrived.**

Participles as Adjectives

Participles as Modifiers

- When a present participle (a verb ending in *ing*) is used as an adjective, it describes the cause of a certain feeling or situation:

  The blinding sparks require eye protection.

  When a past participle (a verb ending in *ed*) is used as an adjective, it describes the effect of a certain feeling or situation.

  A blinded welder would be a tragedy.

Example Participles

Here are more participles that change meaning:

Present (Cause)	Past (Effect)
annoying	annoyed
boring	bored
confusing	confused
depressing	depressed
exciting	excited
fascinating	fascinated
surprising	surprised

Nouns as Adjectives

Nouns as Modifiers

- Nouns sometimes modify other nouns, becoming adjectives. Only singular noun forms can be used as adjectives.

  Mom works as a nurse coordinator.

  She oversees the third-shift team.

  Avoid piling up nouns as adjectives. Such groupings become difficult to read. Use prepositional phrases to add some of the information.

  Difficult: **Mom is the third-shift hospital pediatrics nurse coordinator.**

  Clear: **Mom is the pediatrics nurse coordinator on third shift at the hospital.**

Adverb Placement

Unlike adjectives, adverbs appear in many different places in a sentence.

Adverbs That Modify a Whole Sentence

- **Adverbs that modify a whole sentence** also can go anywhere (except between the verb and direct object), though most often they go at the beginning.

  Fortunately, we correctly packed every shipment and completed the order.

  We correctly packed every shipment and, fortunately, completed the order.

  We correctly packed every shipment and completed the order, fortunately.

Adverbs That Modify Other Adverbs

- **Adverbs that modify other adverbs** should go right before the words they modify.

  It was a very important order for one of our most loyal customers.

Adverbs That Tell *How*

- **Adverbs that tell *how*** can appear just about anywhere in a sentence. The only place such an adverb *cannot* go is between a verb and a direct object.

  Correct: **Quickly we loaded the trucks.**
  Correct: **We quickly loaded the trucks.**
  Correct: **We loaded the trucks quickly.**
  Incorrect: **We loaded quickly the trucks.**

Adverbs That Tell *When*

- **Adverbs that tell *when*** should go at the end of the sentence.

  We should have another rush order like that tomorrow.

Adverbs That Tell *Where*

- **Adverbs that tell *where*** should follow the verbs they modify. Often, prepositional phrases function as *where* adverbs. However, do not place the prepositional phrase between the verb and the direct object.

  All orders are packed downstairs. Workers will load them in the trucks.

Adverbs That Tell *How Often*

- **Adverbs that tell *how often*** should go before an action verb or between a helping verb and an action verb.

  Our packers seldom make an error.

  The department has been frequently praised for consistency.

* The art of being wise

Prepositions

Common Prepositions

- Four little prepositions do a lot of work in English: *by*, *at*, *on*, and *in*.

By means "next to" or "up to a certain place or time."

   by the statue, **by** the river

   by 10:00 p.m., **by** November 2

At refers to a specific place or time.

   at the police station, **at** the corner

   at 3:30 a.m., **at** midnight

On refers to a surface, an electronic medium, or a day or date.

   on the table, **on** the counter

   on the Web site, **on** the DVD

   on July 22, **on** Wednesday

In refers to an enclosed place; a geographical location; a print medium; or an hour, month, or year.

   in the room, **in** the bathtub

   in Chicago, **in** the United States

   in the magazine, **in** the book

   in half an hour, **in** September

Phrasal Prepositions

- Some prepositions are made up of more than one word. They function the same as single-word prepositions.

Phrasal Preposition Examples:

according to	from between	on the side of
across from	from under	on top of
along with	in addition to	outside of
apart from	in back of	owing to
aside from	in behalf of	prior to
away from	in case of	round about
because of	in front of	subsequent to
by means of	in place of	together with
by way of	in spite of	up to
down from	instead of	with respect to
except for	on account of	
from among	on behalf of	

shutterstock.com

is knowing what to overlook. —William James * * * * * * * * * *

30
ELL Sentences

This chapter focuses on the sentence issues that are most challenging for learners of the English language.

Basic Sentence Structure

Structure 1: Subject | Verb

- In English, the order of words indicates their use in the sentence. Subjects generally come before verbs; indirect and direct objects generally follow verbs. In the pattern below, the subject is connected to an intransitive verb—*smiled*. An intransitive verb is complete without any objects.

  Honorato smiled.
  Subject | Verb

Structure 2: Subject | Verb | Direct Object

- In the pattern below, the subject is connected to a transitive verb—*positioned*. A transitive verb requires a direct object to be complete. (Honorato positioned what? The camera.) The direct object receives the action of the verb.

  Honorato positioned the camera.
  Subject | Verb | Direct Object

Structure 3: Subject | Verb | Indirect Object | Direct Object

- In the pattern below, the transitive verb *gave* is completed by an indirect object and a direct object. The direct object receives the action of the verb. (Honorato gave what? An engagement ring.) The indirect object tells to whom or for whom the action was done. (Honorato gave an engagement ring to whom? His girlfriend.)

  Honorato gave his girlfriend an engagement ring.
  Subject | Verb | Indirect Object | Direct Object

Advanced Sentence Structure

Structure 4: Subject | Verb | Direct Object | Object Complement

- In the construction below, the direct object *Lupita* receives the action of the verb *named*. The object complement then renames or describes the direct object. This construction is rare, occurring only with verbs for nominating someone (*named, elected, appointed, nominated, called*) or creating something (*painted, built, made, got*).

  The president named Lupita the
  Subject | Verb | Direct Object |

  Outstanding Student of 2011.
  Object Complement

Mackarus from Flickr

* **Goals are the fuel**

Structure 5: Subject │ Linking Verb │ Subject Complement

- In the construction below, a linking verb (such as *is, are, was, were, will be, seems, appears*) connects the subject *president* with the subject complement *Doctor Allan Schnieder*. A subject complement either renames or describes the subject.

  The president is Doctor Allan Schnieder.
  Subject │ Linking Verb │ Subject Complement

Structure 6: Linking Verb │ Subject │ Subject Complement

- In the construction below, the linking verb comes before the noun, signaling that the sentence is a question.

  Is Doctor Allan Schnieder the president?
  Linking Verb │ Subject │ Subject Complement

Structure 7: Helping Verb │ Subject │ Verb │ Direct Object

- To form a question with an action verb, the sentence below begins with a helping verb followed by the subject and then the main verb.

  Has Doctor Allan Schnieder given his speech?
  Helping Verb │ Subject │ Verb │ Direct Object

Structure 8: Expletive │ Linking Verb │ Subject

- In the construction below, the expletive *there* signals that the subject is delayed until after the verb. (The word *here* is also an expletive.)

  There are twenty-seven past presidents of the school.
  Expletive │ Linking Verb │ Subject

Conditional Sentences

Some sentences express a situation that depends on a certain condition being met. One clause presents the condition (the conditional clause) and the other clause presents the situation (the main clause). Different conditionals are formed differently.

Factual Conditionals

- A factual conditional refers to an actual situation in the present or past tense. The conditional clause starts with a word such as *if, when,* or *whenever,* and the verb in the clause matches the tense of the verb in the main clause (both past tense or both present tense).

Conditional Clause *if, when, whenever* + past tense	+	Main Clause past tense	=	Past Tense

When the members of the band arrived, we cheered.

Conditional Clause *if, when, whenever* + present tense	+	Main Clause present tense	=	Present Tense

Whenever the lead guitarist plays a solo, the crowd goes wild.

shutterstock.com

in the furnace of achievement. —Brian Tracy * * * * * * * * * *

Predictive Conditionals

- A predictive conditional refers to possibilities. The conditional clause starts with the word *if* or *unless* and uses a present tense verb. The main clause uses a modal (*will, can, should, may, might*) and a present-tense main verb.

Conditional Clause *if, unless* + present tense	+	Main Clause modal verb + present tense	=	Future Tense

If all of us receive an invitation, we should attend.

Hypothetical Conditionals

- A hypothetical conditional begins with *if* and refers to a situation that is contrary to fact or is unlikely to happen.

Conditional Clause *if* + past perfect	+	Main Clause *would, could, might* + *have* + past participle	=	Past Tense

If we had ordered sooner, we would have gotten the pizza by now.

Conditional Clause *if* + past tense	+	Main Clause *would, could, might* + base form of main verb	=	Present Tense

If we learned to make pizza, we could eat it any time.

Repeating/Omitting Words

Some languages allow double subjects or double negatives. Others allow subjects to be omitted. These structures aren't permitted in Standard English.

Double Subjects

- Avoid repeating the subject of a sentence or clause.

  Correct: My friend enjoyed the movie.

  Incorrect: My friend, she enjoyed the movie.

Double Negatives

- Avoid using two negatives when forming a negative statement. Two negatives actually cancel each other out, making the sentence positive.

  Correct: I didn't get my paycheck.

  Incorrect: I didn't never get my paycheck.

  I didn't get no paycheck.

  I hardly never got paid.

Omitted Words

- Some languages allow the subject of the sentence to be omitted, but in English, most sentences must have a stated subject. In a command, the subject *you* can be implied. **Wash the car. (You wash the car.)** All other sentences must have a stated subject.

  Correct: It is in the garage.

  Incorrect: Is in the garage.

  Also, make sure not to omit the expletives *there* or *here*.

  Correct: There is a bucket on the shelf.

  Incorrect: Is a bucket on the shelf.

Repeated Object

- In an adjective dependent clause, do not repeat the object.

  Correct: I need the book that I lent to you.

  Incorrect: I need the book that I lent it to you.

* Don't bunt.

Idioms I

An idiom is a commonly used expression whose meaning is different from the meaning of the words in the expression. Here are some common idioms.

Idiom	Meaning	Example
add fuel to the fire	make a bad situation worse	Criticizing your brother for getting upset will only **add fuel to the fire**.
an arm and a leg	a great deal of money	That sleek new convertible costs **an arm and a leg**.
an axe to grind	a dispute with someone	The author had **an axe to grind** with the critic who disliked his book.
back-seat driver	someone who criticizes without being directly involved	I make all the decisions and take all the responsibility, while you're just a **back-seat driver**.
bad apple	someone who causes trouble in a group	That team has a **bad apple** who is destroying morale.
ball in your court	the next act or decision is yours	After we made our proposal, the **ball was in the other company's court**.
beat around the bush	avoid getting to the point	Don't **beat around the bush**. Tell me what you really think.
bend over backward	do anything in order to help	The sales staff **bends over backward** for customer satisfaction.
between a rock and a hard place	between two bad alternatives	The couple could declare bankruptcy or get a second mortgage: They were **between a rock and a hard place**.
bite your tongue	don't say what you want to say	My brother didn't take my advice to get his oil changed. When his engine seized up, I **bit my tongue**.
break the ice	get a group to interact	Let's play a party game to **break the ice**.
chew out	verbally scold	When I showed up late for work, my boss **chewed me out**.
chip on your shoulder	challenging, looking for a fight	My neighbor was never friendly; he always had a **chip on his shoulder**.
chow down	eat heartily	At the buffet, the whole team **chowed down**.

Aim out of the ballpark. —David Ogilvy * * * * * * * * * * * *

Idioms II

Idiom	Meaning	Example
crack up	laugh	When I saw the photo of the dancing dogs, I **cracked up.**
cross your fingers	wish for a positive outcome	Tonight is the vote on the important law. **Cross your fingers**!
cup of joe	cup of coffee	I can't ever focus in the morning until I have a **cup of joe**.
cut to the chase	get to the point	**Cut to the chase:** What happened when the police showed up?
dime a dozen	common, easy to acquire	Bad renditions of Christmas carols are a **dime a dozen**.
drive someone up the wall	annoy someone extremely	The constant dripping from the faucet **drove me up the wall.**
feeding frenzy	an aggressive group attack	The actor's drunk driving arrest set off a media **feeding frenzy.**
get over it	move beyond something troublesome	I know the sales report depressed you, but you have to **get over it.**
get up on the wrong side of the bed	have a bad attitude, feel grumpy	When he slammed the door, I knew he had **gotten up on the wrong side of the bed.**
give someone the cold shoulder	ignore someone	I'm always friendly when I see her, but she **gives me the cold shoulder.**
go for broke	gamble everything	At first I was afraid to ask her out, but I decided to **go for broke.**
go out on a limb	take a chance, take a risky position	I'll **go out on a limb** and suggest that you stop dating people like him.
head over heels	joyful, thrilled, in love	She was **head over heels** about her new boyfriend.
heart on your sleeve	express emotions openly or obviously	You always know how Pedro feels; he wears his **heart on his sleeve.**
hit the hay/sack	go to bed	I'm exhausted. I think I'll **hit the sack.**
hit the nail on the head	do or say something exactly right	When you said we need a new car, you **hit the nail on the head.**
in the bag	completely certain	After preparing for two weeks, I knew my audition was **in the bag.**

* There is no education

Idioms III

Idiom	Meaning	Example
in your face	aggressive, confrontational	The car salesperson was really **in your face**.
kitty-corner/ catty-corner	diagonally across from	The donut shop is **catty-corner** to the gas station.
know the ropes	understand a procedure or location	After a week in the restaurant, I really **knew the ropes.**
let sleeping dogs lie	avoid stirring up an old conflict	Don't remind your brother about losing his necklace: **Let sleeping dogs lie.**
let the cat out of the bag	share a secret	Before I could tell Mom about my job, Dad **let the cat out of the bag.**
lose face	suffer embarrassment	So as not to **lose face**, I quit before they could fire me.
lose your head	go crazy, lose control	When the snowplow blocked my driveway, I **lost my head.**
off on the wrong foot	starting a relationship badly	I spilled my drink on my blind date. We got **off on the wrong foot.**
off the hook	released from a tough situation	When the talent show was canceled, I was **off the hook.**
on pins and needles	anxious or excited	Before our first date, I was **on pins and needles** all day.
on the fence	undecided	I'm **on the fence** about voting Republican or Democrat.
on the same page	in agreement	We're **on the same page** about the new tax: We're against it.
out of the blue	without warning; unexpectedly	We couldn't pay our bills. Then **out of the blue**, I got a job.
over the top	excessive	The complaint letter was scathing and **over the top**.
piece of cake	easily accomplished	I'm good at math, so most equations are a **piece of cake.**
pig out	eat greedily; eat much	At Thanksgiving dinner, the whole family **pigged out**.
pipe down	quiet down; shut up	You'd better **pipe down.** People are tired of your complaints.

like adversity. —Benjamin Disraeli * * * * * * * * * * * * * * *

Idioms IV

Idiom	Meaning	Example
pull your leg	tease, kid, or trick someone	When he said that you won $100, he was **pulling your leg**.
put your foot in your mouth	say something embarrassing	When I criticized the painting, I didn't know I was talking to the artist: I **put my foot in my mouth**.
ride shotgun	sit in the front passenger seat	You can drive, and I will **ride shotgun**.
save face	recover from embarrassment	Paying for the repairs to the pool table helped me **save face**.
start from scratch	do something over from the beginning	We threw out the original files and **started from scratch**.
the last straw	a small burden causing a big breakdown	When my neighbor blocked my drive, that was **the last straw**.
tongue in cheek	joking	The comedy provided a **tongue-in-cheek** view of corporate finance.
toss-up	an unclear situation or result	After all the bids were in, it was a **toss-up** who would get the contract.
under the weather	ill	The talk show host with a scratchy voice seemed **under the weather**.
when pigs fly	never	You can expect me to help you move **when pigs fly**.
zero tolerance	punishing even the smallest crimes	The athletics department has a **zero-tolerance** policy for steroid use.

shutterstock.com

* * * * * * * * * * * * * * * * Problems are only opportunities

31
ELL/Dialect Index

This chapter provides the language-transfer issues common to speakers of various languages and dialects. The issues are named and demonstrated, with cross-references to places where you can learn more about each issue.

Augapafel from Flickr

Tips for Speakers:
European Languages

Tip	Transfer Error	Correction
Don't use *the* with generalizations. (See 330.)	I am studying the politics.	I am studying politics.
Don't use *the* with singular proper nouns. (See 330.)	Warm weather should arrive by the June.	Warm weather should arrive by June.
Do not omit the subject of a sentence. (See 340–341.)	Was a funny story. Is raining outside.	That was a funny story. It is raining outside.
Do not omit *here* or *there* in a sentence with a delayed subject. (See 341.)	Are three recipes. Is a new plan.	Here are three recipes. There is a new plan.
Study progressive tenses. (See 332–333.)	They work here for two years.	They have been working here for two years.
Study the use of infinitives and gerunds as objects. (See 336.)	He wants going along. I regret to call.	He wants to go along. I regret calling.
Follow the order for subjects, verbs, and objects. (See 340–341.)	The pitcher the ball threw. (or) The ball threw the pitcher.	The pitcher threw the ball.
Do not insert an adverb between a verb and its object. (See 338.)	I played very rapidly the piano piece.	I played the piano piece very rapidly.

in work clothes. —Henry J. Kaiser * * * * * * * * * * * * * * * * *

Tips for Speakers: Latin Languages

Tip	Transfer Error	Correction
Place most subjects before the verb. (See 340–341.)	Help got I with my homework.	I got help with my homework.
Avoid double subjects. (See 342.)	Lupe and Juan they enjoy dancing.	Lupe and Juan enjoy dancing.
Avoid double negatives. (See 342.)	We don't have no time.	We don't have any time. _____ (or) _____ We have no time.
Use *don't* or *doesn't* instead of *no* to negate a verb.	He no like the idea. They no want pizza.	He doesn't like the idea. They don't want pizza.
Do not omit the subject of a sentence, even the pronoun *it*. (See 342.)	Was a funny story. Is raining outside.	That was a funny story. It is raining outside.
Do not omit *here* or *there* in a sentence with a delayed subject. (See 341.)	Are three recipes. Is a new plan.	Here are three recipes. There is a new plan.
Do not make adjectives plural. (See 312.)	Thanks for your wonderfuls pies.	Thanks for your wonderful pies.
Do not insert an adverb between a verb and its object. (See 338.)	I played very rapidly the piano piece.	I played the piano piece very rapidly.
Avoid using *which* to refer to people. (See 302.)	My cousin which is a mechanic can fix it.	My cousin who is a mechanic can fix it.
Be careful with *her* and *his*. (See 306.)	My dress matched his dress.	My dress matched her dress.

* All misfortune is

Tips for Speakers:
East Asian Languages

Tip	Transfer Error	Correction
Practice use of plural noun forms. (See 329.)	Please give me three egg.	Please give me three eggs.
Use the adjectival form of nouns. (See 312.)	That is a beauty lamp.	That is a beautiful lamp.
Study the use of articles (*a, an, the*). (See 330.)	I will buy car.	I will buy a car. ———— (or) ———— I will buy the car.
Study the use of infinitives and gerunds as objects. (See 336.)	He wants going along. I regret to call.	He wants to go along. I regret calling.
Use objective case pronouns. (See 306–307.)	Cho threw she the ball.	Cho threw her the ball.
Make sure subjects and verbs agree in number. (See 323–324.)	Your idea have merit.	Your idea has merit. (or) Your ideas have merit.
Carefully form past tenses of verbs. (See 308–309.)	Yesterday I walk to the beach.	Yesterday I walked to the beach.
Study the creation of passive voice. (See 308–309.)	My suggestion adopt by the group.	My suggestion was adopted by the group.
Learn which conjunctions come in pairs and which do not. (See 315.)	Although we arrived on time, but the waiter didn't seat us.	We arrived on time, but . . . ———— (or) ———— Although we arrived on time, the waiter . . .
Avoid repeating the object in a *that* clause. (See 342.)	It's the same radio that I sold you it.	It's the same radio that I sold you.
Do not place too many adjectives before a noun. (See 337.)	I would like the baked with butter on it salmon fillet.	I would like the salmon fillet that is baked with butter.

but a stepping-stone to fortune. —Henry David Thoreau * * *

Tips for Speakers:
Middle Eastern Languages

Tip	Transfer Error	Correction
Study the use of articles (*a*, *an*, *the*). (See 330.)	I will buy car.	I will buy a car. ———— (or) ———— I will buy the car.
Don't use *the* with generalizations. (See 330.)	I am studying the politics.	I am studying politics.
Don't use *the* with singular proper nouns. (See 330.)	Warm weather should arrive by the June.	Warm weather should arrive by June.
Don't omit *be* verbs such as *is*, *are*, *was*, and *were*. (See 308–309.)	This school harder than my last one.	This school is harder than my last one.
Study the creation of past perfect tense. (See 309.)	We were arrived by 3:00 p.m.	We had arrived by 3:00 p.m.
Study progressive tenses. (See 332–333.)	They work here for two years.	They have been working here for two years.
Learn which verbs do not use progressive tense. (See 333.)	I am owning a cat. I am needing a litter box.	I own a cat. I need a litter box.
Use objective case pronouns. (See 306–307.)	Retu threw she the ball.	Retu threw her the ball.
Be careful with *her* and *his*. (See 306.)	My dress matched his dress.	My dress matched her dress.
Study the use of infinitives and gerunds as objects. (See 336.)	He wants going along. I regret to call.	He wants to go along. I regret calling.
Follow the order for subjects, verbs, and objects. (See 340–341.)	The pitcher the ball threw. (or) The ball threw the pitcher.	The pitcher threw the ball.

* * * * * * * * * * * * * * * * * * Commitment leads to action.

Tips for Speakers:
African and Caribbean Languages

Tip	Transfer Error	Correction
Avoid double subjects. (See 342.)	AJ and Sharla they enjoy dancing.	AJ and Sharla enjoy dancing.
Avoid double negatives. (See 342.)	We don't have no time.	We don't have any time. ———— (or) ———— We have no time.
Study the use of articles (*a*, *an*, *the*). (See 330.)	I will buy car.	I will buy a car. ———— (or) ———— I will buy the car.
Make sure subjects and verbs agree in number. (See 323–324.)	Your idea have merit.	Your idea has merit. ———— (or) ———— Your ideas have merit.
Use plural nouns after plural numbers. (See 304.)	We have two cat.	We have two cats.
Study the use of the *be* verb. (See 308.)	The group be meeting.	The group is meeting.
Study the use of past-tense verbs. (See 308–309.)	After Levon arrived, we eat.	After Levon arrived, we ate.

Action brings your dream closer. —Marcia Wieder * * * * *

Tips for Speakers:
English Dialects

Tip	Transfer Error	Correction
Avoid double subjects. (See 342.)	Dave and Lynn they enjoy dancing.	Dave and Lynn enjoy dancing.
Use *an* before a vowel and *a* before a consonant. (See 330.)	Give me a apple. I'd like an banana.	Give me an apple. I'd like a banana.
Use *'s* or *'* to form the possessive of most nouns. (See 270–271.)	I borrowed my dad car.	I borrowed my dad's car.
Use *their* instead of *they* as a possessive. (See 306.)	I went to they concert.	I went to their concert.
Use *himself* instead of *hisself*. (See 305.)	He got hisself a new suit.	He got himself a new suit.
Don't invert the subject-verb order with indefinite pronouns. (See 340–341.)	Hasn't nobody seen the movie yet.	Nobody has seen the movie yet.
Don't use the word *be* for habitual action. (See 308–309.)	He be always fishing.	He is always fishing. _____ (or) _____ He often fishes.
Avoid double negatives. (See 342.)	We don't have no time.	We don't have any time. _____ (or) _____ We have no time.
Use *don't* or *doesn't* instead of *no* to negate a verb.	He no like the idea. They no want pizza.	He doesn't like the idea. They don't want pizza.
Use *isn't* or *aren't* instead of *ain't*.	My friends ain't going.	My friends aren't going.
Use a plural noun after a plural number. (See 304.)	Let me buy two cake.	Let me buy two cakes.

* * * * * Imagination is the eye of the soul. —Joseph Joubert

UP UPWRITE PRESS®
www.upwritepress.com

Our Mission

At UpWrite Press, our mission is to empower individuals and organizations to reach their full potential by improving their writing and communication skills. These gateway skills enhance critical thinking, creativity, and adaptability—essential drivers for success in the modern workplace. To fulfill this mission, UpWrite Press provides engaging products and services designed for the following clients:

- businesspeople seeking professional development
- independent and corporate training professionals
- instructors in high schools, tech/trade schools, community colleges, and universities

Our Company

UpWrite Press is a team of authors, trainers, editors, and designers devoted to helping people write and communicate more effectively in the workplace. Our workplace is a Civil War-era house and barn, where we've created the best-selling Write Source handbooks for teaching writing from kindergarten through college. Now we bring our proven techniques to the business world.

UpWrite Press offers a full suite of materials and services to support and train business writers. From award-winning references such as *Write for Business* to effective training materials such as the *Write Program*, UpWrite Press is your resource for business writing.

shutterstock.com

Our History

UpWrite Press draws upon a long, successful history of teaching effective writing. The company has its roots in Write Source, founded in 1977 by Patrick Sebranek and Verne Meyer, who had together created a writing handbook for their own middle school and high school students.

That handbook soon became such a phenomenon that it drew the attention of Boston-based publisher D. C. Heath, who contracted the authors to create an entire line of books and support materials for kindergarten through high school. When D. C. Heath was in turn acquired by the Houghton Mifflin company, the new publishers created a division named Great Source, largely to manage the multimillion-dollar annual sales of Write Source books.

Having completed the K-12 line in 1999, Write Source went on to create *The College Writer* for Cengage Learning, *The College Writer's Handbook,* and *The Business Writer.* In addition, Write Source authored and developed *COMP: Read, COMP: Write, WRITE1, WRITE2,* and other materials for Cengage's 4LTR Press imprint.

With 25 years of experience running their own business, the founders recognized that business writing has its own unique demands. In 2001, they established UpWrite Press as a sister company to Write Source. UpWrite Press's very first product, *Write for Business,* immediately garnered awards from such organizations as the Chicago Book Clinic.

Since that time, the UpWrite Press team has gone on to create additional books, ebooks, training manuals, Job Aides, and an online testing center, all designed to provide the very best in training materials for business writers such as you. We also maintain a daily blog and bi-monthly *eTips* that offer aid on a variety of business-writing topics.

We appreciate your interest in UpWrite Press. If there is any way we can help with your business writing, don't hesitate to contact us via e-mail at contact@upwritepress.com.

Our Team

Administration

Owner/President: Christopher Erickson
Owner/Vice President: Janae Sebranek
Director of Operations: Steve Augustyn
Customer Service Manager: Jean Varley

Editorial

Editor in Chief: Rob King
Author/Senior Writer: Dave Kemper
Writer/Technologist: Lester Smith
Writer/Editor: Tim Kemper
Copy Editor: Lois Krenzke

Production

Production Manager: Colleen Belmont
Illustrator/Design Consultant: Christian R. Krenzke
Production Designer/Developer: Mark Lalumondier
Production Designer/Developer: April Lindau
Senior Software Developer: Jason Reynolds

shutterstock.com

shutterstock.com